NANTUCKET
OPEN·HOUSE
COOKBOOK

NANTUCKET

OPEN-HOUSE COOKBOOK

by
Sarah Leah Chase

*Illustrations by
Judith Shahn*

*Workman Publishing
New York*

For K.

Who encouraged me to write before he encouraged me to cook, and who has always provided islands of inspiration in both. Thank you for teaching me that clouds may indeed be embraced . . .

Copyright © 1987 by Sarah Leah Chase

Illustrations © 1987 by Workman Publishing Company, Inc.

Library of Congress Cataloging-in-Publication Data
Chase, Sarah Leah.
Nantucket open-house cookbook.
Includes index.
1. Entertaining.   2. Cookery.   3. Que Sera Sarah
(Shop: Nantucket, Mass.)   I. Title.
TX731.C542 1987   641.5′ 68   86-40598
ISBN 0-89480-476-6
ISBN 0-89480-465-0 (pbk.)

Cover and book illustrations: Judith Shahn
Cover Design by Charles Kreloff

Workman Publishing Company, Inc.
1 West 39th Street
New York, NY 10018

Manufactured in the United States of America

First printing June 1987
10 9 8 7 6 5 4 3 2

Acknowledgments

At first glance the name of my food operation—Que Sera Sarah (loosely translated as "whatever will be me")—announces itself as a highly personal venture. Yet, such could never excel without the behind-the-scenes support of a wonderful range of people who lend a most essential substance to my quirky visions and lifestyle. Que Sera Sarah never could have made the leap from dream to reality if it were not for the generous encouragement and patience of my mother, Dun Gifford, Bill Euler, and Andy Oates, fully complemented by the aesthetic talents and innovations of De and Paul Madden, and Todd Winship. A mere thank you does not begin to express my gratitude. Enter Richard Rainwater, whose insatiable culinary curiosity and enthusiasm exist in a class by itself. He deserves a special award for giving my palate a range that roams from the fajitas of Fort Worth to the foie gras of Manhattan's Quilted Giraffe.

The confidence to write this cookbook would have stayed in incubative stages far longer if it were not for the opportunities and New York notoriety so warmly extended to me by Sheila Lukins and Julee Rosso of The Silver Palate. I am most appreciative. Both my agent Reid Boates and my editor Suzanne Rafer deserve rounds and rounds of Champagne toasts for guiding my Nantucket naïveté through the perils of publishing. I am also especially indebted to Suzanne for being able to maintain the unique balance between caring friend and respected mentor.

Though our paths scarcely cross, I am grateful to Sonya Pollack for sharing the sanctuary of her home in Dionis with me through the winters of working on this book. The coziness and isolation have given me many blissful hours of writing and recipe testing.

Last, but certainly not least, there is very deep felt acknowledgment for my Nantucket staff and friends—Sterling, Olga, Candace, Elena, Ann, Ellen, John, and Jerry—who keep me laughing even while chopping onions and make me feel loved through even the worst kitchen calamities. A final P.S. goes to Kitdi Dolce and Richard Meech, two who provide me with the magic of spiritual companionship.

Contents

Que Sera Sarah

*We owe much to the fruitful meditation of our sages, but a sane
view of life is, after all, elaborated mainly in the kitchen.*
—JOSEPH CONRAD

A long time ago, I used to study language philosophy late
into the night. I would lie awake pondering whether language
determined reality, or reality language. I dreamed of becoming a
semiologist, not a chef.

Today, I still possess a restlessness that keeps me awake and
curious at odd hours of the night. Now, however, more often
than not I am lost in a mouthwatering mound of the latest
cooking publications. I worry less about which came first—the
chicken or the egg—and more about the best ways to roast a
chicken, hard boil an egg, roll a grape leaf, or intensify the flavor
of a sorbet. This transformation from the world of ideas to the art
of creating gastronomic delights occurred through nothing more
extraordinary, than falling in love.

But the circumstances were not quite so predictable: an
irresistibly arrogant and nimble French chef didn't whisk me
away to a three-star auberge to live plumply ever after; a dark,
alluring Italian count didn't twirl my tender heart helplessly like
just so many strands of fettuccine; an elegant sushi roller didn't
set my romantic sensibilities blindly ablaze with a fiery blast of
wasabi paste; and a gorgeous, young California Adonis posing as
a culinary star didn't bring about a confusion between passion
fruit and true fulfillment. No, I fell irrevocably in love—not with a
person or an ideal or even a cuisine, but with of all things, an
island—Nantucket Island.

There was absolutely nothing subtle about this seduction, as
Nantucket has it all and almost too much: lucent baby blue skies;
blustery cumulus days; impenetrable fogs and gentle lavender
mists; waters that sparkle, lap, wave, and enchant everywhere in
dramatic cliffside seascapes, cozy harbors, sensuously duned
beaches, and even secluded inland ponds. There is sun that
shines often, hugging people, hydrangeas, and curious old attics
alike and rains that intimidate with fervent but cleansing tan-
trums. Graceful old elms and oaks shade, pine forests remain
hidden secrets, and twisted lanes and cobblestoned streets
captivate with quaintness. Stately old sea captains' homes cluster throughout the town as if to lend historical anchor to the

island's etherealness; but, then, they too are imbued with spirituality as legends of household ghosts are common and whisper of long lost others who could never bear to leave Nantucket, either.

In retrospect, I should have grasped that cooking would become my creative and emotional outlet. I was thirteen years old when I first came to Nantucket to summer as a mother's helper for a favorite aunt and uncle who ran a fascinating antiques business on the island. I was warmly welcomed into their immaculately restored sea captain's house. My sunny golden bedroom served as a microcosm of Nantucket history as it was filled with island treasures—old lightship baskets, whirligigs, seafaring chests, whaling journals, island-loomed blankets, and just-polished brass candlesticks. I loved to gaze down at the wisteria bordered patio below or dream for long hours in front of the sparkling harbor view. But, my very favorite part of the house was the kitchen—a singular blending of early American antiques, state-of-the-art appliances, and irresistible new aromas. My aunt was (and always will be) a fabulous cook. While every little aspect of Nantucket seemed to strike my fancy with magical power, it was in truth the creations and flavors of my aunt's kitchen that were to linger the most indelibly.

My favorite chores as a mother's helper became those of assisting in the family meals and learning hors d'oeuvre assembly for the busy entertaining schedule. As a neophyte, I was initially astounded by the amounts of food my aunt would prepare. My most repeated refrain became, "Auntie Diane, why are you preparing so much food?" It didn't take long to grasp the answer and it was at this point that I learned several essential lessons that were to have a grand influence on the development of my own approach to cooking. First, I noted that imaginative and skilled cooks attract an entertaining array of charismatic and appreciative friends, well versed in the art of spontaneously "dropping by" and loving to be unexpectedly fed. In short, plentiful food and exciting people go together.

Next, I was quick to glean that if one is to expend the effort and emotion required of the best culinary triumphs, it makes sense to prepare generous quantities to cover the next day's inevitable cravings. The third and most important insight for me, however, was realizing that there was something in my aunt's style of cooking that intuitively captured the very essence of Nantucket. Indeed, a meal in my aunt and uncle's Union Street home—the setting, the conversation, and of course the food— was capable of communicating almost all that needed to be known about the highly specialized art of loving Nantucket. In

subtle but unforgettable ways, all the generosity and outrageous-
ness of Nantucket abounded at their dinner table. (Leftovers, if
any, never lasted more than 24 hours.)

It took some maturing to sort out the real significance of all
my impressions. I continued to summer on Nantucket and to
visit whenever possible. In the meantime, I also took the usual
collegiate plunge into exploring the philosophical purpose of life.
A strange but satisfying balance ensued in spending part of my
year searing swordfish steaks and simmering batches of ratatouille and the rest dancing upon Nietzschean tightropes, dipping
into existential abysses, and waiting for Godot. An undeniable
clue to my future occurred when I realized that my stack of
Gourmet magazines had superceded in thickness my senior hon-
ors thesis on language. At that point I concluded I might fare
better by shedding the encumbering words of my abstract essays
and instead confront my love for Nantucket with the seemingly
more supple medium of cooking. Bertrand Russell beckoned no
longer and instead Brillat-Savarin blazed the path to new ways of
communication and fulfillment—"Tell me what you eat, and I will
tell you what you are!"

As I was understandably nervous about my leap from scholar
to shopkeeper, I decided to name my food business "Que Sera
Sarah," reasoning that if one questionable course of life failed, the
name was versatile enough to sustain a few more trial ventures.
Perserverance prevailed and eventually gained me an adorable
and affordable pink (Heaven!) shuttered shop in a former rooming
house in the heart of town.

Once I got the life's investment of kitchen equipment—which
was too wide to pass through the narrow Nantucket doorways—
off the street and into the shop, I hired the artist/tenant on the
floor above me, to help with the chopping, dicing, and dishing of
both salads and people. I also snagged a beautiful wandering
student, who read *Women in Love* during the store's initial slow
moments, to sell the first culinary creations. I had no real scheme
in mind except to cook the foods I liked most, which were
predominantly cold preparations, utilizing Nantucket's ocean
bounty in combination with inspirations from European travels. I
hoped that if I approached this task with enough integrity and
passion, other lovers of Nantucket would share in an appetite for
my personal culinary whims. The transition to the professional
field of cooking was not terribly difficult, as I soon discovered
that my Sabatier chopping knives were almost as dangerous as
collegiate nihilism, and that the very hands that once beheld
being and nothingness so well adjusted amiably to onions and
potatoes.

From the beginning, the Que Sera Sarah shop exuded a cross-section of Nantucket's iconoclastic artistic energy. It was never my policy to hire highly trained professional cooks, as I preferred surrounding myself with an eclectic range of painters, carpenters, writers, designers, philosophers, and entrepreneurs. I found that their interpretation of food as well as their knowledge of passing topics, staved off any forms of culinary drudgery.

For example, Sterling captured on canvas the odd pieces of cake or stray caviar eggs that did not sell and gave the most accurate astrological forecasts daily, predicted according to the ease with which the croissant dough rolled out. Elena would titillate, amuse, and shock with random excerpts from a current writing assignment—about her life with an emotional vampire—while tossing a batch of Kielbasa Vinaigrette. Olga knew every scandalous event that had occurred on the island in the last fifteen years (let alone past fifteen minutes) and possessed a unique talent for making up instant song lyrics. A kitchen favorite began: "I know it's late, I know you're weary. Why don't we bake?" Through all this chatter, Jane could be found quietly kneading peasant bread in a far corner to the rhythmic meter of her next poetry endeavor. And in the midst of these wonderfully inspiring scenes, I would take on the role of kitchen choreographer. I drained Moroccan Carrots, snatched the oatmeal cookies from the oven at the perfect moment, whisked in an egg yolk here and there to bind a mayonnaise back together, and always placed the hearts tenderly on each sausage in brioche. A sane view of life was, after all, elaborated mainly in the kitchen.

The past six years spent cooking have successfully provided the chance to take the beautiful raw ingredients of my beloved island and evoke through taste and personal stylization, many other sensory appeals of my life on Nantucket. I have learned how to cook fish so that it summarizes the sea, to arrange tomatoes in alternating splashes of red and orange in tribute to Madaket sunsets, and to seal memories of September in jars of beach plum jam. The endless hours I devote to the perfection of foods in the Que Sera Sarah shop are seldom questioned because only an environment as generous as that of Nantucket can inspire such devotion and loyalty. The kitchen days that still begin at 6A.M. and end near midnight bring to mind the saying: "Cooking is like love—it should be entered into with abandon or not at all." Such a sentiment seems to go hand in hand with the abandon it takes to live, laugh, and thrive on an island thirty miles out to sea.

Sarah Leah Chase
Nantucket Island, May 1987

Appetizers and Favorite Nibbling Foods

"When shall we live if not now?"
—SENECA

—————

It seems clear to me that those who lead the most enviable lives in a summer retreat are endowed with natural spontaneity and guiltless abandon. When there are warming rays of the sun to absorb, endlessly cresting waves to ride, billowing spinnakers to sail, wild pink roses to inhale, ripening blueberries and raspberries to gather, monumental novels to escape into, cool silver shooting stars to gaze at, and indeed all of summer's sizzling passion to savor, there is little time left to think of meals in a traditional and boringly balanced fashion. Nonetheless the food consumed should have an intensity equal to the life sustained. Nibbling at whim on selective, seductive, and savory morsels has always seemed to me the perfect way to breeze through summer holidays.

The recipes that make up this versatile collection were born out of enjoying many, many summers of plenty on Nantucket Island. Share them with lots of friends or simply secrete them away for private indulgence when the mood strikes.

Scallop Puffs Que Sera

A very favorite Nantucket hors d'oeuvre among friends and customers. The recipe makes twelve dozen puffs, but they need not be made all at once. The scallop mixture keeps for a week in the refrigerator, so that you can make them as needed for spur-of-the-moment entertaining.

3 tablespoons unsalted butter

1 pound bay scallops, quartered

2 teaspoons finely minced lemon zest

3 cloves garlic, minced

3 tablespoons chopped fresh dill

2 cups grated Swiss or Gruyère cheese

2¼ cups Hellmann's mayonnaise

Freshly ground pepper to taste

12 dozen 1-inch bread rounds cut from good-quality commercial white sandwich bread, lightly toasted

Sweet Hungarian paprika

Lemon slices and dill sprigs for garnish

1. Melt the butter in a medium skillet or sauté pan over medium-high heat. Add the scallops, lemon zest, and garlic. Cook, stirring constantly, until the scallops are just barely cooked through, 2 to 3 minutes. Add the dill and cook 30 seconds longer. Let cool to room temperature.

2. Add the cheese, mayonnaise, and pepper to the scallop mixture and stir to combine well. Refrigerate in a covered bowl until ready to use, but no longer than a week.

3. Preheat the broiler.

4. Place the toast rounds ½ inch apart on baking sheets. Top each toast round with a heaping teaspoon of the scallop mixture and sprinkle lightly with paprika.

5. Broil the puffs 5 inches from the heat until puffed and golden, 2 to 3 minutes. Transfer the puffs to platters and garnish with lemon slices and dill sprigs. Serve hot.

Makes 12 dozen.

CAVIAR TARTINES
OR
THE BEST WAY TO EAT CAVIAR

To begin with, the best way to eat caviar is to eat only the best—Russian Beluga. Next, the pomp and circumstance of elaborate caviar paraphernalia must be removed in favor of somewhat more peasanty infusions—fresh crusty bread and slabs of sweet butter. A 125-gram tin of Beluga is the preferred size, for anything smaller is too dainty. The company should be kept to a minimum, perhaps, to just your favorite person in the entire world. There must definitely be drink; either your most coveted bottle of French Champagne or crystal shooters of iced 100-proof vodka would do. Moonlight and the sound of the surf breaking in the background are lovely too but not entirely necessary.

The scene set, the bread must be sliced—about ½ inch thick—and then spread generously with sweet butter. Sterling silver is always appropriate for this action. Then, literally slather the buttered bread with a fortune of the precious eggs—more than you would ever dare be caught consuming in public. This is your basic caviar tartine—a fabulous balance of extravagance and simple peasantry.

Repeat over and over again breaking only for sighs of ecstacy and sips of Champagne or shots of vodka. For the duration of the caviar supply and the period of ensuing afterglow, you will know what it is like to leave the shadowy world of earthly foods and ascend to the purest level of Platonic inception.

Caviar Ceviche

Serve this loosely interpreted ceviche on dainty glass plates as a sophisticated starter at a formal party. Small flutes of iced vodka would make a perfect accompaniment.

1 pound bay scallops	1 jar (30 grams) Sevruga
½ cup fresh lemon juice	caviar
3 tablespoons vodka	Thin lemon slices and
2 teaspoons very finely	fresh parsley or other
grated lemon zest	leafy herb for garnish
¾ to 1 cup crème fraîche	
or sour cream	

1. Toss the scallops, lemon juice, vodka, and lemon zest together in a mixing bowl. Cover and let marinate in the refrigerator for 4 hours.

2. Just before serving, drain the scallops thoroughly and toss with enough crème fraîche to bind. Quickly and gently fold in the caviar, being careful not to break the delicate eggs. Spoon the ceviche on 8 plates and garnish with lemon slices and a sprig or two of parsley.

Makes 8 appetizer servings.

Cornmeal Blinis with Favorite Caviars

These fluffy little golden pancakes make an elegant first course when served on individual plates or quite the decadent nibble when passed hors-d'oeuvre style at parties. I like to top these blinis with three caviars. If you are feeling extravagant, try Beluga, Ossetra, and Sevruga, although a selection of good American caviars such as golden, salmon, and sturgeon will sparkle as well.

1 package (¼ ounce)
  active dry yeast
½ cup warm water (105°
  to 115° F)
1 cup light cream
1 cup unbleached
  all-purpose flour
½ cup yellow cornmeal

3 large eggs, separated
1 teaspoon sugar
½ teaspoon salt
½ cup (1 stick) unsalted
  butter, melted and cooled
1 cup crème fraîche
3 jars (2 ounces each) of
  3 different caviars

1. Sprinkle the yeast over the warm water in a small bowl and let stand for 5 minutes. Pour the yeast mixture into a blender and add the cream, flour, cornmeal, egg yolks, sugar, salt, and melted butter. Blend until smooth. Pour into a large bowl, cover with plastic wrap, and let rise in a warm, draft-free place until doubled in bulk, 1 to 1½ hours.

2. Beat the egg whites in a mixing bowl until soft peaks form. Gently fold the whites into the batter just until incorporated.

3. Heat a griddle over medium-high heat and brush lightly with butter. Drop the batter 2 tablespoons at a time onto the griddle to make little pancakes 1½ inches in diameter. Cook, turning once, until lightly browned on both sides. Transfer the blinis to a baking sheet. Place in a single layer. Repeat with the remaining batter until all are cooked.

4. When you are ready to serve, warm the blinis briefly in a skillet or in a preheated 350°F oven just until warm to the touch. Top each blini with a dollop of crème fraîche and then a small spoonful of one of the caviars. Serve at once.

Makes about 3½ dozen.

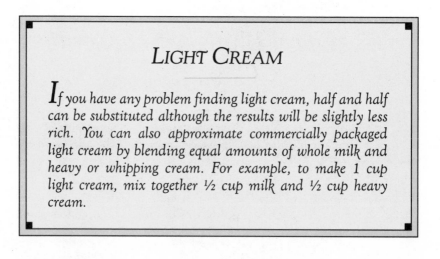

LIGHT CREAM

If you have any problem finding light cream, half and half can be substituted although the results will be slightly less rich. You can also approximate commercially packaged light cream by blending equal amounts of whole milk and heavy or whipping cream. For example, to make 1 cup light cream, mix together ½ cup milk and ½ cup heavy cream.

Steamed Clams Que Sera

Charting the tides, squinting in search of myopic clam holes, and breaking a fingernail or two while furrowing for bivalves are among the simpler summer pleasures of shore living, but cooking up a great feast of one's labor makes the day one of the most rewarding of the lazy sunny season.

5 dozen littleneck or
    steamer clams
⅓ cup olive oil
3 cloves garlic, minced
4 ounces hard Italian
    sausage, cut into
    ¼-inch dice
3 ripe medium tomatoes,
    seeded and cut into
    ½-inch dice
1 tablespoon dried
    oregano

1 teaspoon dried red
    pepper flakes
1 teaspoon fennel seeds
Salt and freshly ground
    pepper to taste
1½ cups dry white wine
3 tablespoons fresh lemon
    juice
3 tablespoons chopped
    fresh basil

1. Scrub and rinse the clams under cold running water to make sure they are free of sand and grit.

2. Heat the oil in a pot large enough for cooking the clams over high heat. Add the garlic, sausage, and tomatoes and cook, stirring constantly, for 5 minutes. Add the oregano, red pepper flakes, fennel seeds, salt, and pepper; cook 1 minute longer.

3. Pour the wine and lemon juice into the pot and then add the clams. Sprinkle the basil over the top and cover the pot tightly. Cook the clams just until they all open.

4. Ladle the clams and cooking liquid into shallow bowls and serve with crusty bread.

Makes 12 to 15 appetizer servings, or 4 to 6 light entrée servings.

Roasted Garlic

T his is a perfect example of very simple food that is purely fabulous. While squeezing the garlic out of the roasted husks can be a bit messy, it is part and parcel of the whole sensual enjoyment of this preparation.

8 whole heads fresh garlic
⅓ cup extra-virgin olive
  oil
1½ teaspoons coarsely
  ground pepper

1½ teaspoons dried
  thyme
1 teaspoon salt

1. Preheat the oven to 350°F.
2. Trim the point off each garlic head to expose the tops of the cloves. Place the heads next to each other in a shallow baking dish, such as a 9-inch pie plate. Drizzle the heads with the oil and sprinkle evenly with the pepper, thyme, and salt.
3. Roast the garlic for 30 minutes. Reduce the temperature to 250°F and cook 1 hour longer.
4. Serve the garlic with slices of crusty French bread, butter, and goat cheese if you like. Pop the cloves out of the skins and spread on the bread.
Makes 8 servings.

French Onion Tart

O ne bite of this delectably rich and savory tart creates instant transport to the sybaritic south of France. It makes a popular party hors d'oeuvre when cut into small squares and garnished with olives and springs of fresh herbs. Cut into large squares, the tart is an indulgent form of luncheon sustenance to fuel a day spent lazing on a sandy beach.

½ recipe Pizza Dough (see page 80)

ANCHOVY PESTO SPREAD:

3 cans (2 ounces each) anchovy fillets (about 20)

3 cloves garlic, minced

2 tablespoons balsamic vinegar

½ cup fresh parsley leaves

1 teaspoon dried thyme

2 large egg yolks

1 cup fresh white bread crumbs

¾ cup olive oil

Freshly ground pepper to taste

1 to 2 tablespoons fresh lemon juice

FILLING:

¼ cup olive oil

4 very large Spanish onions, cut into thin rings

1 tablespoon sugar

2 cloves garlic, finely minced

Niçoise olives and parsley sprigs for garnish

1. Make the pizza dough up to the point it is ready to roll out.

2. Prepare the anchovy pesto spread: Place the anchovies, garlic, vinegar, parsley, and thyme in a food processor fitted with the steel blade. Process to a smooth paste. Add the egg yolks and bread crumbs and process again until smooth. With the machine running, pour the oil through the feed tube in a thin, steady stream and process until the mixture is thick and creamy. Season to taste with pepper and lemon juice.

3. Prepare the filling: Heat the oil in a 4-quart pot over medium-high heat. Add the onions and cook, stirring frequently, for 10 minutes. Reduce the heat to medium-low and continue to cook, stirring frequently, for another 10 minutes. Stir in the sugar and cook 5 minutes longer. Finally, stir in the garlic and cook another 5 minutes. Remove from the heat.

4. Preheat the oven to 375°F. Brush a 15 x 10-inch baking sheet lightly with olive oil.

5. To assemble the tart, roll out the pizza dough to fit the baking sheet. Place the dough in the pan and crimp the edges decoratively. Using a rubber spatula, spread about 1 cup of the anchovy pesto spread in a thin even layer over the dough. (The remaining spread can be stored in the refrigerator up to 2 weeks and used for another tart or as a sandwich spread or vegetable

dip.) Spread the onion filling evenly over the anchovy spread.

6. Bake the tart until the edges are crusty and golden brown, 30 to 40 minutes. Let cool to room temperature. Cut into small or large squares and garnish with Niçoise olives and parsley sprigs.

Makes 15 x 10-inch tart.

Marinated Goat Cheeses

I always have a large platter of these dumplinglike cheeses marinating on one of the store counters. They are so beautiful spattered with brilliant green summer basil and pretty pink peppercorns shimmering under a bath of rich olive oil. The crusty heel of a loaf of French bread and, perhaps, a smear of two of roasted garlic are natural accompaniments.

8 Crottin goat cheeses
   (2 to 3 ounces each) or
   other small, round,
   hard goat cheeses
1½ cups extra-virgin
   olive oil
4 bay leaves
1 tablespoon mixed
   white, black, and green
   peppercorns

1½ tablespoons dried
   thyme
3 large cloves garlic, cut
   into slivers
3 tablespoons slivered
   fresh basil
1 tablespoon dried pink
   peppercorns

1. Place the goat cheeses on an ovenproof platter or flat dish large enough to hold the cheeses without touching. An earthenware pie plate works well.

2. Heat the oil, bay leaves, mixed peppercorns, and dried thyme in a small saucepan over medium-high heat until you hear the mixture begin to sizzle and pop. Immediately remove from the heat and pour over the cheeses.

3. Scatter the slivered garlic in the marinade and sprinkle with the basil and pink peppercorns. Let marinate in the refrigerator overnight to firm up the cheeses. Bring to room temperature before serving.

Makes 8 appetizer servings or 24 hors d'oeuvre servings.

Sausage in Brioche

Decorative and delicious, sausages in brioche are equally popular for an impulse breakfast, lunch, or snack or, sliced into bite-size rounds, as a cocktail nibble. The plump little dough heart adorning each sausage adds great flair.

BRIOCHE DOUGH:

1 package (¼ ounce) active dry yeast
1 tablespoon sugar
⅔ cup milk, heated just until warm to the touch (110 to 115° F)
4 large eggs

4 to 4½ cups unbleached all-purpose flour
1 cup (2 sticks) unsalted butter, melted and cooled
2 teaspoons salt

FILLING:

8 tablespoons Dijon mustard
16 thin slices Provolone cheese

16 cheddarwurst sausages or other plump smoked sausages 5 to 6 inches long

EGG WASH:

1 large egg

1 tablespoon water

1. The day before you plan to serve the sausages, prepare the brioche dough: Place the yeast and sugar in a mixing bowl and pour in the warm milk. Let stand until puffed and foamy, about 5 minutes. Whisk in 2 of the eggs and about ¾ cup flour to make a mixture of the consistency of pancake batter. Cover the bowl with plastic wrap or a damp towel. Let rise in a warm, draft-free place until tripled or more in size, 1½ hours.

2. Transfer the mixture to a heavy-duty mixer fitted with a dough hook or a large mixing bowl if making the dough by hand. Add the remaining 2 eggs, the butter, and salt and mix until well combined. Gradually work in the remaining flour to make a soft (not stiff) elastic dough.

3. Transfer the dough to a clean large bowl. Cover with plastic wrap or a damp towel and let rise overnight in a cool spot or in the refrigerator.

4. The following day, preheat the oven to 375°F. Line 2 large baking sheets with parchment paper.

5. Roll out half the dough ¼ inch thick on a lightly floured surface. Cut the dough into eight 5-inch squares. Reserve the scraps for making the decorations later.

6. Spread ½ tablespoon Dijon mustard down the center of each square. Top with 1 slice of the Provolone. Place a sausage on the cheese. Roll up the sausage in the dough and seal the seam (not the ends) with your fingertips. Place the rolls seam side down and 2 inches apart on the prepared baking sheet. Repeat with the remaining dough, mustard, cheese, and sausages.

7. Mix the egg and water in a small bowl. Using a pastry brush, brush each roll with the egg wash. Gather all the scraps of dough together and roll out ¼ inch thick. Cut out hearts (or another shape) with a 1- to 1½-inch cookie cutter and place 1 heart on the top of each roll. Brush the rolls again with the egg wash.

8. Bake the rolls until light golden brown all over, 25 to 30 minutes. Serve the sausages hot or at room temperature. They can also be reheated in a 350°F oven for 5 to 7 minutes.

Makes 16 servings.

BRIE IN BRIOCHE

*B*rioche dough can also be used to enclose 8 to 10 baby ½-pound wheels or two 1 kilo wheels of Brie. Roll the dough into a circle large enough to completely cover each wheel. Wrap the wheel in dough, trim any excess, and place seam side down on a parchment-lined baking sheet. Brush the top and side of the dough with egg wash and decorate with shapes cut from the scraps of dough. Strips of dough braided or woven into a lattice make pretty designs. Brush the dough again with the egg wash and bake in a preheated 375°F oven until light golden brown about 25 to 30 minutes. Be careful not to overbake; if the Brie melts too much it will ooze out of the dough.

Serve the Brie at room temperature, for if it is hot it will be too runny and messy to eat. The baby wheels make great picnic fare, and the larger wheels always make a dressy and delicious presentation for cocktail parties.

Country Pâté with Beer and Fennel

This recipe has been a longtime favorite. It is a rather coarse-textured pâté packed with strong, distinctive flavors. While delightful served in the traditional manner with a crock of tart cornichons, it is even more irresistible when tucked into a crusty loaf of French bread with lots of mustard. The best part of making this pâté is that a good swig or two of the cooking beer always seems to make the assembly of the recipe seem almost effortless.

5 tablespoons unsalted butter

2 large onions, chopped

5 cloves garlic, minced

1 bunch scallions (white bulbs and green stalks), sliced

1½ cups fresh parsley leaves, minced

½ cup shelled pistachios

2 tablespoons fennel seeds

3 pounds sweet Italian sausage, removed from casings

2 cups beer, preferably imported

1 pound lean ground veal

1 pound sliced bacon

1 package (8 ounces) Pepperidge Farm's herb-seasoned crumb stuffing

4 or 5 large eggs

Salt and freshly ground pepper to taste

6 whole bay leaves

1. Melt the butter in a large skillet over medium-high heat. Add the onions, garlic, and scallions and cook until soft and translucent, about 7 minutes, stirring occasionally. Transfer the onion mixture to a large mixing bowl. Stir in the parsley, pistachios, and fennel seeds.

2. Sauté the sausage in 2 batches in the same skillet over medium-high heat. Cook each batch for 2 or 3 minutes, crumbling the sausage into smaller pieces with the back of a wooden spoon. Add ½ cup of beer to each batch and cook just until the sausage is no longer pink. Add each batch to the mixing bowl and stir to combine with the onions.

3. Add the ground veal to the same skillet and cook with another ½ cup beer just until the veal is no longer pink. Add to the mixing bowl.

4. Cut 6 slices of bacon into ½-inch dice. Cook in the same skillet until the bacon renders some of its fat; do not let it begin to become crisp. Add the crumb stuffing and the remaining ½ cup beer. Cook, stirring constantly, for 30 seconds and then add to the mixing bowl.

5. Add 4 eggs to the pâté mixture and beat to make a moist, but not wet, meat-loaf–like mixture. Add the last egg if necessary to bind the mixture. Season with salt and freshly ground pepper.

6. Preheat the oven to 350°F.

7. Place 3 bay leaves in a row down the center of each of two 9 x 3-inch loaf pans. Line each pan with the remaining bacon slices by arranging the strips crosswise in the pan to line both the sides and bottom. Let the ends of the slices hang over the edges of the pan.

8. Pack the pâté mixture very tightly into the pans, pressing down firmly with the back of a spoon or your hands. Fold the overhanging bacon over the top of each pâté. Completely wrap each pan tightly with aluminum foil. Place the pans in a larger baking pan and fill the pan with enough hot water to come halfway up the sides of the pâté pans.

9. Bake the pâtés for 1½ hours. Remove the pâtés from the oven and weight for several hours with a heavy object (such as a 5-pound bag of flour or a large can of tomatoes) placed on each pâté. Refrigerate for several hours.

10. To unmold the pâtés, run a knife around the sides of each pan and invert the pâté onto a clean surface.

11. The pâté will keep up to 2 weeks, tightly wrapped in the refrigerator. The pâté can also be frozen, tightly wrapped in plastic wrap and then in aluminum foil, up to 2 months.

Makes two 9 x 3-inch pâtés.

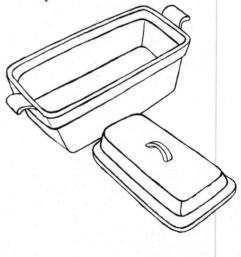

Sicilian Loaf

I used to make this recipe years ago as a hot meat leaf when it was my turn to cook a family meal. Over the years my fanaticism for cold foods has given reincarnation to Sicilian Loaf as one of my shop's most popular chilled pâtés. When sliced thinly, the roulade effect of the baked prosciutto and provolone makes a very pretty presentation. Leftovers make robust sandwiches layered with strong mustard, lettuce, and sliced garden tomatoes.

1½ pounds ground beef
   sirloin
1 pound ground veal
1 medium onion, chopped
4 cloves garlic, minced
2 tablespoons dried
   Italian herb blend
½ cup chopped fresh
   parsley
2½ cups fresh bread
   crumbs

2 large eggs
1 cup tomato juice
1 tablespoon salt
2 teaspoons freshly
   ground pepper
8 ounces thinly sliced
   ham or prosciutto
12 ounces sliced
   Provolone cheese

1. Place the sirloin, veal, onion, garlic, Italian herbs, parsley, and bread crumbs in a large mixing bowl and mix it together with your hands. Add the eggs and tomato juice and blend it in with your hands to bind the mixture. Season to taste with salt and freshly ground pepper.

2. Preheat the oven to 350°F.

3. Place a large sheet of parchment or waxed paper on a work surface. Shape the meat mixture into a 15 x 10-inch rectangle on the paper. Arrange the ham in an even layer over the meat mixture. Cover the ham with 8 ounces of the sliced cheese. Starting from one long side of the rectangle, roll up the meat loaf like a jelly roll and pat the ends gently to make a good loaf shape.

4. Pulling on the paper, carefully slide the meat loaf onto a large baking sheet. Bake for 50 minutes. Arrange the remaining cheese over the top of the meat loaf and bake until the cheese is lightly browned and bubbling, about 10 minutes longer.

5. Let the loaf cool to room temperature, then wrap it in aluminum foil and refrigerate for several hours or overnight. Using a serrated knife, slice it into ¼-inch slices.

Makes 8 entrée servings or 20 to 25 hors d'oeuvre servings.

Smoked Bluefish Pâté

A popular and very Nantucket appetizer.

1 pound smoked bluefish, skinned and flaked

12 ounces cream cheese, at room temperature and cut into small chunks

6 tablespoons unsalted butter, at room temperature and cut into bits

1 medium red onion, minced

¼ cup chopped fresh dill

2 tablespoons capers, drained

3 tablespoons fresh lemon juice

2 tablespoons Cognac

Freshly ground pepper to taste

Lemon wedges and capers for garnish

French Toast Rounds (recipe follows)

1. Beat the bluefish, cream cheese, and butter in a mixing bowl with a hand mixer just until combined. Add the onion, dill, capers, lemon juice, and Cognac; beat until blended but do not overbeat so that the pâté will have some texture. Season to taste with pepper.

2. Pack the pâté into small crocks or 1 large one. Cover and refrigerate for a few hours to mellow the flavors. Garnish with lemon wedges and capers and serve at room temperature with toast rounds.

Makes about 3 cups.

French Toast Rounds

While these toasts were invented simply as a way to use up stale bread, they have developed such a devoted following that we now have to bake extra bread just to meet the demand. One customer from Connecticut is so addicted to these that we have named him "Mr. Toast." The toast rounds do add a nice homemade look when serving cheeses and pâtés, and I must admit these are indeed quite delicious.

2 loaves day-old French
    bread, cut into ¼-inch-
    thick slices
½ cup olive oil

1½ tablespoons fines
    herbes or Italian herb
    blend

1. Preheat the oven to 350°F.

2. Arrange the bread slices in a single layer on baking sheets. Lightly brush 1 side of each slice all over with oil, then sprinkle lightly with the herbs.

3. Bake just until crisp and light golden brown, 12 to 15 minutes. Let cool to room temperature and store in an airtight container.

Makes 4 to 5 dozen.

Pastel Chicken Pâté

This pâté is full of the complex flavors of other pâtés but is lighter in texture and summery in color.

8 whole boneless, skinless
    chicken breasts, cut
    into ½-inch chunks
1 cup plus 3 tablespoons
    snipped fresh chives
5 tablespoons chopped
    fresh tarragon
1¼ cups diced thinly
    sliced baked ham
½ cup shelled pistachios
5 tablespoons pink
    peppercorns

⅔ cup Cognac
2 teaspoons salt, or more
    to taste
1 teaspoon freshly ground
    black pepper, plus
    additional
2 large eggs
2 large egg whites
½ teaspoon grated
    nutmeg
2½ cups heavy or
    whipping cream

1. Place one-quarter of the chicken breasts in a large mixing bowl. Add 1 cup chives, 3 tablespoons tarragon, the ham, pistachios, pink peppercorns, ⅓ cup Cognac, 2 teaspoons salt, and 1 teaspoon black pepper; toss together. Let the mixture marinate at room temperature for 30 minutes.

2. Meanwhile, place the remaining chicken breasts in a food processor fitted with the steel blade and process until the meat is ground. Add the eggs and egg whites and process until smooth.

Add the remaining ⅓ cup Cognac, 3 tablespoons chives, 2 tablespoons tarragon, and the nutmeg and process until blended. With the machine running, pour the heavy cream through the feed tube and process until thoroughly blended.

3. Preheat the oven to 350°F. Brush a 16 x 5-inch loaf pan with vegetable oil.

4. Add the processed mixture to the marinated mixture in the mixing bowl and stir until well combined. Spoon the pâté mixture into the prepared pan. Cover with aluminum foil. Place the pan in a larger baking pan and fill the larger pan with enough hot water to come halfway up the sides of the pâté pan. Bake until the top of the pâté is just firm to the touch, about 1 hour. Let cool to room temperature. Invert onto a clean surface, wrap in plastic wrap, and refrigerate until ready to serve.

Makes 16 x 5-inch pâté.

June Taylor Chicken Legs

I was at first dismayed when I realized that of all the esoteric fare available at the store these simple chicken drumsticks were one of the most popular items. Then I thought of the little legs in a chorus line, and that infused enough humor into the daily preparation of trays and trays to make it enjoyable.

20 to 24 chicken
   drumsticks
⅓ cup vegetable oil
½ cup Dijon mustard
⅓ cup dry white wine

Salt and coarsely ground
   black pepper to taste
1½ cups fresh bread
   crumbs

1. Preheat the oven to 350°F.

2. Arrange the drumsticks in rows on a large baking sheet. Using a pastry brush, brush each drumstick lightly with oil. Whisk the mustard and wine together in a small bowl and brush this mixture generously over each drumstick. Sprinkle the drumsticks with salt and pepper, then sprinkle the bread crumbs evenly over all the drumsticks.

3. Bake the drumsticks for 50 to 60 minutes. Cover the drumsticks with aluminum foil if they seem to be getting too brown. Serve the drumsticks warm or at room temperature arranged on a large platter in a chorus line.

Makes 10 to 12 hors d'oeuvre servings.

Summer Steak Tartare

This wonderful rendition of classic steak tartare captures the flavors and fragrances of summer and takes a delicious bit of license with the standard presentation.

1½ pounds finely ground very lean beef tenderloin

3 shallots, minced

1 clove garlic, minced

1½ tablespoons capers, drained

½ cup chopped fresh basil

½ cup chopped fresh parsley

10 sun-dried tomatoes, packed in oil, drained and minced

2½ tablespoons Dijon mustard

2 tablespoons Cognac (optional)

2 large egg yolks

Salt and freshly ground pepper to taste

1 bunch arugula

2 ounce wedge Parmesan cheese

2 hard-cooked egg yolks, pressed through fine sieve

1. Using your hands, thoroughly combine the beef, shallots, garlic, capers, basil, parsley, sun-dried tomatoes, mustard, and Cognac in a mixing bowl. Blend in the raw egg yolks and season the mixture with salt and pepper.

2. Line a serving plate with arugula leaves. Mound the steak tartare on the center of the plate. Shave the wedge of Parmesan cheese with a vegetable peeler to make thin shards and scatter them over the steak tartare and arugula leaves. Sprinkle the sieved egg yolks over all to create a fine spattered effect. Serve at once with toast points.

Makes 8 servings.

Orange Rosemary Muffins with Sliced Duck Breast

The pronounced flavors in these savory bite-size sandwich hors d'oeuvres capture the essence of summer lushness.

ORANGE ROSEMARY MUFFINS:

½ cup (1 stick) unsalted butter, at room temperature
1 cup sugar
2 large eggs
2 cups unbleached all-purpose flour
1 teaspoon baking soda
½ teaspoon salt
1 cup sour cream or well-shaken buttermilk
1 cup golden raisins
1 large orange, zest grated, orange juiced
1 tablespoon dried rosemary

DUCK BREASTS:

3 whole boneless duck breasts
¼ cup fresh orange juice
2 tablespoons orange-flavored liqueur
¼ cup fruity olive oil
Salt and freshly ground pepper to taste
Honey mustard

1. Prepare the muffins: Preheat the oven to 375°F. Lightly grease miniature muffin cups, 1½ inches in diameter.

2. Using an electric mixer, beat the butter and sugar in a mixing bowl until smooth and creamy. Beat in the eggs, one at a time, then continue beating until light and fluffy.

3. Sift the flour, baking soda, and salt together. Add the flour mixture to the butter mixture alternately with the sour cream, blending thoroughly after each addition.

4. Place the raisins, orange zest, and rosemary in a food processor fitted with the steel blade and process until finely minced. Stir the raisin mixture into the batter.

5. Spoon the batter into the muffin cups, filling each cup almost to the top. Bake until light golden brown, 10 to 12 minutes. Remove the muffins from oven and brush the tops lightly with the orange juice. Turn out onto a wire rack and let cool completely. You will have enough batter for about 5 dozen muffins.

6. Prepare the duck breasts: Grill the duck on an outdoor grill, preferably over mesquite or another flavorful wood chip.

Grill the breasts, skin side down, until the skin is well browned, 4 to 5 minutes. Turn the duck and grill 2 minutes longer for rare meat. Let the duck cool, then cut diagonally into thin slices.

7. Place the meat in a shallow bowl. Add the orange juice, liqueur, oil, salt, and pepper and toss to combine. Let marinate for at least 1 hour.

8. To serve, split each muffin in half and spread the bottoms with a generous dab of honey mustard. Fold a slice of marinated duck breast in half and place over the mustard. Replace the top on each muffin and when all are assembled, arrange in a flat basket or on a serving platter. These will hold unrefrigerated for to 2 to 3 hours if covered with a lightly dampened cloth.

Makes 5 dozen.

Sweet-Potato and Peanut Chips

A simple and irresistible nosh that finds its inspiration way down in the land of Dixie. When not serving them as a fast-to-disappear party hors d'oeuvre, try them as an accompaniment to barbecued ribs or Southern fried chicken.

¾ cup honey roasted peanuts
2 large sweet potatoes, peeled and sliced ⅛ inch thick

½ cup (1 stick) unsalted butter, melted
Salt to taste

1. Preheat the oven to 475°F. Line 2 large baking sheets with aluminum foil. Lightly butter the foil.

2. Process the peanuts in a food processor fitted with the steel blade until finely chopped but not powdered; transfer to a bowl. Dip the potato slices in the melted butter to coat both sides. Arrange the slices on the prepared pans in rows that are close together but not overlapping. Sprinkle the top of each potato slice generously with peanuts.

3. Bake the chips until the tops are lightly browned and the potatoes are just tender, 15 to 20 minutes. Watch carefully that they do not burn. Transfer the chips to paper towels to drain off any excess butter. Let cool 5 minutes. Taste and sprinkle with additional salt if desired. Arrange the chips on trays and serve.

Makes about 4 dozen.

Baby Chiles Rellenos

Although quite a bit of work to make, the delectable results make it all worthwhile. I love these.

2 cans (4 ounces each)
  whole green chiles
1 can (8 ounces) whole
  pimientos
8 ounces Monterey Jack
  cheese

8 ounces Monterey Jack
  cheese with jalapeño
  peppers

BATTER:

2 cups unbleached
  all-purpose flour
1 tablespoon ground
  cumin

2 teaspoons salt
2 cups beer, preferably
  imported

CORIANDER DIPPING SAUCE:

3 cloves garlic, minced
8 canned whole tomatillos
1 cup fresh coriander
  leaves
½ cup whole or slivered
  blanched almonds

⅓ cup fresh lime juice
½ cup olive oil
Salt and freshly ground
  pepper to taste

Vegetable oil for deep frying

1. Drain the cans of green chiles and pimientos. Cut the chiles and pimientos into ½-inch-wide strips. Cut both cheeses into ½-inch cubes. Wrap the green chile strips around the plain Monterey Jack cheese and the pimiento strips around the jalapeño Jack cheese, securing each with a wooden toothpick. Place them all on a tray and refrigerate for a few hours.

2. Meanwhile, prepare the batter: Stir the flour, cumin, and salt together in a mixing bowl. Add the beer and whisk until smooth. Let stand at room temperature for at least 1 hour.

3. Prepare the dipping sauce: Place the garlic, tomatillos, coriander, and almonds in a food processor fitted with the steel blade; process until smooth. Add the lime juice and olive oil and process until blended. Season with salt and pepper. Transfer to a small bowl.

4. Pour 1 inch vegetable oil into a large skillet and heat to 400°F. Dip the chilled cheese morsels, one at a time, in the beer batter and immediately drop in the hot oil. Do not crowd the pan. Fry, turning once, until light golden brown. Drain on paper towels. Serve immediately with the dipping sauce. (The chiles rellenos can be fried up to 3 hours in advance and reheated in a 375°F hot oven for 5 minutes, just before serving.)

Makes 4 to 4½ dozen.

Stuffed Grape Leaves (Dolmas)

I like my grape leaves cold or at room temperature and therefore prefer a filling without ground meat. These are done in the Persian tradition with the sweet addition of currants, cinnamon, and nutmeg balancing the saltiness of the brine-packed grape leaves in mysterious ways. The only problem with grape leaves is the time-consuming labor of rolling each individual one. During the late summer cocktail party frenzy, I often think I would trade all my food processors, attachments included, for an automatic grape-leaf roller. Short of that, friends' Greek mothers are always welcomed with open arms in late August.

FILLING:
½ cup plus 3 tablespoons olive oil
1 medium onion, minced
1½ cups converted rice
4 cups chicken stock, preferably homemade
½ cup dry white wine
⅔ cup currants
2 tablespoons ground cinnamon
1 teaspoon grated nutmeg
½ cup pine nuts, lightly toasted
1 cup minced fresh parsley
Salt and freshly ground pepper to taste

1 jar (16 ounces) grape leaves packed in brine (preferably from California, for they tend to be better than the imported Greek brands)
½ cup fresh lemon juice
½ cup water
Lemon slices and fresh mint sprigs for garnish

1. Heat 3 tablespoons oil in a large skillet over medium-high heat. Add the onion and cook for 4 minutes. Stir in the rice and cook 2 minutes longer, stirring to coat the rice well with the oil.

2. Reduce the heat to medium and pour in 2 cups of the chicken stock and the wine. Add the currants and simmer uncovered, stirring occasionally, for 10 minutes. Add 1½ cups more chicken stock and simmer 5 minutes longer. Add the remaining ½ cup chicken stock and cook another 5 minutes, watching the rice carefully throughout and stirring occasionally to prevent burning.

3. Reduce the heat to low, stir in the cinnamon and nutmeg, and cook 1 minute. Let cool, stirring occasionally to fluff the rice. Add the pine nuts and parsley and toss to combine. Season to taste with salt and pepper. (Be careful not to salt heavily as the grape leaves are quite salty.)

4. Rinse the grape leaves under cold running water and pat dry. Place 1 leaf, vein side up, on a dry working surface. Place about 1 tablespoon filling at the center stem end of the leaf. Shape the filling into a compact log, about 1 inch long, and roll up the leaf as tightly as possible, folding in the sides as you roll to make a compact bundle. Repeat with the remaining grape leaves and filling.

5. Line the bottom of a 4-quart pot with any torn grape leaves to prevent the stuffed leaves from burning and sticking to the pot. Pack the stuffed leaves in concentric circles in the pot, making as many layers as necessary.

6. Pour the lemon juice, ½ cup olive oil, and the water over the grape leaves. Place a heatproof plate on top of the grape leaves with a heavy can (such as tomatoes) on top. Simmer the grape leaves over medium heat for 40 minutes. Let cool completely with the plate and can still on top.

7. Arrange the grape leaves on a platter and garnish with lemon slices and sprigs of mint. Serve at room temperature or slightly chilled. Store any extra or leftover grape leaves in the refrigerator.

Makes about 60.

Sunny Sauces, Sips, and Skinny Dips

Those languorous spells of hot, hot, and hazy summer days call for effortless sustenance in a soothing variety of cooling liquid forms. The splendid selection of sauces in this chaper can all be made ahead and either dolloped on an entanglement of pasta or splashed atop sizzling fare from the grill at the last minute. The dips require just a flick or two of the food processor blade or, at most, a rhythmic flexing of the chopping knife. The sips—the most cooling enticement of all—demand only a good supply of ice, a liberal pouring hand, and a few choice libations spiked with a dash or two of island mixing secrets.

Great Guacamole

While it is not difficult to make authentic tasting Mexican guacamole, I find that few people north of Texas seem to develop the instincts for such. To be truly transported to the land of tequila, tacos, and *mañana*, a scoop of guacamole should be chunky in texture, balanced perfectly between the fire of jalapeño peppers and the soothing cool of lime juice, and spiced liberally with aromatic fresh coriander leaves. This much admired version is made daily in my shop.

8 Haas avocados (dark green small) or 4 large, smooth-skinned Florida avocados, at the peak of ripeness

4 ripe medium tomatoes, seeded and cut into ¼-inch dice

1 small red onion, coarsely chopped

2 fresh jalapeño peppers, seeded and finely chopped

½ cup fresh lime juice

3 tablespoons chopped fresh coriander leaves

Salt to taste

3 tablespoons Hellmann's mayonnaise

⅓ cup sour cream

1. Peel and pit the avocados and mash the pulp in a medium mixing bowl to a chunky consistency. A large wooden spoon or potato masher works well, but do not use a food processor or blender or the mixture will become too smooth.

2. Add the tomatoes, onion, and jalapeño peppers to the avocados and stir to combine. Stir in the lime juice, coriander, and salt. Fold in the mayonnaise to keep the guacamole from discoloring. Transfer the guacamole to an earthenware or ceramic serving dish; make an indentation in the center and spoon in the sour cream. Serve with plenty of your favorite corn tortilla chips.

Makes 4 to 4½ cups.

Tomatillo Salsa

A slippery green version of the more traditional red salsa. Use as a dip for tortilla chips or as a sauce with cold poached chicken or shellfish.

3 cups whole tomatillos,
 fresh or canned, peeled
2 ripe medium tomatoes,
 seeded and finely
 chopped
1 small red onion,
 minced
1 clove garlic, minced
2 fresh jalapeño peppers,
 seeded and finely chopped
½ yellow bell pepper,
 seeded and finely
 chopped
½ cup fresh lime juice
¼ cup fruity olive oil
¼ cup freshly chopped
 coriander
Salt and freshly ground
 pepper to taste

Purée the tomatillos in a blender or food processor fitted with the steel blade until smooth. Transfer to a mixing bowl. Stir in the remaining ingredients. Refrigerate a few hours to allow the flavors to blend, then serve.

Makes about 1 quart.

Mexican Salsa

This salsa bears little resemblance to the red sauce served in typical American Mexican restaurants. I believe this to be the perfect summer dip.

1 bunch scallions,
 chopped
3 ripe large tomatoes,
 seeded and chopped
2 fresh jalapeño peppers,
 seeded and minced
1 green bell pepper,
 seeded and diced
½ red bell pepper, seeded
 and diced
½ yellow bell pepper,
 seeded and diced
1 can (35 ounces) whole
 tomatoes, puréed with liquid
½ cup water
½ cup fresh lime juice
2 tablespoons fruity olive oil
2 tablespoons chopped coriander
Salt and freshly ground
 pepper to taste

Combine the scallions, fresh tomatoes, and peppers in a large mixing bowl. Stir in the puréed tomatoes, water, and lime juice. Stir in the oil and coriander and season with salt and pepper. Refrigerate covered until ready to serve. Serve with your favorite corn tortilla chips.

Makes 8 cups.

WIDOW'S WALK COCKTAILS

Stuffed Grape Leaves
Roasted Garlic
Marinated Goat Cheeses • French Toast Rounds
Sicilian Loaf
Hummus bi Tahini

Lillet Martinis
Hammie Heard's Bloody Marys

Hummus bi Tahini

The Que Sera version of hummus acquires more devoted followers every summer season. It is no wonder, for this recipe for hummus is by no means the bland chick-pea paste you may have tasted elsewhere, but a voluptuous spread with lots of garlic, lemon, and cumin. It is perfect and versatile fare to pack for the beach, to dip into in the late afternoon, or to serve with pre-dinner cocktails. Accompaniments are simple—fresh pita triangles for scooping and, perhaps, some deep purple Mediterranean olives.

3 large cloves garlic,
  minced
½ cup fresh lemon juice
1 cup sesame tahini paste
1 cup water
6 cups canned chick-peas,
  rinsed and drained
1½ tablespoons ground
  cumin

Salt to taste
3 tablespoons fruity olive
  oil
Sweet Hungarian paprika
Lemon slices, Greek
  olives, and fresh mint
  or parsley sprigs for
  garnish

1. Place the garlic, lemon juice, and tahini in a food processor fitted with the steel blade; process to a smooth paste.

2. Add the water and chick-peas and process until the mixture is very smooth, almost fluffy. Season with the cumin and salt to taste.

3. Transfer the hummus to an earthenware bowl. Pour the oil over the top and swirl lightly with the tip of a knife. Sprinkle with the paprika, and garnish with lemon slices, olives, and mint or parsley sprigs.

Makes about 6 cups.

Baba Ghanouj

A close cousin to hummus, this Middle Eastern dip is often referred to as eggplant caviar.

2 medium eggplants
¾ cup sesame tahini
  paste
½ cup fresh lemon juice
2 cloves garlic, minced
Salt and freshly ground
  pepper to taste
1 small red onion,
  minced

2 ripe medium tomatoes,
  seeded and finely diced
¾ cup chopped fresh
  parsley
2 tablespoons fruity olive
  oil

1. Preheat the oven to 375°F.

2. Place the whole eggplants on a lightly oiled baking sheet. Roast the eggplants, turning once halfway through cooking, until the flesh is quite soft, about 45 minutes. Let stand until cool enough to handle.

3. Cut off the stems and peel the skin from the eggplants. Place the pulp in a food processor fitted with the steel blade and process until smooth. Add the tahini, lemon juice, and garlic and process again until smooth. Season to taste with salt and pepper.

4. Transfer the eggplant mixture to a mixing bowl. Add the onion, tomatoes, ½ cup of the parsley, and the oil and stir until blended. Refrigerate a few hours to mellow the flavors. Garnish with the remaining ¼ cup chopped parlsey and serve with fresh pita triangles for dipping.

Makes about 3 cups.

Roasted Red Pepper Dip

Save this sunset-colored dip for the ripest of summer's vegetables plucked warm from the vine.

2 red bell peppers,
    roasted, peeled, and
    seeds removed
1 whole head roasted
    garlic (see page 20),
    pulp squeezed and
    skins discarded
8 ounces Montrachet or
    other mild, soft goat
    cheese, without ash

3 tablespoons fruity olive
    oil
5 tablespoons minced
    fresh basil
1 tablespoon chopped
    fresh rosemary
Pinch cayenne pepper
Salt and freshly ground
    pepper to taste

Place the red peppers, garlic, and cheese in a blender or food processor fitted with the steel blade; purée until smooth. Transfer the mixture to a mixing bowl and stir in the oil, basil, rosemary, and cayenne. Season to taste with salt and pepper. Refrigerate covered to firm the dip. Serve with your favorite dipping vegetables.

Makes about 1½ cups.

Tomato Béarnaise Mayonnaise

A fabulous accompaniment to both cold sliced tenderloin and whole poached salmon, this mayonnaise also adds extra zest to spur-of-the-moment sandwiches.

4 shallots, minced
3 heaping tablespoons
    dried tarragon
⅓ cup tarragon vinegar
⅓ cup dry white wine
3 large egg yolks
2½ tablespoons Dijon
    mustard

2 tablespoons fresh lemon
    juice
1¼ cups vegetable oil
1 cup olive oil
¼ cup tomato paste
Salt and freshly ground
    pepper to taste

1. Place the shallots, tarragon, vinegar, and wine in a small saucepan. Heat to boiling over high heat and reduce until just 1 tablespoon liquid remains. Set aside.

2. Process the egg yolks, mustard, and lemon juice in a food processor fitted with the steel blade for 10 seconds. With the machine running, add the oils in a thin, steady stream through the feed tube to make a thick emulsion. Add the tomato paste and the shallot mixture; process until blended. Season to taste with salt and pepper. Refrigerate covered until ready to serve.

Makes about 4 cups.

Basil Parmesan Mayonnaise

This pesto-inspired mayonnaise was developed as a salad binder when working with The Silver Palate on the *Good Times Cookbook*. As it was soon discovered to be sensational just on its own, I decided to adapt the recipe into a crudite dip. The fresh green color and clear basil flavor provide instant transport to the middle of a garden patch and the mayonnaise contrasts beautifully with Roasted Red Pepper Dip on large vegetable platters.

1 large egg	3 tablespoons fresh lemon
2 large egg yolks	juice
2 tablespoons Dijon	2 cups olive oil
mustard	1½ cups vegetable oil
½ cup finely grated	Salt and freshly ground
Parmesan cheese	pepper to taste
½ cup minced fresh basil	

Place the egg, egg yolks, mustard, Parmesan, basil, and lemon juice in a food processor fitted with the steel blade; process for 10 seconds. With the machine running, add the oils in a thin, steady stream through the feed tube to make a thick emulsion. Season the mayonnaise to taste with salt and freshly ground pepper. Refrigerate covered until ready to serve.

Makes about 4 cups.

Aioli

I think almost everything tastes better with a little dab of aioli on it. Two of my most favorite dippers are blanched green beans and chunks of steaming lobster meat.

1 thick slice day-old
  French bread
3 tablespoons light cream
  (see Index) or half and
  half
5 or 6 cloves garlic,
  minced
2 large egg yolks

1 tablespoon Dijon
  mustard
1 cup vegetable oil
¾ cup olive oil
2 to 3 tablespoons fresh
  lemon juice
Salt and freshly ground
  pepper to taste

1. Trim the crust from the bread and tear the bread into irregular pieces. Combine the bread and cream in a small bowl and let stand for 5 minutes. Gather the bread into a ball and squeeze out as much liquid as possible.

2. Place the bread, garlic, egg yolks, and mustard in a food processor fitted with the steel blade; process until smooth. With the machine running, pour the oils in a thin, steady stream through the feed tube to make a thick emulsion.

3. Season to taste with lemon juice, salt, and pepper. Refrigerate covered until ready to serve.

Makes about 2 cups.

Remoulade Sauce

One of the most flavorful homemade mayonnaises: Besides being the perfect accompaniment to codfish cakes, remoulade sauce is great dolloped on top of grilled hamburgers, spread on your favorite club sandwich, or tossed with a julienne of fresh celeriac to make the classic version of the French bistro salad, celeriac remoulade.

1 large egg
2 large egg yolks
6 anchovy fillets, drained
2 tablespoons capers,
   drained
4 cornichons, minced
2 cloves garlic, minced
2 tablespoons Dijon
   mustard
⅓ cup minced fresh
   parsley

2 tablespoons minced
   fresh tarragon or 1
   tablespoon dried
   tarragon
2 tablespoons balsamic
   vinegar
2 tablespoons fresh lemon
   juice
1¾ cups olive oil
Salt and freshly ground
   pepper to taste

Place the egg, egg yolks, anchovies, capers, cornichons, garlic, mustard, parsley, tarragon, vinegar, and lemon juice in a food processor fitted with the steel blade; process to combine, 15 seconds. With the machine running, pour the oil through the feed tube in a thin, steady stream to make a thick emulsion. Season the sauce with salt and pepper to taste. Store covered in the refrigerator for up to 1 week.

Makes about 2½ cups sauce.

Cold Pine Nut Sauce for Seafood

This sunny yellow sauce adds a new dimension to the accompaniments usually served with cold poached seafood. The inspiration for this recipe is of obscure Mexican origins.

⅓ cup pine nuts, toasted
3 hard-cooked large egg
   yolks
1 cup sour cream
¼ cup Hellmann's
   mayonnaise

2 tablespoons fresh lime
   juice
2 tablespoons minced
   fresh coriander
Salt to taste

Place the pine nuts and egg yolks in a food processor fitted with the steel blade; process until finely minced. Add the sour cream, mayonnaise, and lime juice and process until smooth. Stir in the coriander and season with salt. Refrigerate covered until cold. Serve with your favorite cold poached seafood.

Makes 1½ cups.

Tomato Cognac Sauce for Chilled Mussels

An elegant hors d'oeuvre sauce to be spooned over cold steamed mussels that have been nestled back into the half shell.

¼ cup tomato paste
2 tablespoons fresh lemon juice
1 tablespoon dry sherry
3 tablespoons Cognac
2 cloves garlic, minced
1 small Bermuda onion, minced

½ cup water
1½ cups Hellmann's mayonnaise
½ cup sour cream
2 heaping tablespoons (or to taste) prepared horseradish with beets

1. Place the tomato paste, lemon juice, sherry, Cognac, garlic, onion, and water in a small saucepan and cook, stirring occasionally, over medium heat until the mixture is reduced by half. Be careful not to let the mixture burn on the bottom of the pan. Transfer to a mixing bowl and let cool to room temperature.

2. Fold the mayonnaise, sour cream, and horseradish into the tomato mixture. Refrigerate the sauce for a few hours to allow the flavors to blend and mellow.

Makes about 2¼ cups.

Liptauer

This delicious Hungarian spread is an excellent accompaniment to sliced smoked salmon with dark bread.

8 ounces cream cheese, cut into small pieces
4 tablespoons (½ stick) unsalted butter, cut into small pieces
1 small onion, minced
1 tablespoon capers, drained

1½ tablespoons sweet Hungarian paprika
1 teaspoon Dijon mustard
1 teaspoon anchovy paste
2 teaspoons caraway seeds

Place the cream cheese, butter, onion, capers, paprika, mustard, and anchovy paste in a food processor fitted with the steel blade; process until combined but not smooth or puréed. Add the caraway seeds and process quickly just to combine. Transfer the mixture to a small serving bowl and refrigerate for several hours to allow the flavors to mellow.

Makes about 1½ cups.

Red Clam Sauce

A traditional Italian sauce for pasta, but try it also as a base for a seafood pizza.

¼ cup olive oil
1 large onion, chopped
6 cloves garlic, minced
2 cans (28 ounces each)
  Italian plum tomatoes,
  undrained
¼ cup (or as needed)
  tomato paste
½ cup (or as needed) dry
  red wine
¾ cup bottled clam juice

1 teaspoon dried red
  pepper flakes
3 tablespoons dried
  oregano
Salt and freshly ground
  pepper to taste
3½ cups minced cooked
  clams, fresh or canned
¼ cup chopped fresh basil
¼ cup chopped fresh
  parsley

1. Heat the oil in a large pot over medium-high heat. Add the onion and garlic and cook, stirring frequently, for 10 minutes. Add the tomatoes, paste, wine, clam juice, red pepper, and oregano. Simmer 30 minutes, adding more wine if the sauce seems too thick or more tomato paste if too thin. Season to taste with salt and pepper.

2. Stir the clams, basil, and parsley into the sauce and simmer 10 minutes longer.

Makes about 3 quarts.

White Clam Sauce·

An easy sauce that always wins raves from friends and guests.

¾ cup dry white wine
4 dozen littleneck clams,
   scrubbed
½ cup fruity olive oil
6 cloves garlic, minced
1 tablespoon dried
   oregano

3 tablespoons minced
   fresh parsley
½ cup chopped fresh basil
Salt and freshly ground
   pepper to taste
1 pound linguine, cooked
   al dente

1. Pour the wine into a large pot. Add the clams and cook covered over high heat until the clams open. Remove the clams from the pot with a slotted spoon. Remove the meat from the shells and set aside. Discard the shells. Strain the cooking liquid through a fine mesh sieve and reserve.

2. Heat the oil in a large skillet over medium heat. Add the garlic, reduce the heat to low, and cook, stirring frequently, just until the garlic is light golden. Add the oregano and the reserved cooking liquid. Heat to boiling, then simmer for 10 minutes.

3. Stir the clams, parsley, and basil into the sauce. Season to taste with salt and pepper. Simmer 5 minutes longer. Serve the sauce tossed with the linguine.

Makes 4 to 6 servings.

Onion Marmalade

This is fantastic on top of grilled hamburgers or as an accompaniment to other summer barbecue fare.

2 extra large yellow
   onions (2½ to 3
   pounds), each cut into
   10 wedges
1½ cups chicken stock
½ cup medium-dry sherry

2 tablespoons sherry
   vinegar
2 teaspoons sugar
Salt and freshly ground
   pepper to taste
½ cup crème fraîche

Place the onions in a medium saucepan. Add the chicken stock, sherry, sherry vinegar, and sugar. Heat to boiling. Reduce the heat and simmer covered, stirring occasionally, until most of the liquid evaporates, about 45 minutes. Season to taste with salt and pepper. Stir in the crème fraîche and cook over low heat 10 minutes longer. Serve warm or at room temperature. Store any extra covered in the refrigerator. It will keep for up to 1 week.

Makes about 2½ cups.

Elena's Grandfather's Peasant Sauce

My close friend Elena escaped the trials and tribulations of writing magazine articles and reading screenplays in New York one summer and blessed my kitchen with her unique sense of humor and some treasured old family recipes. Both my staff and customers fell madly in love with a very simple and straightforward recipe for her grandfather's meatless tomato sauce. The secret to its unique appeal lies in the large ratio of onions to tomatoes and the resulting smoky sweet taste that the slow sautéing of the onions in fruity olive oil imparts to the overall taste of the sauce. While always comforting in its traditional use on pasta, I'm also partial to a spoonful or two of Peasant Sauce over charcoal grilled hamburgers.

½ cup fruity olive oil
3 large yellow onions, chopped medium fine
1 tablespoon salt
2½ tablespoons tomato paste
1 can (35 ounces) Italian plum tomatoes, undrained

1 pound vermicelli or capellini, cooked al *dente*
Freshly grated Parmesan or Romano cheese

1. Heat oil in a large saucepan over high heat until sizzling hot. Add the onions and sauté, stirring frequently, for 5 minutes. Reduce the heat to medium and cook the onions, stirring frequently, just until beginning to turn golden brown, about 25 minutes.

2. Stir in the salt and tomato paste. Stir in the canned tomatoes and simmer the sauce uncovered for 30 minutes.

3. Toss the hot pasta with just enough of the sauce to keep it from sticking together. Serve the remaining sauce on the side and pass the cheese.

Makes 4 to 6 servings.

ELENA'S STORY

"My grandfather grew up in San Polo di Cavalieri, a tiny hill town outside of Rome where Italian messengers were sent for an ancient version of rest and relaxation. When he came to this country, he brought with him many treasures, none of which were packed in his small valise. Among my favorites is his recipe for a sauce that made meatless Catholic Fridays a joy.

When visiting his family in Rome last summer, I offered to make this sauce which I had always thought of as his creation. But the very next day his niece prepared—la pranza—the midday meal—and lo and behold, it was my grandfather's sauce! More than any history or stories that we shared, this sauce said we were family."

Hammie Heard's Bloody Mary

Years ago I was invited to a Sunday afternoon picnic on the sunny deck of Hammie Heard's Hulbert Avenue home. He served absolutely the best Bloody Mary I have ever tasted. Hammie graciously offered to share his blending secrets provided that we could test the recipe together and perfect it several times over!

6 ounces Beefamato
Dash Jane's Crazy
   Mixed-Up Salt
Few grinds of the
   peppermill
Few shakes Tabasco sauce

Few drops Worcestershire
   sauce
1 generous shot vodka
Ice cubes
Juice of ½ lime

Stir the Beefamato, salt, pepper, Tabasco, and Worcestershire together in a large glass. Stir in the vodka and then add enough ice to fill the glass. Stir like crazy. Squeeze some of the lime juice around the rim of the glass and squeeze the rest over the drink. Savor!

Makes 1 drink.

CHAMPAGNE

Champagne is a luxury for the unluxurious moment, the moment of monetary, or, worse, emotional poverty. When despair has tightened your throat so, you can't swallow anything, and you have to speak by hand signals. When no human comfort can reach you, and you must rely, helpless, on the beneficience of the generous sound of pouring wine. When the kindest hand would be too heavy. The voice of sympathy, abrasive as a badly stroked cello. When the heartache you've always read about in the distance turns out to be your own. When love has been mistaken, gone, died. Champagne is for laughing-in-spite-of-your-tears, a shout of defiance, an act of faith, a promise of renewal. Champagne is best when your world is falling apart.

—JEANINE LARMOTH
The Passionate Palate

Pink Bellinis

Those who have traveled to Venice are no doubt familiar with the magical Venetian cocktail, the Bellini—a quenching froth of fresh peach juice and Italian Prosecco. While it is hard to find good Prosecco in this country and our peaches differ in intensity from those grown in Italy, I feel I have devised a rather irresistible facsimile using dry pink Champagne and orchard ripe peaches.

Every summer I spend an annual Bellini afternoon on the

beach with my special friend and children's author, Joan Walsh Anglund. We swim in the surf, nibble on grapes and olives, get lost in deep spiritual conversation, and usually end up sipping this sunset-colored cocktail right into the moonlight.

2 ripe large peaches
2 tablespoons fresh lemon
   juice
3 tablespoons fresh orange
   juice

1 cup small ice cubes
1 bottle (750 ml) dry
   pink Champagne, cold

Drop the peaches into a small saucepan of boiling water, blanch for 2 minutes, and drain. Remove the skins and pits from the peaches. Purée the peaches, lemon and orange juices in a blender. Add the ice and Champagne and blend until smooth and frothy. Pour into 8 chilled champagne flutes and serve.

Makes 8 Bellinis.

Lillet Martini

The French aperitif Lillet is the light drink I prefer to sip through the summer. However, for those days when something far more potent than the traditional Lillet and soda is needed I have devised this outrageous martini.

1¼ cups vodka
¼ cup Lillet Blanc
2 large strips (2 inches
   wide) orange zest

2 thin strips orange zest
   for garnish

1. The day before you think you might need a strong martini, mix the vodka and Lillet and pour into a freezer container. Add the 2 large strips of orange zest. Freeze covered for at least 12 hours.

2. When ready to serve, remove the orange zest from the martini and pour into 2 chilled martini glasses. Garnish with the thin strips of orange zest. For added drama, twist the thin zest strips to release the oils and ignite them with a match before dropping into the martini glass.

Makes 2 very strong martinis.

Las Palmas

In the early days of Que Sera when the shop was tucked into a pink shuttered cubbyhole at 21 Federal Street, and town zoning regulations were still lax enough to allow a creative soul to open a business spontaneously, my neighbor in the apartment above my shop opened a free-spirited clothing store named Zecchino. To infuse a touch of established class into this ephemeral operation, she decided that she needed two locations printed on her sign. She chose Nantucket and Las Palmas—the latter being the warmest possible spot she might long for deep in the raw chill of a Nantucket winter. That summer she and her roommate, my artist friend Sterling, collaborated on tropical rum concoctions and sent them floating down to my shop in the late afternoon. In memory of Zecchino and in honor of her wonderful spirit, here is the drink recollected.

½ cup Mount Gay or
   other good-quality dark
   rum
1½ tablespoons brown
   sugar
1 can (6 ounces)
   pineapple juice
Juice of 3 limes

½ cup diced ripe
   cantaloupe, peach, or
   nectarine
½ ripe banana
⅓ cup fresh raspberries
1 cup ice cubes
Lime slices for garnish

Place all the ingredients, except the garnish, in a blender and blend until smooth and frothy. Pour into 3 glasses, garnish with lime slices, serve, and savor.

Makes 3 drinks.

Soup
Sorcery

When she knew that he [Denys] was coming she would have his favorite dish for him. This was "clear soup," Kamante's exquisite consommé. Perhaps the making of this soup taught Karen Blixen something about writing stories. The recipe calls for you to keep the spirit but to discard the substance of your rough ingredients: eggshells and raw bones, root vegetables and red meat. You then submit them, like a storyteller, to the "fire and patience." And the clarity comes at the end, a magic trick."

Isak Dinesen: The Life of a Storyteller
—JUDITH THURMAN

I believe that soup making is one of the most gratifying experiences of all in the vast spectrum of culinary activities. Tender stirring and simmering cannot help but bring forth the loving and nurturing instinct of every soup maker, but it is the finished product that contains the power to assuage the parched palate or soul in truly magical ways.

On New England islands such as Nantucket, where old tourist brochures would boast that "Summer is five Septembers long," soup sorcery takes on many different forms. Chilled soups are in demand on the hot, high noon days when even chewing seems too difficult, while creamy rich soups are needed when pure self-indulgence is in order. The heartier soups, bursting with hominess and nourishment, acknowledge the first signs of summer's fading and the invigorating chill in the air. This coveted collection of soup recipes, ranging from a silky avocado to peasanty potato and kale, is guaranteed to provide many sips of contentment, whatever the climate or occasion.

Smoky Clam Chowder

Every cook harbors secret inexplicable idiosyncracies. One of mine is that making clam chowder sends me into a state of pure rapture. I always rely on my instincts to add extra generous amounts of my favorite chowder ingredients and believe this particular version is made extraordinary by the addition of smoky finnan haddie to the usual clam base.

8 slices bacon, cut into ½-inch dice
2 tablespoons unsalted butter
1 large onion, chopped
2 quarts water
2 cups dry white wine
3 large boiling pototoes, peeled and cut into ½-inch dice (about 4½ cups)
1 pound finnan haddie
2 cups milk
4 cups canned or fresh clams with juice
2 cups half and half
1 cup heavy or whipping cream
2 teaspoons dried thyme
1 teaspoon paprika
Salt and freshly ground pepper to taste

1. Fry the bacon in a large stockpot over medium-high heat, stirring frequently, until crisp. Using a slotted spoon, transfer the bacon to paper towels to drain. Set aside.

2. Add the butter to the bacon fat in the pot and heat over medium heat. Add the onion and cook, stirring occasionally, for 10 minutes.

3. Pour the water and wine into the pot, then add the potatoes. Simmer uncovered until the potatoes are tender, about 25 minutes. Measure 3 cups of the soup with potatoes into a blender and process until smooth. Return the purée to the soup and stir.

4. While the soup is simmering, cut the finnan haddie in half and place it in a saucepan. Cover with the milk. Heat to boiling. Reduce the heat and simmer for 20 minutes. Pour the poaching liquid into the soup. Flake the finnan haddie into small pieces. Add the fish and clams with juice to the soup.

5. Stir the half and half and cream into the soup. Add the thyme and paprika and season with salt and pepper to taste. Simmer 10 to 15 minutes. Stir in the bacon just before serving.

Makes about 3½ quarts.

My Aunt's Cold Clam Chowder

As with most of the fabulous and abundant creations of my aunt's Nantucket kitchen, we would discover the next day that we loved the leftovers cold from the refrigerator. I became so fond of this clam chowder that whole batches were frequently made just for chilling.

5 ounces salt pork, cut into ¼-inch dice
1 large onion, diced
4 cups clam juice (combination bottled and fresh from the shucked clams)
1 cup dry white wine
4 cups peeled potato cubes (bite size)
2 pounds shelled fresh clams, chopped, drained, juice reserved

½ teaspoon dried thyme
½ teaspoon dried dill
Few shakes Tabasco sauce
2½ cups heavy or whipping cream
Salt to taste
⅓ cup Dry Sack sherry or other good-quality dry sherry
Chopped pimiento and fresh parsley for garnish

1. Fry the salt pork in a large stockpot over medium-high heat until browned and crisp. Remove with a slotted spoon and save for another use or discard.

2. Add the onion to the fat in the pot and cook, stirring occasionally, over medium-high heat until tender, 10 to 15 minutes. Add the clam juice, wine, and potatoes. Simmer just until the potatoes are tender, about 25 minutes.

3. Add the clams, thyme, dill, and Tabasco to taste to the soup. Simmer 5 minutes longer. Stir in the cream and season with salt to taste. Heat the soup almost to a boil, then stir in the sherry. Remove from the heat and let cool.

4. Purée the soup in a food processor fitted with the steel blade. Refrigerate until cold, about 3 hours. Ladle the cold chowder into soup bowls and garnish with a sprinkling of chopped pimiento and fresh parsley.

Makes about 3 quarts.

Meursault and Escargot Bisque

Two of Burgundy's famed products star in this truly graceful bisque. I like to make this soup when I am longing for my days spent bicycling through the vineyards of the Côte d'Or.

3 dozen canned escargot (snails), rinsed under cold water
1 bottle (750 ml) Meursault wine
12 tablespoons (1½ sticks) unsalted butter
4 shallots, minced
½ cup unbleached all-purpose flour
2 quarts fish stock (recipe follows)
2 teaspoons dried thyme
2 carrots, peeled and cut into fine julienne strips, 2 inches long
2 leeks, rinsed, dried, and cut into fine julienne strips, 2 inches long

2 ribs celery, cut into fine julienne strips, 2 inches long
1 yellow bell pepper, seeded and cut into fine julienne strips, 2 inches long
2½ cups heavy or whipping cream
2 large egg yolks
1 tablespoon fresh lemon juice
Salt and freshly ground white pepper to taste
Finely chopped fresh parsley for garnish

1. Place the escargot in a saucepan and cover with the Meursault. Heat just to boiling. Reduce the heat and simmer for 5 minutes. Remove from the heat. Drain the snails, reserving the cooking wine.

2. Melt 10 tablespoons of the butter in a large stockpot over medium-high heat. Add the shallots and cook for 5 minutes. Whisk in the flour and cook, stirring constantly, for 2 minutes. Gradually whisk in the fish stock, the reserved cooking wine, and the thyme. Reduce the heat to low and simmer the soup uncovered for 30 minutes.

3. Meanwhile, melt the remaining 2 tablespoons butter in a large skillet over medium-low heat. Add all the julienned vegetables and toss to coat with the butter. Cook, stirring occasionally,

just until the vegetables are tender, about 5 minutes. Remove the vegetables from the heat and set aside.

4. Stir 2 cups of the cream into the soup. Whisk the remaining ½ cup cream with the egg yolks and lemon juice in a small mixing bowl. Whisk ½ cup of the hot soup into the egg yolk mixture, then whisk it back into the soup. Add the escargot and julienned vegetables to the soup. Season the soup to taste with salt and white pepper. Serve the soup hot in wide soup bowls. Garnish with a sprinkling of finely chopped parsley.

Makes 10 to 12 servings.

Fish Stock

Bottled clam juice may provide a convenient substitute for recipes calling for fish stock, but it cannot replace the rich ocean flavors achieved from making fish stock from scratch. I suggest making a big batch and storing pint containers in the freezer to defrost and use as needed.

1 large Spanish onion, thinly sliced
1½ cups minced fennel bulb or celery ribs
2 carrots, peeled and sliced into rounds
2 cloves garlic, peeled
1 lemon, sliced
6 sprigs fresh parsley
2 teaspoons dried thyme
3 bay leaves
1 tablespoon black peppercorns
4 cups dry white wine
1 tablespoon salt
4 pounds fish heads, bones, and trimmings
2½ quarts cold tap water

Place all of the ingredients in a large heavy stockpot. Bring to a boil over medium-high heat and then lower the heat and simmer, uncovered, for 45 minutes. Strain the stock through a fine sieve, discarding all of the solids. Store in covered plastic containers in the refrigerator for 2 to 3 days or in the freezer for up to 3 months.

Makes about 3 quarts.

Mexican Corn Soup with Shrimp and Cilantro Purée

I always felt that corn chowder was about the most unpleasant looking dish ever invented. Then all of a sudden hot restaurants across the country began making smooth corn soups swirled with a variety of contrasting purées. While the soups were certainly more pleasing to the eye, I was still disappointed by the bland flavor. I became determined to invent a corn soup that even I could adore. This recipe is the result. The contrast between the pastel yellow of the soup, the coral of the shrimp, and the vibrant green of the cilantro is spectacular.

1 bottle (12 ounces) beer preferably imported
3½ cups water
1 bay leaf
½ teaspoon dried red pepper flakes
1 pound medium (24 to 35 per pound) shrimp, shelled and deveined
5 tablespoons unsalted butter
1 large onion, minced
3 ribs celery, minced
2 carrots, peeled and minced
½ yellow bell pepper, seeded and diced

1 tablespoon dried oregano
1 tablespoon ground cumin
1 teaspoon dried thyme
3 tablespoons unbleached all-purpose flour
1½ cups bottled clam juice or fish stock (see facing page)
4½ cups fresh corn kernels (6 to 8 ears)
1½ cups heavy or whipping cream
1 cup milk
¼ cup fresh lime juice
Salt and freshly ground pepper to taste

CILANTRO PURÉE:
1 can (4 ounces) green chiles, drained
1 cup fresh cilantro (coriander) leaves

¼ cup olive oil

1. Heat the beer, 2 cups of the water, the bay leaf, and red pepper flakes in a 2-quart saucepan to boiling. Add the shrimp and cook just until done, 2 to 3 minutes. Drain the shrimp and

return the cooking liquid to the saucepan. Boil the cooking liquid over high heat until reduced by one-half.

2. Meanwhile, melt the butter in a large stockpot over medium heat. Add the onion, celery, carrots, and bell pepper. Cook, stirring frequently, for 15 minutes. Stir in the oregano, cumin, thyme, and flour. Cook and stir for 2 minutes.

3. Add the reduced cooking liquid, the clam juice, remaining 1½ cups water, and the corn to the pot. Simmer uncovered for 20 minutes.

4. Cut each shrimp into 4 pieces and add half the shrimp to the soup. Remove from the heat and stir in the cream, milk, and lime juice. Purée the soup in batches in a blender. Press through a sieve or food mill back into the pot. Season to taste with salt and pepper. Stir in the remaining shrimp and keep warm over low heat.

5. Prepare the cilantro purée: Place the chiles, cilantro, and oil in a food processor fitted with the steel blade and process until smooth.

6. Ladle the soup into serving bowls and swirl a couple tablespoons of the cilantro purée on top of each serving.

Makes 8 to 10 servings.

Cream of Sweet Onion and Sauternes Soup

My very favorite way to enjoy Georgia's famous Vidalia onion.

½ cup (1 stick) unsalted butter

4 Vidalia onions, sliced lengthwise into thin slivers

2 medium red onions, sliced lengthwise into thin slivers

3 tablespoons sugar

¼ cup unbleached all-purpose flour

4 cups Sauternes wine

2 quarts chicken stock, preferably homemade

2½ cups heavy or whipping cream

Salt and freshly ground white pepper to taste

Snipped fresh chives and whole chive blossoms for garnish

1. Melt the butter in a stockpot over medium-high heat. Stir in the onions and cook, stirring constantly, for 5 minutes. Reduce the heat to low. Place a sheet of waxed paper on top of the onions and sweat the onions until very tender and translucent, about 20 minutes.

2. Remove and discard the waxed paper. Stir in the sugar and cook the onions for 3 minutes to caramelize them. Stir in the flour and cook for another 2 minutes. Gradually whisk in the wine and chicken stock. Simmer the soup uncovered for 10 minutes.

3. Stir the cream into the soup and season to taste with salt and pepper. Keep the soup warm over low heat until ready to serve. Garnish with a few snipped chives and a purple chive blossom in the center of each serving.

Makes 8 to 10 servings.

Cream of Cauliflower Soup

My friend Elena, known for her grandfather's peasant sauce (see Index) among other things, believes that some food is meant for blonds only. Being a blond myself, I happen to agree. To my mind cream of cauliflower soup is quintessential blond food.

5 tablespoons unsalted
  butter
1 leek, rinsed, dried, and
  minced
1 medium onion, chopped
1 carrot, peeled and
  minced
1 teaspoon dried tarragon
½ teaspoon dried thyme
¼ cup unbleached
  all-purpose flour
1 cup dry white wine

6 cups chicken stock,
  preferably homemade
Salt and freshly white
  ground pepper to taste
1 head cauliflower,
  steamed just until
  barely tender, then
  broken into small
  flowerets
1 cup milk
1 cup heavy or whipping
  cream

1. Melt the butter in a stockpot over medium-high heat. Add the leek, onion, and carrot and cook, stirring occasionally, for 10 minutes. Stir in the tarragon and thyme and cook 1 minute longer.

2. Add the flour and cook, stirring constantly, for 1 minute. Reduce the heat to medium and gradually stir in the wine and chicken stock. Season the soup with salt and white pepper and add the cauliflower flowerets. Simmer the soup uncovered, stirring occasionally, for 30 minutes.

3. Purée the soup in batches in a blender and return to the pot. Stir in the milk and cream. Gently heat just until heated through. Taste and adjust the seasonings. Serve the soup hot.

Makes about 2½ quarts.

VARIATION

CAULIFLOWER CHEESE SOUP Stir 2½ cups grated Swiss cheese into the soup after the milk and cream have been added and heat until the cheese is melted.

Roasted Yellow Pepper Soup with Parmesan Gremolata

This sunshine-colored soup is laden with the smoky sweet flavor of roasted peppers. The gremolata—a traditional Italian mixture of lemon zest, garlic, and parsley—adds harmonious contrast.

6 tablespoons extra-virgin
  olive oil
1 large yellow onion,
  chopped
2 carrots, peeled and
  minced
2 ribs celery, minced
2 cloves garlic, minced
4 sun-dried tomatoes,
  packed in oil, drained
  and minced
8 yellow bell peppers,

roasted, peeled, seeded,
  and chopped
2 quarts chicken stock,
  preferably homemade
1 cup dry white wine
5 tablespoons chopped
  fresh basil
½ cup light cream (see
  Index)
Salt and freshly ground
  pepper to taste

PARMESAN GREMOLATA:

Finely chopped zest of
 2 lemons
4 cloves garlic, minced
5 tablespoons chopped
 fresh basil

1 bunch parsley, stems
 trimmed and leaves
 minced
5 ounces Parmesan
 cheese, freshly grated

1. Heat the oil in a stockpot over medium-high heat. Stir in the onions, carrots, celery, garlic, and tomatoes; cook, stirring frequently, for 5 minutes. Reduce the heat to medium and cook, stirring occasionally, 15 minutes longer.

2. Stir in the yellow peppers, chicken stock, and white wine and simmer for 15 minutes.

3. Stir in the basil and simmer for 2 minutes. Remove from the heat and stir in the cream. Purée the soup in batches in a blender and return to the pot. Season to taste with salt and pepper. Bring the soup just to a simmer.

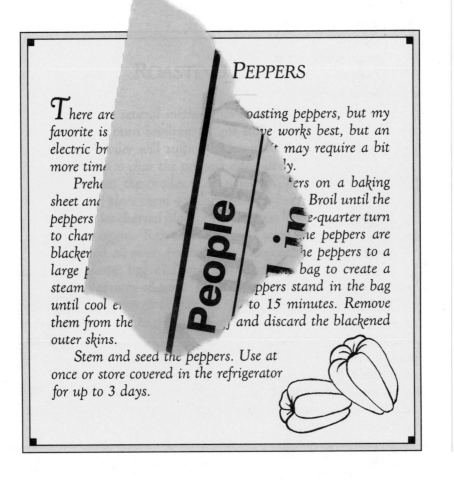

PEPPERS

There are ____ ____ ____ oasting peppers, but my favorite is ____ ____ ____ ve works best, but an electric br____ ____ ____ may require a bit more time ____ ____ ____ ly.

Preh____ ____ ____ ers on a baking sheet and ____ ____ Broil until the peppers ____ ____ e-quarter turn to char ____ ____ he peppers are blacken ____ ____ he peppers to a large ____ ____ bag to create a steam ____ ____ ppers stand in the bag until cool e____ ____ to 15 minutes. Remove them from the ____ and discard the blackened outer skins.

Stem and seed the peppers. Use at once or store covered in the refrigerator for up to 3 days.

4. Prepare the gremolata: Toss together in a small mixing bowl all the ingredients until mixed.

5. Ladle the hot soup into bowls and top each serving with a heaping spoonful of the gremolata.

Makes 10 to 12 servings.

Tomato Soup Provençal

An uninhibitedly flavorful interpretation of tomato soup—great for September lunches served with lots of crusty bread.

⅓ cup fruity olive oil
4 leeks, rinsed, dried, and minced
3 carrots, peeled and minced
1 medium red onion, chopped
3 cloves garlic, minced
Grated zest of 1 orange
1 tablespoon dried thyme
1 teaspoon fennel seeds
1 teaspoon saffron threads

12 ripe large tomatoes, seeded and diced
3 cans (35 ounces each) Italian plum tomatoes, undrained
2 quarts chicken stock, preferably homemade
1 cup orange juice
Salt and freshly ground pepper to taste
1 cup chopped fresh basil
Crumbled goat cheese for garnish

1. Heat the oil in a large stockpot over high heat. Add the leeks, carrots, onion, and garlic and cook, stirring frequently, for 15 minutes.

2. Add the orange zest, thyme, fennel seeds, and saffron; cook, stirring frequently, for 3 minutes.

3. Add the fresh and canned tomatoes, chicken stock, and orange juice and stir to combine. Simmer the soup uncovered over medium heat for 30 minutes. Remove from the heat and purée in batches in a blender or food processor fitted with the steel blade. Season to taste with salt and pepper.

4. Return the soup to the pot and bring just to a simmer. Just before serving, stir in the basil. Garnish each serving with a little goat cheese.

Makes 4 quarts.

Potato Soup with Quattro Formaggi

The Italians have a wonderful way of making starchy excess ever so satisfying. Here I have borrowed their *quattro formaggi* (four cheese) concept for pasta and melted it into a smooth and comforting potato soup.

6 tablespoons (¾ stick) unsalted butter

1 large yellow onion, chopped

2 quarts chicken stock, preferably homemade

2 cups dry white wine

2 large boiling potatoes, peeled and diced

1½ cups milk

2 cups heavy or whipping cream

4 ounces shredded mozzarella

4 ounces shredded Italian Fontina cheese

4 ounces crumbled Gorgonzola

4 ounces freshly grated Parmesan cheese

2 large egg yolks

½ teaspoon grated nutmeg

Salt and freshly ground white pepper to taste

Croutons for garnish (see page 117)

1. Melt the butter in a stockpot over medium-high heat. Stir in the onion and cook until softened, about 10 minutes. Add the chicken stock, wine, and potatoes; simmer uncovered until the potatoes are tender, about 25 minutes.

2. Stir in the milk and 1½ cups of the cream. Purée the soup in batches in a blender, then return it to the pot.

3. Heat the soup over medium-low heat. Add all the cheese and heat, stirring frequently, until the cheese is completely melted.

4. Whisk the egg yolks and remaining ½ cup cream in a small bowl until blended. Whisk ½ cup of the hot soup into the cream mixture, then whisk this mixture into the hot soup. Stir in the nutmeg and season to taste with salt and pepper. Be careful not to let the soup boil, or it will separate. Ladle the hot soup in earthenware crocks and garnish with croutons.

Makes 10 to 12 servings.

Portuguese Kale Soup

Everyone in New England coastal towns has a favorite recipe for the hearty Portuguese specialty, kale soup. Knowing how to make this soup well can increase one's chances of acceptance in the local community from summer tourist to nearly native. The soup keeps well and even improves with age, so I think it best to make a large pot full.

6 tablespoons fruity olive oil

3½ to 4 pounds beef neck bones or other meaty soup bones

2 large onions, coarsely chopped

6 cloves garlic, minced

3 carrots, peeled and cut into ¼-inch dice

1 cup minced fresh fennel or celery

4 quarts water

1 cup dry red wine

1 can (35 ounces) whole tomatoes, coarsely chopped, with juice

2 bay leaves

Salt and freshly ground pepper to taste

4 large potatoes, peeled and cut into ¾-inch dice

1½ pounds linguica sausage

1½ pounds Polish kielbasa

1½ pounds fresh kale, rinsed and cut into long thin strips

Freshly grated Parmesan cheese and olive oil for garnish

1. Heat 4 tablespoons of the oil in a large stockpot over medium-high heat. Add the beef bones and brown on all sides, about 15 minutes. Remove the bones from the pot.

2. Add the onions to the pot and cook, stirring occasionally, for 10 minutes. Add the remaining 2 tablespoons oil and then the garlic, carrots, and fennel. Cook, stirring occasionally, for 10 minutes.

3. Return the beef bones to the pot. Add the water, wine, tomatoes, bay leaves, salt, and pepper. Simmer the soup uncovered over low heat for 2 hours. Remove the bones from the pot again and let stand until cool enough to handle.

4. Meanwhile, add the potatoes to the pot and simmer the soup 30

minutes longer, stirring occasionally.

5. Place the *linguica* and kielbasa in a separate pot, add water to cover, and heat to boiling. Reduce the heat and simmer 5 minutes. Drain.

6. Tear the beef from the bones into fine shreds. Cut the sausages into ¼-inch-thick slices. Add the beef and sausage to the soup.

7. Stir in kale and simmer the soup for 1 hour. If the soup seems to be too thick, thin it with water.

8. Serve the soup steaming hot in large deep bowls. Sprinkle the top with a healthy amount of Parmesan and drizzle a little fruity olive oil over the top too.

Makes about 6 quarts.

Mushroom and Hazelnut Soup

This is an outrageous soup that is velvety rich and soothing. Serve it in precious portions to your most elegant and appreciative friends.

6 cups chicken stock,
  preferably homemade
5 tablespoons sweet
  Marsala wine
7 tablespoons unsalted
  butter
½ cup unbleached
  all-purpose flour
12 ounces fresh white
  mushrooms, cleaned
2 tablespoons fresh lemon
  juice

1 cup milk
½ cup hazelnuts, lightly
  toasted and finely
  ground
2 large egg yolks, at room
  temperature
1 cup light cream (see
  Index)
Pinch grated nutmeg
Salt and freshly ground
  pepper to taste

1. Heat the chicken stock and 3 tablespoons of the Marsala in a medium saucepan until quite hot to the touch.

2. Meanwhile, melt 4 tablespoons of the butter in a heavy stockpot over medium heat. Whisk in the flour and cook, stirring constantly, until the roux is light golden, 3 to 4 minutes. Gradually add the hot stock mixture, whisking until smooth. Heat to boiling. Reduce the heat to low and simmer uncovered, stirring occasionally, for 40 minutes.

3. Finely chop the mushrooms by hand or in a food processor fitted with the steel blade. Toss with the lemon juice to prevent discoloration. Melt the remaining 3 tablespoons butter in a skillet over medium-high heat. Add the mushrooms and cook, stirring constantly, until all the moisture evaporates. Remove from the heat.

4. Stir the mushrooms into the stock. Stir in the milk and then the hazelnuts over low heat.

5. Whisk the egg yolks and light cream together in a small bowl. Whisk in 1 cup of the hot soup, then gently whisk it back into the soup. Be careful at this point not to let the soup boil or it will curdle. Stir in the remaining 2 tablespoons Marsala and season with the nutmeg, salt, and pepper. Serve hot.

Makes 6 to 8 small servings.

Olga's Avgolemono Soup

It is far easier to describe's Olga's *avgolemono* than it is to describe Olga. No person has ever made me laugh as long and as much; at the same time, no person has ever made me see, feel, and appreciate life as much as Olga. Our lives intertwined very closely during the initial years of Que Sera Sarah. Without Olga's presence, neither my shop nor my life on Nantucket would have been the same. While I would really like her recipe for life, I have settled momentarily for her recipe for this refreshing Greek soup.

2 small chickens, cut into serving pieces	½ cup (1 stick) butter, melted
1 tablespoon salt	½ cup white rice
1 tablespoon freshly ground pepper	6 large eggs, separated
1 tablespoon dried oregano	1 cup water
	Juice of 3 lemons

1. Place the chickens in a stockpot and add water to cover. Sprinkle with salt and pepper to taste. Heat to boiling. Reduce the heat and simmer covered for 1 hour.

2. Preheat the oven to 350 F.

3. Remove the chickens from the pot and place in a roasting pan. Sprinkle with the oregano and more salt and pepper and drizzle with the melted butter. Roast for 30 minutes.

4. Meanwhile, strain the chicken broth and spoon off the fat. Taste and adjust the seasoning. Heat the broth in the stockpot to boiling. Stir in the rice and simmer covered just until the rice is tender, about 15 minutes. Remove from the heat.

5. Beat the egg whites in a large mixing bowl until fluffy but not stiff. Gradually beat in the egg yolks and then the water. While still beating, slowly drizzle in the lemon juice. Beat in the hot broth, 1 ladle at a time, until all is added (The rice will sink to the bottom of the pot and should not be ladled in with the broth.) Return the soup to the pot, stir up the rice, and serve immediately with the chicken alongside.

Makes 4 to 6 servings.

Olga Writes:

Sitting around on a rainy day brings out the best and worst in people. Some find good books and other sit and lament the state of their lives. As a friend, you can either give advice or be smart and get up and make this soup. It soothes, it nourishes, and it keeps you out of trouble!

If you or your friend are feeling particularly infantile or fragile it's okay to add shredded pieces of chicken to the soup.

Some of my best memories are of standing at my mother's stove whisking an Avgolemono. Wonderful conversations would spring up—secrets exchanged or announcements made.

Minestrone Freddo

Several years ago I slipped into a little Florentine restaurant tucked away on a side street near the busy Ponte Vecchio and discovered this fabulous cold version of classic Italian minestrone. I make at least one big batch of this healthy vegetable soup every summer. It seems to improve with age and is perfect sustenance on hot days.

3 tablespoons olive oil
4 ounces pancetta, cut
  into small dice
4 ounces prosciutto, cut
  into small dice
1 large onion, minced
4 cloves garlic, minced
2 carrots, peeled and cut
  into ¼-inch dice
1 large zucchini, rinsed
  and cut into ½-inch
  dice
1 large yellow summer
  squash, rinsed and cut
  into ½-inch dice
2 baking potatoes, peeled
  and cut into ¼-inch
  dice
5 tomatoes, seeded and
  cut into ½-inch chunks
3 quarts plus 3 cups (15
  cups) chicken stock,
  preferably homemade

1 cup dry white wine
1 pound green beans,
  trimmed and cut into
  2-inch lengths
1 small green cabbage,
  cored and shredded
1 pound fresh spinach,
  stems trimmed, and
  leaves cut into thin
  strips
1 large can (1 pound 3
  ounces) cannellini
  beans, rinsed and
  drained
2 cups cooked Italian
  short-grain rice
  (Arborio) or converted
  rice
½ cup chopped fresh basil
Salt and freshly ground
  pepper to taste
Freshly grated Parmesan
  cheese

1. Heat the oil in a large stock pot over medium-high heat. Add the pancetta and prosciutto and cook just until crisp and light brown, 7 to 10 minutes.

2. Stir in the onion, garlic, carrots, zucchini, summer squash, and potatoes; cook, stirring frequently, for 10 minutes. Stir in the tomatoes and cook 5 minutes longer. Pour in the chicken stock and wine, then add the green beans, cabbage, and spinach. Simmer the soup uncovered, stirring occasionally, for 45 minutes.

3. Stir the cannellini beans, rice, and basil into the soup. Season to taste with salt and pepper. Simmer for 10 minutes.

4. Let the soup cool completely, then store covered in the refrigerator. Remove about 30 minutes before serving. The soup should be slightly chilled and served in large bowls with plenty of Parmesan cheese.

Makes 14 to 16 servings.

Peruvian Avocado Soup

This soup was inspired by the brilliant Peruvian chef at The Ballroom Restaurant in New York City. It is the best and most unusual avocado soup I have ever tasted.

4 Haas avocados (dark green small) at the peak of ripeness
1 tablespoon fresh lemon juice
6 tablespoons (¾ stick) unsalted butter
1 large onion, chopped
3 cloves garlic, minced
2 small fresh jalapeño peppers, seeded and minced
1 cup minced celery
1 tablespoon chopped fresh tarragon
1 tablespoon ground cumin
½ teaspoon grated nutmeg

3 tablespoons unbleached all-purpose flour
2 quarts chicken stock, preferably homemade
Salt and freshly ground pepper to taste
½ yellow bell pepper, seeded and diced
1 red bell pepper, seeded and diced
3 tablespoons chopped fresh coriander
3 tablespoons chopped fresh basil
2 tablespoons chopped fresh mint

HYDRANGEAS AND HIGH NOON

Peruvian Avocado Soup

Classic Chicken and Grape Salad
Moroccan Carrots
Green Beans in Dill Walnut Sauce

Lace Cookies

Iced Tea

1. Peel and pit the avocados and put them in a bowl of cold water mixed with the lemon juice to keep them from discoloring.

2. Melt the butter in a stockpot over medium-high heat. Add the onion, garlic, jalapeño peppers, and celery; cook, stirring frequently, for 5 minutes. Reduce the heat to low and cook, stirring occasionally, until the vegetables are soft, 15 minutes.

3. Stir in the tarragon, cumin, and nutmeg and cook a few minutes longer. Stir in the flour and cook 1 minute. Gradually stir in the chicken stock. Increase the heat and heat to boiling. Reduce the heat and simmer uncovered for 15 minutes. Remove from the heat and let cool for 15 minutes.

4. Drain the avocados, cut into pieces, and add to the soup. Process the soup in batches in a blender until smooth. Season to taste with salt and freshly ground pepper. Refrigerate until cold.

5. Ladle the soup into bowls and sprinkle with the yellow and red peppers and the fresh herbs.

Makes 8 to 10 servings.

Que Sera Gazpacho

While gazpacho lost its sense of foreign intrigue years ago, it is still one of the most irresistible summer soups. The secret of making the best gazpacho is to start with a bread-crumb base and only make the soup when intensely flavored farm vegetables are available.

3 slices fresh white bread, preferably homemade, crusts removed

5 cloves garlic, peeled

3 tablespoons fresh lemon juice

10 ripe large tomatoes, seeded and cut into ¼-inch dice

2 bunches scallions, minced

3 cucumbers, peeled, seeded, and cut into ¼-inch dice

2 green bell peppers, seeded and diced

1 red bell pepper, seeded and diced

1 yellow bell pepper, seeded and diced

1 large can (46 ounces) V-8 juice

3 tablespoons balsamic vinegar

5 tablespoons fruity olive oil

Salt and freshly ground pepper to taste

Croutons for garnish (see page 117)

1. Place the bread, garlic, and lemon juice in a blender or food processor fitted with the steel blade and process to a smooth paste. Transfer to a large mixing bowl.

2. Add all the vegetables to the bread paste and toss to combine. Stir in the V-8, then the vinegar, oil, salt, and pepper.

3. Purée half the soup in the food processor or blender and combine with the remaining soup. Refrigerate until very cold. Serve the soup garnished with a couple of croutons.

Makes 12 to 15 servings.

Chilled Potato, Pear, and Arugula Soup

The rather strange-sounding combination of ingredients work together in this exceptional cold soup.

4 tablespoons (½ stick) unsalted butter

1 medium red onion, minced

3 ribs celery, minced

2 quarts chicken stock, preferably homemade

1 cup dry white wine

2 large potatoes, peeled and cut into small dice

5 ripe pears, peeled, cored, and sliced

4 cups arugula, rinsed and stems removed, plus additional for garnish

1 cup light cream (see Index)

1 cup heavy or whipping cream

2 teaspoons ground coriander seeds

Salt and freshly ground white pepper to taste

1. Melt the butter in a stockpot over medium-high heat. Add the onion and celery and sauté, stirring frequently, for 7 minutes.

2. Add the chicken stock, wine, and potatoes. Simmer the soup just until the potatoes are tender, about 25 minutes.

3. Add the pears and arugula to the soup and simmer 5 minutes longer. Remove from the heat and stir in the light and heavy creams. Stir in the coriander. Process the soup in batches in a blender until smooth. Season to taste with salt and white pepper.

4. Refrigerate the soup until cold. To serve, ladle the cold soup into bowls and garnish each serving with a whole arugula leaf.

Makes 10 to 12 servings.

Beet and Beaujolais Soup

This soup has an intense deep ruby color but a light texture. The beets, pear, and raspberry vinegar all blend wonderfully with the fruitiness of Beaujolais wine. The soup is most refreshing during the hot summer months, but the color makes it an elegant choice to serve throughout the holidays. Try making it with Beaujolais Nouveau after mid-November.

8 medium beets, peeled
  and cut into ½-inch
  dice
1 small red onion,
  chopped
1 ripe medium pear,
  peeled, cored, and cut
  into ½-inch dice
3 tablespoons raw white
  rice

4½ cups water
1 tablespoon sugar
3 tablespoons raspberry
  vinegar
2 cups Beaujolais wine
Salt and freshly ground
  pepper to taste
2 teaspoons finely grated
  lemon zest
Crème fraîche for garnish

1. Place the beets, onion, pear, and rice together in a large saucepan. Add the water and heat to boiling over high heat. Reduce the heat and simmer uncovered until the beets are very tender, about 30 minutes.

2. Stir the sugar, vinegar, and wine into the soup. Purée the soup in batches in a blender. Season to taste with salt and pepper.

3. Strain the soup through a fine-mesh sieve to make it very smooth. Stir in the lemon zest. Serve the soup hot or very chilled. Garnish each serving with a small dollop of crème fraîche.

Makes 8 to 10 servings.

Summer
Savories

This chapter contains the recipes for the most irresistible food baked at Que Sera Sarah: pizzas, frittatas, calzones, turnovers and empanadas. California health crazes and Perrier preachings aside, East Coast saltwater seasons inspire hearty appetites and unrelenting cravings for carbohydrates. Every morning one entire counter of my shop is aromatically overladen with this collection of savories still sizzling from the oven. The hand-formed crusts are filled with nooks and crannies that support an almost unbearable amount of temptation: luscious local vegetables, shiny and smoky black Mediterranean olives, splashes of fiesta-colored peppers, fragrant green herbs, spicy cured meats and sausages, and spatters of pungent melted cheeses.

Whether these guilt-inducing specialties go on board boats, to the beach, nearest park bench, or are stashed furtively for bedtime snacks, I do not know. But I do know that by midafternoon of any given summer day, there is scarcely a stray pepperoni from a pizza or lone olive from a empanada left resting on the counter.

Deep-Dish Broccoli Pizza

Once upon a sunny summer morning in the early days of Que Sera Sarah, I found that I had a surplus of broccoli. I consulted local chef Marian Morash's superb *Victory Garden Cookbook* for inspiration; this recipe was the delicious best-selling result. I now make at least one of these outrageous pizzas every single day in the store, and, more often than not, I find I never have enough broccoli to keep up with the deep-dish devotees.

Olive oil and yellow cornmeal for the pan
1 recipe Pizza Dough (recipe follows)
1½ cups Pizza Sauce (recipe follows)
8 sweet Italian sausage (about 1 pound), casings removed
1 tablespoon fennel seeds
2 cups sliced fresh mushrooms

⅓ cup dry white wine
½ teaspoon coarsely ground pepper
2 quarts water
2 large bunches broccoli
4½ cups shredded mozzarella cheese
3 to 4 tablespoons olive oil

1. Brush a 14-inch deep-dish pizza pan lightly with olive oil and dust with cornmeal. Roll out two-thirds of the pizza dough into an 18-inch circle on a lightly floured surface. Fit the dough into the prepared pan, letting the excess dough hang over the edges.

2. Spread the pizza sauce evenly over the dough in the bottom of the pan.

3. Brown the sausage, crumbling it with a wooden spoon, and the fennel seeds in a large skillet over medium-high heat. Remove the sausage but keep the fat in the skillet. Add the mushrooms, wine, and pepper to the fat and cook, scraping up any browned bits on the bottom of the pan, just until the mushrooms are cooked through and most of the liquid has evaporated.

4. Preheat the oven to 400°F.

5. While the sausage and mushrooms are cooking, heat the water to boiling in a large pan. Trim off and discard the tough lower stalks on the broccoli. Slice the remaining stalks ½ inch thick. Separate the flowerets. When the water boils, add the

broccoli stalk pieces and cook for 4 minutes. Then add the flowerets and cook until barely tender, 2 to 3 minutes. Drain well in a colander.

6. Spread the cooked mushrooms over the pizza sauce in the pan. Top with 2 cups of the mozzarella.

7. Roll the remaining one-third of the dough into a 14-inch circle and place on top of the cheese layer. Press the edges into the dough-lined sides of the pan to secure. Slash the dough a few times with a sharp knife to create steam vents.

8. Spoon the sausage over the dough and top with all the broccoli. Sprinkle with the remaining 2½ cups mozzarella. Drizzle the top with the olive oil. Fold the edge of the dough over and crimp to form a thick rim.

9. Bake the pizza until the crust is browned and the cheese is bubbling, 40 to 45 minutes. Let stand for 5 to 10 minutes before cutting into wedges. The pizza is also delicious served at room temperature.

Makes 10 to 12 hearty slices.

Pizza Dough

I make pizza dough at least once a day in the shop and it is much more sturdy than most people would imagine. While it is often hard to make just the right amount of dough needed for a given recipe, I have found that trimmings and leftovers are amazingly resilient when tucked away in the refrigerator or freezer in anticipation of the next craving.

1 package active dry yeast	4½ teaspoons fruity olive oil
3 cups warm water (105° to 115°F)	¼ cup rye flour
2 teaspoons salt	8 to 9 cups unbleached all-purpose flour

1. Sprinkle the yeast over the warm water in a large bowl or heavy-duty mixer bowl and let stand for 5 minutes. Stir in the salt and oil, then the rye flour. By hand or machine, gradually mix in enough of the unbleached flour to make a moderately stiff dough. Knead the dough until smooth and satiny, 10 to 15 minutes.

2. Place the dough in a large bowl. Cover with plastic wrap or a damp towel and let rise in a warm place for 2 hours or in a cool spot overnight. Punch the dough down and use as called for

in the recipes. Any remaining dough can be double-wrapped in plastic wrap and stored in the refrigerator for 2 to 3 days or in the freezer up to 1 month. Let the dough come to room temperature before using.

Makes enough dough for two 15x10-inch pizzas or twelve 6-inch pizzas.

Pizza Sauce

A versatile, all-purpose, aromatic tomato sauce. In a pinch it can be used over spaghetti or in making lasagne.

¼ cup olive oil
1 large Spanish onion,
    chopped
6 cloves garlic, minced
2 cans (28 ounces each)
    Italian plum tomatoes,
    with juice
1 can (14½ ounces)
    whole tomatoes, with
    juice

5 tablespoons tomato
    paste
¾ cup dry red wine
¼ cup dried Italian herb
    blend
Salt and freshly ground
    pepper to taste

1. Heat the oil in a large saucepan over medium-high heat. Add the onion and garlic and cook, stirring frequently, for 10 minutes.

2. Stir in the canned tomatoes, tomato paste, and red wine. Season the sauce with the Italian herbs, salt, and pepper. Simmer, uncovered, over medium heat, stirring occasionally with a large spoon to break up the tomatoes, for about 45 minutes.

Makes 2 quarts.

Pizza Bianca

The crispness and saltiness of this pale pizza balances beautifully with Champagne bubbles. I often pass it on silver trays at the beginning of a wedding reception or other festive Champagne occasion.

Yellow cornmeal for the
  baking sheet
½ recipe Pizza Dough
  (see page 80)
½ cup extra-virgin
  olive oil
2 teaspoons coarse or
  kosher salt

3 tablespoons chopped
  fresh rosemary
1 dozen whole fresh sage
  leaves
3 cloves garlic, minced
½ cup finely chopped (not
  grated) Parmesan
  cheese

1. Preheat the oven to 400°F. Lightly sprinkle one 18 x 12-inch baking sheet with cornmeal.

2. Roll out the pizza dough as thinly as possible into a rough rectangle, 18 x 12 inches, on a lightly floured surface. Place the dough on the prepared baking sheet, stretching a bit if necessary.

3. Spread the olive oil evenly over the dough with a pastry brush. Sprinkle evenly all over with the salt and rosemary. Arrange the sage leaves artistically over the dough, then sprinkle with the garlic and Parmesan.

4. Bake pizza until crisp and light golden brown, 20 to 25 minutes. Let the pizza cool to room temperature, then cut into small irregular squares to serve.

Makes one 18 x 12-inch pizza.

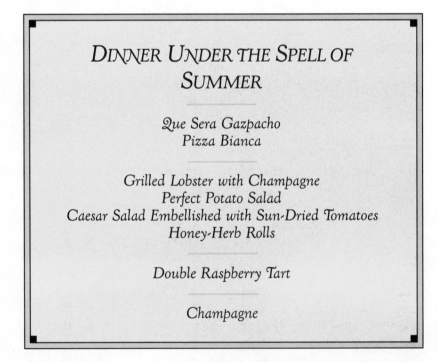

DINNER UNDER THE SPELL OF SUMMER

Que Sera Gazpacho
Pizza Bianca

Grilled Lobster with Champagne
Perfect Potato Salad
Caesar Salad Embellished with Sun-Dried Tomatoes
Honey-Herb Rolls

Double Raspberry Tart

Champagne

Pizza with a Few of My Favorite Things

Yellow cornmeal for the
  baking sheet
½ recipe Pizza Dough
  (see page 80)
1 cup Pizza Sauce
  (see page 81)
4 ounces prosciutto,
  thinly sliced
4 ounces crumbled
  Gorgonzola or blue
  cheese

8 sun-dried tomatoes
  packed in oil, drained
  and cut into slivers
½ cup pitted Niçoise olives
½ cup chopped fresh basil
½ cup freshly grated
  Parmesan cheese
2 tablespoons pine nuts,
  lightly toasted
3 tablespoons extra-virgin
  olive oil

1. Preheat the oven to 375°F. Lightly sprinkle cornmeal on a 15 x 10-inch baking sheet.

2. Roll out the dough into a 16 x 11-inch rectangle on a lightly floured surface. Place on the baking sheet and crimp the edges.

3. Spread the pizza sauce over the dough. Top with the prosciutto, then scatter the Gorgonzola, tomatoes, and olives over the prosciutto. Sprinkle with the basil, Parmesan, and pine nuts. Drizzle the oil evenly over the top.

4. Bake the pizza until the crust is golden brown and the topping is bubbling, 40 to 45 minutes. Let the pizza cool slightly, then cut into 8 squares and serve.

Makes 8 servings.

Pizza Rustica

This peasanty layered pizza makes perfect picnic fare. The colored stratified layers are an impressive sight, and the pizza will tote easily for an afternoon sail or a day's beach excursion.

*Olive oil and yellow
  cornmeal for the pan*
1 recipe Pizza Dough
  (see page 80)
4 tablespoons olive oil
1 medium red onion,
  minced
2 cloves garlic, minced
2 packages (10 ounces
  each) frozen spinach,
  thawed, steamed,
  squeezed dry, and
  chopped
2 tablespoons dry white
  wine
2 tablespoons heavy or
  whipping cream

¼ cup freshly grated
  Parmesan cheese
Salt and freshly ground
  pepper to taste
4 ounces mozzarella
  cheese, thinly sliced
¾ pound prosciutto,
  thinly sliced
1 can (16 ounces) whole
  pimientos, drained
12 ounces Provolone
  cheese, thinly sliced
10 sun-dried tomatoes,
  packed in oil, drained

1. Preheat the oven to 375°F. Lightly oil a 9½-inch springform pan and dust with cornmeal. Line 2 baking sheets with parchment paper.

2. Roll out half of the dough into 2 thin 9½-inch circles on a lightly floured surface. Transfer the circles to the lined baking sheets. Bake until lightly browned, 10 to 15 minutes. Let cool.

3. Meanwhile, heat 2 tablespoons of the oil in a medium skillet over medium-high heat. Add the onion and garlic and sauté, stirring occasionally, for 10 minutes. Stir in the spinach, wine, and cream and simmer until most of the liquid evaporates. Stir in the Parmesan and heat just until melted. Season to taste with salt and pepper and remove from heat.

4. Roll out two-thirds of the remaining dough into a 15-inch circle. Line the prepared springform pan with the dough and trim any overhanging dough.

5. Arrange all the mozzarella over the bottom of the dough and cover with one-third of the spinach mixture. Top with a layer of the prosciutto and then half the pimientos spread out flat. Top with a layer of the Provolone and follow with 1 of the baked dough circles. Press the layers lightly as you work.

6. Top the baked dough with another third of the spinach mixture and follow with a layer of prosciutto, all the sun-dried tomatoes, and then Provolone. Top with the second baked dough circle.

7. Make final layers with the remaining spinach mixture, prosciutto, pimientos, and Provolone.

8. Roll out the remaining dough into a 11-inch circle. Place over the top of the torte and join and decoratively crimp the edges to seal. Cut a few steam vents in the dough and brush with the remaining 2 tablespoons oil.

9. Place the torte on a baking sheet to catch any drips and bake until the top is light golden brown, 50 minutes to 1 hour. Let the pizza cool for at least 20 minutes. Remove the pizza from the pan. Serve, cut into wedges, warm or at room temperature.

Makes 8 to 10 servings.

Baby Pizzas

No pizza parlor can ever match the flavor or personality of these hand-formed miniature pizzas.

Olive oil and yellow
  cornmeal for the
  baking sheets
½ recipe Pizza Dough
  (see page 80)
2½ cups Pizza Sauce
  (see page 81)
1 small summer squash,
  sliced into thin rounds
6 thin slices prosciutto
1 green bell pepper, sliced
  into thin rings
1 can (14½ ounces)
  artichoke hearts,
  drained and thinly
  sliced
6 whole basil leaves
3 tablespoons olive oil
2½ cups shredded
  mozzarella

1. Preheat the oven to 375°F. Lightly oil two 15 x 10-inch baking sheets and sprinkle lightly with cornmeal.

2. Divide the pizza dough into 6 equal pieces. Roll out each piece into a 6- to 7-inch circle on a lightly floured surface. Place 3 dough circles on each baking sheet.

3. Spread a thin coating of the pizza sauce over each dough circle. Arrange the summer squash over one-quarter of each circle, the prosciutto over another quarter, the bell pepper over another quarter, and the artichoke hearts over the remaining quarter. Place 1 basil leaf in the center of each pizza and drizzle lightly with the oil.

4. Bake the pizzas until the crusts have just begun to color, 12 to 15 minutes. Scatter the cheese evenly over the pizzas and bake until the cheese is melted and bubbling, another 5 to 7 minutes. Serve hot or at room temperature.

Makes 6 baby pizzas.

Goat Cheese Calzones

A great filling for this hearty Italian turnover.

2 pounds ricotta cheese
8 ounces Montrachet
   goat cheese, without
   ash
4 ounces prosciutto,
   minced
2 ripe medium tomatoes,
   seeded and chopped
1 cup finely chopped
   mushrooms, squeezed
   dry in kitchen towel
¼ cup pine nuts, lightly
   toasted

1 cup grated mozzarella
   cheese
½ cup freshly grated
   Parmesan cheese
1 tablespoon dried Italian
   herb blend
3 tablespoons chopped
   fresh basil
Salt and freshly ground
   pepper to taste
½ recipe Pizza Dough
   (see page 80)
3 tablespoons fruity olive oil

1. To make the calzone filling, place the ricotta and goat cheese in a mixing bowl and beat until light and fluffy. Stir in the prosciutto, tomatoes, mushrooms, and pine nuts. Fold in the grated cheeses. Season the mixture with the Italian herb blend, basil, salt, and pepper.

2. Preheat the oven to 400°F. Line 2 baking sheets with parchment paper.

3. Divide the dough into 9 equal pieces and roll out each piece into a thin circle, about 5 inches in diameter, on a lightly floured surface. Place a heaping spoonful of the filling on half of each circle. Fold the dough over and moisten the edges with a little water to seal. Crimp the edges together as you would a pie shell.

4. Place the calzones on the lined baking sheets and brush with oil. Bake until puffed and lightly golden, 25 to 30 minutes. Serve hot or at room temperature.

Makes 9 calzones.

Tex-Mex Turnovers

These are one of my personal favorites. I love the way the creaminess of the cheese soothes the fire of the jalapeños. Some summer mornings when caffeine alone doesn't get me going, a nibble or two on a spicy turnover seems to do the trick. For more conventional noshing, make these for lunch or in miniature for a cocktail party.

CREAM CHEESE DOUGH:

12 ounces cream cheese, cold

1½ cups (3 sticks) unsalted butter, cold

¼ teaspoon salt

3 cups unbleached all-purpose flour

TEX-MEX FILLING:

12 ounces cream cheese, at room temperature

1 boneless skinless whole chicken breast, poached and diced

2 fresh jalapeño peppers, seeded and minced, or 1 can (4 ounces) chopped green chiles, drained

½ red bell pepper, seeded and diced

5 scallions, chopped

4 ounces Cheddar or Monterey Jack cheese, shredded

1 tablespoon ground cumin

Salt and freshly ground pepper to taste

EGG WASH:

1 large egg

1 tablespoon water

1. Prepare the dough: Cut both the cream cheese and butter into small pieces and place in a food processor fitted with the steel blade. Add the salt and the flour. Process the mixture just until it sticks together and begins to gather into a ball. Remove the dough from the machine, wrap in plastic wrap, and refrigerate at least 1 hour.

2. Prepare the filling: Place all the filling ingredients in a mixing bowl and beat with an electric mixer until well blended.

3. Preheat the oven to 350°F. Line 2 baking sheets with aluminum foil or parchment paper.

4. Divide the dough in half and roll out 1 piece ⅛ inch thick on a lightly floured surface. Using a pastry cutter or knife, cut out as many 5-inch squares as possible. Reserve the dough scraps.

5. Place 2 heaping tablespoons of the filling on half of each square. Fold each square neatly in half to form a triangle. Seal by

pressing around the edges with the tines of a fork. Place the turnovers on the lined baking sheets.

6. Repeat with the remaining dough and filling. You should have about 16 turnovers.

7. Make the egg wash by beating the egg and water together. Brush the egg wash over the turnovers. Roll out the dough scraps and cut out using a small star cookie cutter. Place a star on top of each turnover and brush again with the egg wash.

8. Bake the turnovers until lightly browned all over, 25 to 30 minutes. Serve hot or at room temperature.

Makes about 16 turnovers.

Empanadas

Oil for the baking sheets	*2 large eggs*
2 packages (17¼ ounces	*2 tablespoons water*
each) frozen puff	*Lamb and Pine Nut*
pastry	*Filling or Picadillo*
Flour for the pastry sheets	*Filling (recipes follow)*

1. Thaw the puff pastry according to package directions. Line two 15 x 10-inch baking sheets with parchment paper. Place each sheet of pastry on a lightly floured surface and roll lightly in all directions to smooth the dough and expand the size slightly.

2. Cut 3 of the puff pastry sheets into 6 equal squares each; reserve the fourth sheet for decorations. Beat the egg and water together and brush lightly around the edges of each square. Place a heaping spoonful of either filling on half of each square. Fold dough squares over to make triangles and seal the edges by pressing together with the tines of a fork. Place the empanadas a couple inches apart on the baking sheets.

3. Lightly flour the remaining sheet of puff pastry and cut out using a 2-inch star cookie cutter or other cutter of your choice. Place a star on each turnover. Brush the turnovers all over with the egg wash and refrigerate for 20 minutes.

4. Preheat the oven to 400°F.

5. Bake the empanadas until toasty brown all over, 25 to 30 minutes. Serve hot or at room temperature.

Makes 18 empanadas.

Note: Baked empanadas can be frozen in plastic bags. Heat frozen empanadas on baking sheets in a 400°F oven. Additionally, baby empanadas make great hors d'oeuvres and can be made in the same manner using 2-inch squares of puff pastry.

Lamb and Pine Nut Filling

2 tablespoons olive oil
1 medium red onion,
  minced
3 cloves garlic, minced
1½ pounds ground lean
  lamb
½ cup currants
½ cup dry red wine

¼ cup pine nuts, lightly
  toasted
1 cup crumbled feta
  cheese
3 tablespoons chopped
  fresh mint
Salt and freshly ground
  pepper to taste

1. Heat the oil in a large skillet over medium-high heat. Stir in the onion and garlic and sauté for 5 minutes. Add the lamb to the skillet and cook, crumbling the meat with a fork or the back of a wooden spoon, just until the meat is no longer pink.

2. Stir in the currants and wine. Simmer uncovered for 20 minutes.

3. Stir in the pine nuts and feta and cook 2 minutes longer. Remove from the heat. Stir in the mint and season with salt and pepper.
Makes 6 cups.

Picadillo Filling for Empanadas

3 tablespoons olive oil
2 green bell peppers,
  seeded and diced
1 red bell pepper, seeded
  and diced
1 large onion, chopped
1½ pounds ground lean
  beef
3 cloves garlic, minced

1 cup tomato sauce
1 cup dry red wine
1 cup dark raisins
1 cup Spanish olives,
  sliced
½ cup capers, drained
Salt and freshly ground
  pepper to taste

1. Heat the oil in a large skillet over medium-high heat. Add the peppers and onion and sauté for 10 minutes.

2. At the same time, cook the ground beef in another skillet,

just until it is no longer pink. Add to the pepper mixture, then stir in the garlic, tomato sauce, wine, raisins, olives, and capers. Season with salt and pepper. Simmer uncovered, stirring occasionally, for 40 minutes.

Makes 6 cups.

Frozen Puff Pastry

In the process of writing this cookbook, I have realized that there are certain ingredient revelations that might shock devoted customers and serious cooks. One example is the fact that I make my empanadas with frozen rather than homemade puff pastry. Although I am fanatically opinionated about all sorts of food preparations, tastes, and techniques, I am not so holy that I will not nab a good convenience product when it comes along. My three favorites are Hellmann's mayonnaise, Pepperidge Farm Herb Stuffing crumbs, and frozen puff pastry.

In the case of puff pastry, I find that my empanada fillings are so flavorful that they would overpower the delicacy of the best and most time-consuming homemade puff pastry. While I would never dream of using frozen puff pastry for making feathery light Napoleons or Feuilletés, it makes little qualitative difference in a hearty empanada recipe. And I must confess that as intimately engrossed as I am with food preparation, I don't mind saving a little time here and there to allow for a perusal of a current best-seller or a sunny siesta at the beach.

September Stuffed Cabbage

I always herald September in the shop by placing one of these fabulous peasanty stuffed cabbages on a pedestal next to all the pizzas. Making this brings out all my Polish instincts.

1 head Savoy or other
  leafy green cabbage
  (about 2½ pounds)
3 tablespoons unsalted
  butter
1 medium onion, chopped
2 leeks, rinsed, dried,
  and chopped
3 cloves garlic, minced
12 ounces sweet Italian
  sausage, casings removed
1 pound Polish kielbasa,
  cut into ¼-inch dice

1 tablespoon caraway seeds
1½ cups Riesling wine
2 packages (10 ounces each)
  frozen chopped spinach,
  cooked and drained
1½ cups cooked rice
1½ cups grated Gruyère
2 large eggs
2 teaspoons dried thyme
Pinch grated nutmeg
Salt and freshly ground
  pepper to taste
4 slices bacon

1. Heat a large pot of water to boiling. Remove the outer leaves from the cabbage that come off easily and remain whole. Blanch the leaves in the boiling water for 3 minutes and remove to cool and drain. Add the remaining cabbage in 1 piece to the boiling water and cook until tender, 7 to 10 minutes. Drain, cool, and slice the cabbage into thin strips.

2. Melt the butter in a large skillet over medium-high heat. Add the onion, leeks, and garlic and sauté for 5 minutes. Add the Italian sausage and cook, crumbling with the back of a wooden spoon, until the meat is no longer pink. Stir in the kielbasa and the caraway seeds. Add ½ cup of the wine and cook until most of the liquid evaporates, about 10 minutes.

3. Transfer the meat mixture to a large mixing bowl and combine with the shredded cabbage, spinach, rice, and cheese. Beat in the eggs to bind the mixture. Season with the thyme, nutmeg, salt, and pepper.

4. Preheat the oven to 375°F. Lightly butter a 9-inch round ovenproof bowl.

5. Cross 2 slices of the bacon over the bottom of the bowl. Line the bowl with the whole cabbage leaves, letting the edges hang over the edge of the bowl and reserving 1 leaf for the top. Gently pack the meat mixture into the bowl. Top with the reserved cabbage leaf and fold the hanging leaves toward the center. Crisscross the remaining bacon over the top.

6. Pour the remaining wine over the top and let it seep between the sides of the bowl and the cabbage leaves. Cover the top of the cabbage with a piece of buttered aluminum foil and bake for 1 hour. Remove from the oven and let stand for 15 minutes. Carefully invert onto a platter and serve.

Makes 8 servings.

Mexican Torta

This impressive savory torte is a Mexican-food lover's dream come true.

3 tablespoons olive oil
2 cloves garlic, minced
1 medium onion, chopped
3 small fresh jalapeño
  peppers, seeded and
  minced
1 green bell pepper,
  seeded and minced
1 red bell pepper, seeded
  and minced
1½ pounds lean ground
  beef
2 tablespoons ground
  cumin

1 tablespoon chili powder
½ cup fresh lime juice
½ cup dry red wine
½ cup raisins
½ cup slivered almonds, toasted
1 can (16 ounces) refried beans
2 tablespoons chopped
  fresh coriander
Salt and freshly ground
  pepper to taste
1½ pounds Monterey
  Jack cheese, thinly sliced
Butter for the aluminum foil

1. Heat the oil in a large skillet over medium-high heat. Stir in the onion and garlic and cook 2 minutes. Add the jalapeños, and green and red peppers and cook, stirring occasionally, 5 minutes.

2. Add the ground beef and cook, crumbling with a wooden spoon, just until the meat is no longer pink. Stir in the cumin and chili powder and cook 1 minute. Stir in the lime juice, wine, and raisins; simmer uncovered for 20 minutes.

A great many people, to be sure, visit the Island every summer for quite other purposes. They go to have a good time at a summer resort. But like the case of the man who went to church to scoff and remained to pray, the Island lays its spell over every one of them; they come to love best of all its ancient flavor; they choose by preference its oldest houses to live in; they resent every suggestion that the cobblestones be removed from Main Street in favor of asphalt; they walk at sunset down the ancient, crooked streets and call Nantucket "home."

—Guide to Nantucket 1932

3. Stir in the almonds, beans, and coriander. Season to taste with salt and pepper and remove from the heat.

4. Preheat the oven to 350°F.

5. Line the bottom and sides of a 3-quart soufflé dish with the sliced Monterey Jack. Pack one-third of the meat mixture into the dish and top with a layer of the cheese. Repeat the layers 2 more times, ending with cheese.

6. Cover the dish with a buttered sheet of aluminum foil. Place the dish in a larger baking pan and pour enough hot water into the pan to come halfway up the side of the dish. Bake until firm, 50 minutes. Remove the dish from the water bath and let stand for 15 minutes. Unmold the torta onto a serving platter. Cut into wedges and serve at once.

Makes 8 servings.

Italian Ricotta Pie

Every once in a while I crave the robust quality of Italian pastries. They're the thing to eat when I want to feel like I've really eaten something. I particularly like the combination of sweet, savory, and smoky in this recipe, which traces its origins to cooking traditions of the Renaissance.

CRUST:

2¼ cups unbleached all-purpose flour

⅓ cup sugar

½ teaspoon salt

1 cup lard, cold, cut into small pieces

3 large egg yolks, lightly beaten

3 tablespoons cold water

FILLING:

2 pounds ricotta cheese

5 large eggs

12 ounces fresh mozzarella cheese, cut into ¼-inch dice

5 ounces prosciutto, minced

½ cup freshly grated Pecorino Romano cheese

1 tablespoon dried oregano

Salt and freshly ground pepper to taste

EGG WASH:

1 large egg

1½ tablespoons water

1. Prepare the crust: Place the flour, sugar, salt, and lard in a food processor fitted with the steel blade. Process until the mixture resembles coarse meal. Add the egg yolks and cold water and process just until the dough begins to gather into a ball. Wrap the dough in plastic wrap and refrigerate at least 1 hour.

2. Prepare the filling: Beat the ricotta and eggs together in a large mixing bowl until smooth. Stir in the mozzarella, prosciutto, and Pecorino Romano. Season with the oregano, salt, and pepper.

3. Preheat the oven to 350°F.

4. Roll out two-thirds of the dough into a 12-inch circle on a well-floured surface. Carefully fit the dough into a 9½-inch springform pan. Pour the filling into the pan. Roll out the remaining dough into a 10½-inch circle and place on top of the pie. Crimp the edges together and trim in a decorative fashion.

5. Make the egg wash by beating the egg and water together. Brush the egg wash over the top of the pie with a pastry brush. You can decorate the top of the pie with cutouts from the dough scraps. Brush the decorations with egg wash.

6. Bake the pie until golden brown, 1¼ hours. Let cool at least 30 minutes before cutting into wedges. Serve warm or at room temperature.

Makes 12 servings.

Lobster Frittata

A more sumptuous rendition of the Vegetable Frittata!

3 tablespoons olive oil
1 medium red onion, thinly sliced
2 cloves garlic, minced
3 summer squash, sliced ¼ inch thick
1 yellow bell pepper, seeded and cut into ¼-inch-thick strips
2 red bell peppers, seeded and cut into ¼-inch-wide strips
6 large eggs
¼ cup heavy or whipping cream
1 teaspoon saffron threads
3 tablespoons chopped fresh basil
Salt and freshly ground pepper to taste
2 packages (5 ounces each) Boursin cheese
1 pound cooked fresh lobster meat, cut into bite-size chunks
2 cups grated Gruyère cheese

1. Preheat the oven to 350°F. Butter the bottom and sides of a 10-inch springform pan.

2. Heat the oil in a large pot over medium-high heat. Add the onion, garlic, squash, and peppers; sauté, stirring frequently, until crisp-tender, 10 to 15 minutes.

3. While the vegetables are cooking, whisk the eggs and cream together in a large mixing bowl. Whisk in the saffron, basil, salt, and pepper. Crumble the Boursin into small pieces and stir into the egg mixture. Stir in the lobster meat and sautéed vegetables. Then add the Gruyère and stir well to combine. Pour the mixture into the prepared pan.

4. Place the pan on a baking sheet to catch any leaks. Bake just until firm throughout, 45 to 60 minutes. Let cool for 10 minutes and then cut into wedges.

Makes 6 to 8 servings.

Vegetable Frittata

This spectacular vegetable frittata is more dramatic than most because it is baked in a springform pan for added height and richness. Depending on the weather or the occasion, it is equally delicious hot, at room temperature, or cold—for a lazy summer brunch, a boat picnic, or late night alfresco nibble.

3 tablespoons olive oil
1 large Spanish onion, thinly sliced
3 cloves garlic, minced
3 medium summer squash, sliced ¼ inch thick
3 medium zucchini, sliced ¼ inch thick
1 red bell pepper, seeded and cut into ¼-inch-wide strips
1 yellow bell pepper, seeded and cut into ¼-inch-thick strips
1 green bell pepper, seeded and cut into ¼-inch-thick strips

8 ounces fresh mushrooms, sliced
6 large eggs
¼ cup heavy or whipping cream
2 teaspoons salt
2 teaspoons freshly ground pepper
2 cups stale French bread cubes (½-inch pieces)
8 ounces cream cheese, crumbled into small bits
2 cups grated Swiss cheese

1. Preheat the oven to 350°F. Grease the bottom and sides of a 10-inch springform pan.

2. Heat the oil in a large pot over medium-high heat. Add the onion, garlic, summer squash, zucchini, peppers, and mushrooms; sauté, stirring and tossing the vegetables occasionally, until crisp-tender, 15 to 20 minutes.

3. While the vegetables are cooking, whisk the eggs and cream together in a large mixing bowl. Season with salt and pepper. Stir in the bread, cream cheese, and Swiss cheese.

4. Add the sautéed vegetables to the egg mixture and stir until well combined. Pour into the prepared pan and pack the mixture tightly.

5. Place the pan on a baking sheet to catch any leaks. Bake the frittata until firm to the touch, puffed, and golden brown, about 1 hour. If the top of the frittata is getting too brown, cover it with a sheet of aluminum foil.

6. Serve the frittata hot, at room temperature, or cold. It can also be reheated in a 350°F oven until warmed through, about 15 minutes.

Makes 8 servings.

Nantucket Farm Vegetables

*If thou art wise, lay thee down now and steep thyself
in a bowl of summer-time.*
—Virgil

One of the very first things that lured me to living on Nantucket was the spectacular array of locally grown vegetables abundantly displayed on rickety old carts throughout the morning on Main Street. To this day I remain convinced that I will never taste more intensely flavored and perfect vegetables anywhere in the world.

Farm vegetables have come to symbolize for me the essence of what it means to live on and love Nantucket. The cascading heads of light and leafy lettuces refresh like the froth of the ocean waves, the deep purple eggplants brood like the early morning fog of the moors, the dusty beets and potatoes concentrate the earthy taste of the salt-misted shores, the plump red and yellow tomatoes overwhelm as the most brillant of Madaket sunsets, and the baskets of fresh herbs intoxicate in the way of all the best of Nantucket.

Tian of Just Picked Vegetables

A tian is a large round earthenware dish used in Provence for baking gratins. Vegetable tians make great accompaniments to grilled foods.

3 medium zucchini, sliced ¼ inch thick
Salt
3 medium summer squash, sliced ¼ inch thick
1 large eggplant, sliced ¼ inch thick
5 ripe medium tomatoes, sliced ¼ inch thick
¾ cup olive oil
2 large yellow onions, chopped

4 cloves garlic, minced
1½ cups fresh bread crumbs
Freshly ground pepper to taste
1 bunch fresh parsley, minced
Very finely chopped zest of 1 lemon
1 cup freshly grated Parmesan cheese

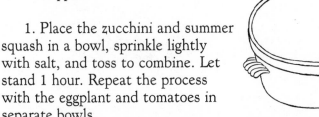

1. Place the zucchini and summer squash in a bowl, sprinkle lightly with salt, and toss to combine. Let stand 1 hour. Repeat the process with the eggplant and tomatoes in separate bowls.

2. Meanwhile, heat ¼ cup of the oil in a large skillet over medium-high heat. Add the onions and sauté, stirring frequently, for 5 minutes. Stir in the garlic, reduce the heat to medium, and cook, stirring occasionally, 10 minutes longer.

3. Remove the onion mixture from the heat. Stir in the bread crumbs. Season to taste with salt and pepper. Sprinkle half the mixture over the bottom of a 12-inch round or oval gratin dish.

4. Drain the zucchini and summer squash and pat dry with paper towels. Repeat with the eggplant and tomatoes.

5. Preheat the oven to 350°F.

6. Alternately layer the vegetables over the bread mixture in the dish. Sprinkle each layer with salt and pepper and drizzle with the remaining oil. Top with the remaining bread mixture.

7. Cover the dish tightly with aluminum foil and bake for 30 minutes. Combine the parsley, lemon zest, and Parmesan cheese.

Remove the foil from the dish and sprinkle the parsley mixture evenly over the top. Bake uncovered until the top is nicely browned and the vegetables are tender, 20 to 25 minutes. Let stand several minutes and then serve.

Makes 8 to 10 servings.

Oil-Roasted Farm Vegetables

This is one of the simplest, most colorful, and absolutely ravishing ways I know of preparing summer vegetables warm from the vine.

3 large or 12 small red
    potatoes, scrubbed
¾ to 1 cup olive oil
Coarse (kosher) salt and
    freshly ground pepper
    to taste
1 medium eggplant
2 medium zucchini
2 medium summer
    squash

2 yellow bell peppers
2 red bell peppers
2 medium red onions,
    peeled
3 ripe medium tomatoes,
    seeded and cut into
    ½-inch wedges
¼ cup chopped fresh basil

1. Cut the potatoes into ⅛-inch-thick slices. Arrange the slices in a single layer in a 12 x 9-inch baking dish and drizzle lightly with some of the oil. Sprinkle lightly with salt and pepper.

2. Cut the unpeeled eggplant into ½-inch-thick slices, then cut the slices crosswise in half. Slice the zucchini and summer squash in the same manner. Core and seed the peppers, cut into ½-inch-thick rings, and then in half to make half rings. Finally, cut the red onion into ¼-inch-thick half circles.

3. Preheat the oven to 375°F.

4. To form a rainbow of colors, arrange all the vegetables over the potatoes in compact, alternating rows, each vegetable slice standing balanced on its straight edge. Drizzle the vegetables with about ½ cup oil and sprinkle with salt and pepper.

5. Cover the dish very tightly with aluminum foil. Bake for 1¼ hours. Remove the foil and insert the tomato wedges ran-

domly between the rows of vegetables. Sprinkle the basil over the top and drizzle with a bit more olive oil if the vegetables seem to be drying out. Bake the vegetables uncovered 30 to 40 minutes longer. Serve the vegetables warm or at room temperature.

Makes 8 to 10 servings.

Summer Squash Casserole

This was one of my favorite things to make and eat during the summers I spent with my aunt and uncle on Nantucket. It is still, in my opinion, the most delicious way to savor summer squash.

2 tablespoons olive oil
10 medium summer
  squash, sliced ¼ inch
  thick
2 medium red onions,
  thinly sliced
Salt and freshly ground
  pepper to taste
Fines herbes or your
  favorite blend of salad
  herbs to taste

10 ounces sharp Cheddar
  cheese, sliced ¼ inch
  thick
8 ounces Havarti,
  Monterey Jack, or
  Swiss cheese, sliced ¼
  inch thick

1. Preheat the oven to 375°F.
2. Brush a 10-inch round casserole or soufflé dish with the oil. Arrange a layer of summer squash slices evenly in the bottom of the casserole. Top with a layer of onion and sprinkle with salt, pepper, and herbs. Dot with slices of Cheddar cheese. Repeat the layers, alternating the Havarti and Cheddar. Finish with a layer of cheese. Cover the casserole with aluminum foil.
3. Bake for 35 minutes. Remove the foil and continue to bake until the squash is tender and the cheese is bubbly and browned, 15 to 20 minutes. Let stand 5 minutes before serving.

Makes 8 to 10 servings.

Stuffed Summer Tomatoes

I first discovered baked stuffed tomatoes in Rome and couldn't wait to try the recipe using Nantucket tomatoes. I am happy to report that the dish loses none of its delectable appeal in translation. Serve on a patio as a summer luncheon entrée or as a peasanty first course at dinner time.

6 firm ripe large tomatoes
Coarse (kosher) salt and
   freshly ground pepper
   to taste
3 tablespoons olive oil
1 medium yellow onion,
   chopped
3 cloves garlic, minced
6 sweet Italian sausages
   (about ½ pound),
   casings removed
2 tablespoons balsamic
   vinegar
1 cup cold cooked
   long-grain or
   Arborio rice

3 tablespoons chopped
   fresh basil
3 tablespoons chopped
   fresh parsley
1 large egg
¼ cup pine nuts, lightly
   toasted
½ cup shredded
   mozzarella cheese
½ cup freshly grated
   Parmesan cheese

1. Slice the tops off the tomatoes and discard. Using a spoon or small paring knife, remove the pulp from the tomatoes and reserve. Sprinkle the inside of each tomato shell with salt and pepper. Invert the shells onto paper towels and let drain for 20 minutes.

2. Meanwhile, heat the oil in a medium skillet over medium-high heat. Add the onion and garlic and sauté for 5 minutes. Add the sausage and cook, crumbling the meat with a fork or wooden spoon into small pieces, just until the meat begins to lose its pink color. Stir in the reserved tomato pulp and the vinegar; simmer uncovered for 15 minutes.

3. Reduce the heat to low and stir in the rice, basil, and parsley. Season to taste with salt and pepper. Cook 2 minutes and remove from the heat. Lightly beat the egg and stir it into the filling mixture. Stir in the pine nuts, half the mozzarella, and half the Parmesan.

4. Preheat the oven to 375°F.

5. Place the tomato shells in a baking dish just large enough

to hold them. Spoon the filling into the shells, mounding it slightly on top. Sprinkle with the remaining mozzarella and Parmesan. Bake the tomatoes for 25 to 30 minutes. Serve slightly warm or at room temperature.

Makes 6 servings.

Bruschetta

Bruschetta is a simple but superb Italian appetizer of thick slices of toasted bread spread with a garden-fresh topping of marinated deep red tomatoes, basil, and olive oil. This is my friend Elena's version, learned from her relatives in Italy but made with the local Nantucket tomatoes and Portuguese bread.

3 cups diced, seeded,
  peeled ripe tomatoes
5 tablespoons chopped
  fresh basil
1 tablespoon minced
  garlic
¼ cup extra-virgin
  olive oil

Salt and freshly ground
  pepper to taste
6 thick (½ to ¾ inch)
  slices Italian or
  Portuguese bread,
  toasted

1. Combine the tomatoes, basil, garlic, and oil in a mixing bowl. Season to taste with salt and pepper. Let the mixture marinate at room temperature for 45 minutes.

2. Spoon the mixture generously over the toasted bread. Serve with a knife and fork as an appetizer or antipasto.

Makes 6 servings.

Just Tomatoes

I have never been quite certain whether there is something in the salt-misted air or mysterious elements in the soil, but I think that the Nantucket tomatoes of August and September are the best-tasting tomatoes in the entire world. I eat them every single day of their short season and find that they need very little embellishment. This is how I like to prepare them.

---

4 vine-ripened very large tomatoes	Coarse (kosher) salt and freshly ground black pepper to taste
3 to 4 tablespoons extra-virgin olive oil	3 tablespoons thinly slivered fresh basil
1½ tablespoons balsamic vinegar	

About 30 minutes before serving, cut the tomatoes into thick ½-inch slices and arrange them on a flat platter. Drizzle with the oil and vinegar and sprinkle with salt and pepper. Scatter the basil over the top. Let stand at room temperature for 30 minutes. Then savor and understand why tomatoes were created.

Makes 4 servings.

Tomato Relish

My aunt makes this relish every September with the ripest summer tomatoes. We love it as a condiment with red meat, game, grilled sandwiches, or even spooned directly from the jar onto the tip of the tongue.

---

21 pounds ripe red tomatoes	4 pounds sugar
2 pints white distilled vinegar	4 bottles (6 ounces each) liquid pectin
½ cup fresh lemon juice	4 cinnamon sticks
	1 cup bourbon

1. Core the tomatoes and chop them into coarse chunks. Place the tomatoes, vinegar, and lemon juice in a large non-aluminum stockpot. Heat to boiling. Reduce the heat and simmer uncovered for 30 minutes. Remove from the heat and drain the liquid from the tomatoes in a colander.

2. Return the tomatoes to the pot and stir in the sugar, pectin, and cinnamon. Simmer 20 minutes. Stir in the bourbon and simmer 10 minutes longer. Let the tomato relish cool for several hours or overnight.

3. Ladle the relish into sterilized jars and seal according to manufacturer's instructions.

Makes about 12 pints.

Ratatouille

Ratatouille is the perfect dish to make when all of summer's vegetables are at their peak. It is a wonderful warm accompaniment to grilled fare and a refreshing cold salad the next day. However, my very favorite way to enjoy ratatouille is to stir in cubes of mozzarella just after the mixture has finished cooking and pack it into a pocket of fresh Syrian bread. It makes a luscious, though slightly messy, stuffed sandwich.

½ cup olive oil
4 large Spanish onions,
    thinly sliced
6 cloves garlic, minced
2 medium eggplants,
    unpeeled, cut into 1- to
    1½-inch cubes
2 green bell peppers,
    seeded and cut into
    ½-inch-wide strips
2 red bell peppers, seeded
    and cut into ½-inch-
    wide strips
3 medium zucchini,
    sliced ¼ inch thick
3 medium summer
    squash, sliced ¼ inch
    thick

3 tablespoons dried
    oregano
1 tablespoon dried
    marjoram
Salt and freshly ground
    pepper to taste
4 ripe medium tomatoes,
    seeded and cut into
    ¾-inch dice
1 pound fresh small
    mushrooms
½ cup chopped fresh basil
½ cup chopped fresh
    parsley
12 ounces mozzarella
    cheese, cut into
    ½-inch dice

1. Heat the oil in a very large pot over medium-high heat. Add the onions and sauté, stirring occasionally, until soft and translucent.

2. Add the garlic and eggplant to the pot and cook until the eggplant begins to soften, about 10 minutes. Add the bell peppers, zucchini, summer squash, oregano, marjoram, and salt and pepper to taste. Stir and cover the pot. Reduce the heat and simmer for 30 minutes.

3. Stir in the tomatoes and mushrooms and cook uncovered, stirring occasionally, 10 minutes longer. Stir in the basil and parsley and cook 5 more minutes. Remove from the heat and let cool a bit. Stir in the diced mozzarella and serve.

Makes 12 servings.

Green Beans with Warm Mustard Vinaigrette

A perfect last-minute accompaniment for many summer dishes. Use only the most tender green beans.

2 pounds fresh green beans, ends trimmed	½ cup olive oil
2 shallots, minced	Salt and freshly ground pepper to taste
2 tablespoons Dijon mustard	¼ cup chopped fresh dill
2 tablespoons balsamic vinegar	

1. Heat a large pot of water to boiling. Add the green beans and cook until crisp-tender, 2 to 4 minutes. Drain well.

2. While the beans are cooking, place the shallots, mustard, vinegar, oil, salt, and pepper in a small saucepan. Heat, whisking constantly, just until the mixture is hot to the touch.

3. Toss the hot green beans with the dressing to coat. Quickly add the dill and toss to combine. Serve at once.

Makes 6 to 8 servings.

Baby Carrots with Dill and Capers

The bunches of baby Nantucket carrots with their feathery green tops always look so adorable that I have a hard time deciding between using them decoratively on the table or delectably on the dinner plate.

Salt
1 pound baby carrots,
    trimmed and lightly
    peeled

4 tablespoons (½ stick)
    unsalted butter, melted
¼ cup chopped fresh dill
1½ tablespoons minced capers

1. Heat a pot of salted water to boiling. Add the carrots and cook just until barely tender. Drain well and return to the pot.

2. Toss the hot carrots with the butter, dill, and capers. Keep warm on the stove until ready to serve.

Makes 6 servings.

Fresh Peas with Prosciutto

When fresh peas are available on Nantucket, I can rarely restrain myself from popping them raw from the shell directly into my mouth. When I can muster up enough discipline, this is the way I like to cook farm peas.

4 tablespoons (½ stick)
    unsalted butter
1 small red onion,
    minced
4 cups (4 pounds in the
    pod) shelled fresh peas
1 tablespoon sugar
1 cup chicken stock,
    preferably homemade

4 ounces thinly sliced
    prosciutto, cut into
    thin strips
Salt and freshly ground
    pepper to taste
2 tablespoons chopped
    fresh parsley

1. Melt the butter in a medium saucepan over medium-high heat. Add the onion and cook, stirring occasionally, just until softened, about 5 minutes.

2. Stir in the peas, sugar, and chicken stock and simmer covered until the peas are barely tender, about 5 minutes. Stir in the prosciutto and cook 1 minute longer.

3. Using a slotted spoon, transfer the peas and prosciutto to a warmed serving bowl. Reduce the liquid remaining in the saucepan over high heat to a thin syrupy glaze. Pour the glaze over the peas and season with salt and pepper. Sprinkle with parsley and serve at once.

Makes 6 to 8 servings.

Corn Pudding

A while ago I was researching old Nantucket recipes and came across many for corn pudding. This is my updated version. It is a creamy and comforting way to enjoy corn off the cob.

8 to 10 ears fresh corn
1 large egg
½ cup light cream (see Index)
½ cup heavy or whipping cream
1 tablespoon brown sugar
2 tablespoons snipped fresh chives

Pinch grated nutmeg
Salt and freshly ground pepper to taste
½ cup plus 3 tablespoons crumbled Ritz crackers
4 tablespoons (½ stick) unsalted butter, melted

1. Preheat the oven to 350°F. Butter a 6- to 8-cup casserole.
2. With a sharp knife, split each row of corn kernels on each ear of corn down the center. Scrape enough kernels off the cobs to measure 2½ cups.
3. Beat the egg, light cream, heavy cream, and brown sugar in a mixing bowl just until blended. Stir in the chives and nutmeg. Season to taste with salt and pepper. Stir in the corn.
4. Toss ½ cup cracker crumbs with 3 tablespoons of the melted butter in a large mixing bowl, then stir in the corn mixture. Pour the corn mixture into the prepared casserole. Toss the remaining 3 tablespoons cracker crumbs with remaining 1 tablespoon butter. Sprinkle the crumbs over the top of the pudding.
5. Bake the pudding uncovered until light golden brown and slightly firm to the touch, 45 to 50 minutes.
Makes 6 servings.

Brussels Sprouts with Poppy Seeds and Sherry

A quick and delicious way to prepare this plump little autumn vegetable.

1½ pounds Brussels
  sprouts, trimmed and
  cut with X on bottom
3 tablespoons unsalted
  butter
2 tablespoons sherry

1½ tablespoons poppy
  seeds
Pinch grated nutmeg
Salt and freshly ground
  pepper to taste

1. Steam the Brussels sprouts in a vegetable steamer over boiling water just until crisp-tender. Drain.

2. Meanwhile, melt the butter in a small saucepan. Stir in the sherry and the poppy seeds and simmer for 3 minutes. Stir in the nutmeg, salt, and pepper to taste. Pour the butter over the hot Brussels sprouts in a serving bowl; toss to coat well. Serve at once.

Makes 6 servings.

Broccoli with Balsamic Butter

The rich tang of Balsamic vinegar splashed over vibrant green summer broccoli makes for an irresistible vegetable.

1 large head broccoli,
  trimmed and broken
  into large flowerets
2 tablespoons balsamic
  vinegar
2 tablespoons dry
  red wine

6 tablespoons unsalted
  butter, cold and cut
  into small pieces
Salt and freshly ground
  pepper to taste

1. Steam the broccoli in a vegetable steamer over boiling water just until crisp-tender.

2. Meanwhile, combine the vinegar and wine in a small saucepan and cook over medium-high heat until reduced by half. Remove from the heat and whisk in the butter, bit by bit until all is incorporated and the sauce is creamy. Season to taste with salt and pepper.

3. Pour the balsamic butter over the broccoli and toss to coat well. Serve at once.

Makes 4 to 6 servings.

Braised Cauliflower

One evening I was discussing favorite foods with a group of friends. One person mentioned that his favorite vegetable was cauliflower cooked in chicken stock. As I am a great lover of the vegetable, I decided to experiment and discovered the method to be a nice enrichment to the subtle flavor of cauliflower.

1 large head or 2 small
   heads cauliflower
4 tablespoons unsalted
   butter
1 carrot, peeled and
   minced

2 shallots, minced
1 cup chicken stock,
   preferably homemade
3 tablespoons dry vermouth
Salt and freshly ground
   pepper to taste

1. Prepare the cauliflower by discarding the outer green leaves and cutting out the thick center core. Break the head into flowerets, then cut each floweret into ½-inch-thick slices. Set aside.

2. Melt the butter in a large skillet over medium-high heat. Add the carrots and shallots and sauté for 3 minutes. Stir in the cauliflower pieces and toss to coat with the vegetables and butter. Pour in the chicken stock and vermouth. Reduce the heat to medium, cover the pan, and braise the cauliflower just until crisp-tender, about 7 minutes. Season with salt and pepper to taste. Serve at once.

Makes 6 servings.

Beets with Raspberry Vinegar

The taste of these raspberry-infused beets makes them a passion, but I also love the intense burst of color they bring to the dinner table.

12 medium beets,
   trimmed, washed, and
   peeled
3 tablespoons unsalted
   butter

2 tablespoons raspberry
   vinegar
Salt and freshly ground
   pepper to taste

Place the beets in a large saucepan and cover with water. Bring to a boil over medium-high heat, then reduce the heat and simmer uncovered until the beets are just tender. Drain and return the beets to the saucepan. Add the butter and raspberry vinegar. Cook over low heat until the butter is melted and the beets are lightly glazed, about 5 minutes. Season with salt and pepper to taste and serve at once.

Makes 6 servings.

Purée of Fresh Beets with Horseradish

While color alone makes me adore this recipe, the taste is quite sensational as well.

8 medium beets,
  trimmed, washed,
  peeled, and diced
5 tablespoons unsalted
  butter, cut into
  tablespoons
½ cup heavy or whipping
  cream
1 teaspoon sugar

2 teaspoon fresh lemon
  juice
3 tablespoons prepared
  horseradish
Salt and freshly ground
  pepper to taste
Fresh dill sprigs and
  pink peppercorns
  for garnish

1. Place the beets in a medium saucepan and add cold water to cover. Heat to boiling, then reduce the heat and simmer uncovered until quite tender. Drain.

2. Purée the beets in a blender or food processor fitted with the steel blade. Add the butter, cream, sugar, lemon juice, horseradish, salt, and pepper and process until blended. Strain the purée through a sieve into the saucepan.

3. Gently reheat over very low heat, stirring frequently to prevent it from sticking to the bottom of the pan. Spoon the purée onto serving plates and garnish each serving with a sprig of dill and a few pink peppercorns.

Makes 6 servings.

Kale au Gratin

I made this one evening in a little seaside cottage that was provisioned with an interesting range of odd seasonings, though lacking in the most common herbs and spices. The results were serendipitous and instantly made confirmed kale eaters of the guests. It is an excellent accompaniment to pork or any red meat.

*2 pounds fresh kale,
stems removed and
leaves rinsed
4 tablespoons (½ stick)
unsalted butter
1 small red onion,
coarsely chopped
1 cup heavy cream
½ teaspoon ground
cumin*

*½ teaspoon Chinese
five-spice powder
½ cup grated Gruyère
cheese
Salt and freshly ground
pepper to taste
1½ cups coarse fresh
bread crumbs
¼ cup freshly grated
Parmesan cheese*

1. Heat a large pot of water to boiling. Add the kale and cook for 10 minutes. Drain well, then squeeze out any remaining water with your hands. Remove the tough center rib from each kale leaf and tear the leaves into irregular pieces.

2. Preheat the oven to 350°F. Butter a 7-inch soufflé or gratin dish.

3. Melt 2 tablespoons butter in a small skillet over medium-high heat. Add the onion and sauté 5 minutes. Stir in the cream and heat to boiling. Reduce the heat and simmer for 5 minutes to reduce the cream slightly. Stir in the cumin and five-spice powder. Stir in the Gruyère cheese and heat, stirring constantly, just until it melts. Season with salt and pepper.

4. Stir the kale and cream sauce together and place it into the prepared dish. Sprinkle with the bread crumbs, dot with the remaining 2 tablespoons butter, and sprinkle with the Parmesan.

5. Bake until bubbling and the top turns a light golden brown, 30 to 35 minutes. Serve immediately.

Makes 4 to 6 servings.

Potato Gratin with Minced Black Truffle

This recipe takes the extravagant liberty of infusing earthy Nantucket potatoes with a hint of precious black truffle. It is a wonderful accompaniment to steak and lamb entrées.

4 tablespoons (½ stick) butter, melted

6 medium red-skinned potatoes

1 canned black truffle, ¾ to 1 inch in diameter, finely minced

3 tablespoons minced fresh chives

Salt and freshly ground pepper to taste

⅔ cup heavy cream

1. Preheat the oven to 350°F. Brush a little of the butter in a 4- to 6-cup soufflé dish.

2. Scrub the potatoes well and cut into ⅛-inch-thick slices. Make a double layer of the potato slices in the prepared dish. Drizzle with a little butter and scatter some of the truffle and chives over the top. Sprinkle lightly with salt and pepper. Repeat the layers. Pour the heavy cream over the top.

3. Bake the potato gratin until the potatoes are tender and the top is lightly browned, about 1 hour.

Makes 6 servings.

Potatoes Persillade

The French parsley sauce—Persillade—infuses little new potatoes with a rich flavor and provides a striking contrast to their rosy-hued skins. They team up beautifully with grilled fish.

24 small red-skinned potatoes, scrubbed

4 tablespoons unsalted butter

1 shallot, minced

3 cloves garlic, minced

1 bunch fresh parsley, stems trimmed, minced

¾ cup fresh bread crumbs

Salt and freshly ground pepper to taste

1. To make the potatoes look decorative, peel a stripe of skin around the center of each potato with a paring knife or vegetable peeler, leaving the rest of the skin intact. Place the potatoes in a large saucepan, cover with water, and bring to a boil over high heat. Lower the heat and simmer the potatoes just until tender, 25 minutes.

2. Meanwhile, prepare the persillade: Melt the butter in an 8-inch skillet over medium heat. Add the shallot and garlic and sauté for 3 minutes. Stir in the parsley and bread crumbs and continue to cook, stirring frequently, until the bread crumbs turn light golden brown, about 10 minutes. Season the mixture with salt and pepper to taste.

3. Drain the potatoes very well. Transfer them to a mixing bowl or clean saucepan and toss with the persillade mixture to coat thoroughly. Serve at once.

Makes 6 to 8 servings.

Basic Herb Vinaigrette

This is a good and flavorful dressing to have on hand during the salad season.

4 cloves garlic, finely minced	½ cup vegetable oil
3 tablespoons Dijon mustard	3 tablespoons dried Italian herb blend
¾ cup red wine vinegar	Salt and freshly ground pepper to taste
2 cups olive oil	

1. Whisk the garlic and mustard together in a mixing bowl. Whisk in the vinegar.

2. While continuing to whisk, pour in the olive and vegetable oils in a thin, steady stream. Season with the herbs and salt and pepper to taste. Let stand at room temperature for several hours to allow the flavors to mellow. Store covered in the refrigerator. Let warm to room temperature before using.

Makes about 4 cups.

Lemon Leek Salad Dressing

This is a favorite salad dressing that is both rich and tart. It combines well with most green salads. Because I love eating salads every day in the summertime, I make lots of dressing at one time and keep it in the refrigerator, where it actually improves with age as the flavors mellow. Remember to bring the dressing to room temperature before serving.

1 large egg yolk
2 tablespoons Dijon
  mustard
½ cup fresh lemon juice
3 tablespoons tarragon
  vinegar
1 leek, rinsed well, white
  bulb and green stalk
  finely minced

3 tablespoons dried
  tarragon
1½ cups vegetable oil
2 cups extra-virgin olive
  oil
Salt and lots of freshly
  ground pepper to taste

1. Whisk the egg yolk and mustard together in a mixing bowl, then whisk in the lemon juice and vinegar. Add the leek and tarragon and whisk to combine.

2. While continuing to whisk, pour in the vegetable and olive oils in a thin, steady stream. Season to taste with salt and pepper. Store covered in the refrigerator.

Makes 5 cups.

Lemon Dill Vinaigrette

I often poach a variety of farm vegetables until barely tender, arrange them on a large platter, and drizzle with this vinaigrette. Just looking at this vegetable garden on the table makes me feel healthy.

½ cup fresh lemon juice
2½ tablespoons Dijon
  mustard
1¾ cups olive oil

½ cup chopped fresh dill
Salt and freshly ground
  pepper to taste

Whisk the lemon juice and Dijon mustard together in a mixing bowl. Gradually whisk in the oil, then whisk in the dill and season to taste with salt and pepper. Let stand at room temperature several hours to allow the flavors to mellow.

Makes about 2¼ cups.

Warm Port Vinaigrette

This is a great autumn salad dressing for greens mixed with crumbled blue or Stilton cheese and perhaps a crunchy apple or pear.

3 shallots, minced   2½ tablespoons honey
2½ cups extra-virgin   2 tablespoons fresh lemon
   olive oil   juice
½ cup port   Salt and freshly ground
¼ cup balsamic vinegar   pepper to taste

1. Place the shallots in a skillet and pour the oil over them. Heat over medium-high heat just until it starts to sizzle. Reduce the heat and simmer for 2 minutes and remove from the heat.

2. Meanwhile, whisk the port, vinegar, honey, and lemon juice together in a mixing bowl. Whisk in the hot oil and shallots. Season with salt and pepper to taste.

3. When ready to use the dressing, heat the amount you need in a small skillet until it starts to sizzle. Pour the dressing over the salad, toss, and serve at once. Store the dressing covered in the refrigerator. It will keep for several weeks.

Makes about 3 cups.

Cream Dressing

With all the fancy salad ingredients available in today's market, there is often a tendency to make overly elaborate salads. I believe the art of restraint could stand a bit of reviving in order to rediscover the joys of a simple green salad. This is the dressing I like to drizzle over silky leaves of Boston or butter lettuce. Feel free to substitute minced shallot for the garlic if you prefer a milder dressing.

1 clove garlic, minced
2 teaspoons Dijon
    mustard
2 tablespoons white wine
    vinegar
1 tablespoon fresh lemon
    juice
½ cup extra-virgin
    olive oil

½ cup heavy or whipping
    cream
Salt and freshly ground
    pepper to taste
2 tablespoons snipped
    fresh chives

Purée all the ingredients except the chives in a blender until smooth and thick. Stir in the chives. Toss your favorite greens with just enough dressing to coat the leaves lightly. Store the dressing covered in the refrigerator.

Makes about 1 cup.

Salad Croutons

Learning the subtle art of sautéing a batch of crunchy, garlicky croutons should be a prerequisite for every aspiring salad maker.

3 tablespoons olive oil
3 tablespoons unsalted
    butter
4 cups day-old ½-inch
    bread cubes
1 clove garlic, minced
2 teaspoons mixed dried
    herbs (your favorite
    blend)

Salt and freshly ground
    pepper to taste
½ cup freshly grated
    Parmesan cheese

1. Heat the oil and butter in a large skillet over medium heat. Add the bread cubes and toss to coat with the oil and butter. Reduce the heat to low and sauté the bread, stirring frequently, until toasted light golden brown, 15 to 20 minutes.

2. Stir in the garlic, herbs, and salt and pepper to taste; sauté 5 minutes longer. Remove from the heat and transfer to a mixing bowl. Add the Parmesan and stir until the croutons have cooled. Refrigerate in an airtight container or bag. The croutons can be recrisped on a baking sheet in a 275°F oven for 10 minutes or so.

Makes 4 cups.

Beach Plum Jam

While beach plums are certainly not a vegetable, I couldn't resist including this recipe here because they are a special Nantucket treat. Indeed, gathering dusty blue, purple, and ruby beach plums while surrounded by windswept ocean vistas is one of the great pleasures of September seashore living. Hunting for a plentiful picking spot can be great sport, although pitting all the berries is quite tedious. But there is nothing that can come close to the sweet-tart flavor of beach plum jam which compensates for the intensive work of making an annual batch of this Cape and Island specialty.

Don't limit this jam to the usual morning toast or croissant routine as it is a delicious condiment with grilled lamb chops or finishing glaze for roasted chicken.

12 cups beach plums,
*   stems and leaves*
*   removed*
1 cup water

1½ cups Grand Marnier
Finely chopped zest of 2
*   oranges*
4 to 4½ cups sugar

1. Rinse the beach plums under cold running water. Place in a large saucepan and add the water along with 1 cup of the Grand Marnier. Heat to boiling over medium-high heat. Reduce the heat and simmer uncovered for 15 minutes. Remove from the heat and let cool to room temperature.

2. Remove the pits from the beach plums by squeezing them out individually with your fingers. (It will help to be engrossed in some riveting television mini-series or movie while doing this.) Discard the pits and place the pulp and any remaining liquid in a clean saucepan.

3. Stir in the orange zest. Simmer uncovered, stirring occasionally, over medium-low heat until the mixture is quite thick, about 45 minutes. Stir in 4 cups sugar, taste, and add more sugar if needed. Stir in the remaining ½ cup Grand Marnier and simmer 15 minutes longer.

4. Ladle the jam into sterilized jam jars and seal according to manufacturer's instructions.

Makes 6 cups.

Open-House Salads

Paprika-perfumed Moroccan carrots, rich red cabbage and Roquefort, slender green beans feathered with dill pesto, plump garden vegetables splashed with citronnade, perfect potato salad, a Caesar enriched with sun-dried tomatoes, or a spicy blend of crunchy Oriental pods and sprouts—these are among the lighter salads that celebrate lazy summer days at Que Sera Sarah.

More often than not, vacation-style entertaining is casual—a sunset barbecue, a shady picnic, boating expedition, or deckside potluck supper—where guests are asked to contribute a favorite side dish to the feasting. This chapter, with its vast array of portable salads, adds just the right pizzazz to such open-air, open-house occasions. At first glance, these recipes may seem to yield rather large quantities, but experience has proven that the spontaneous gatherings of unpredictable numbers of family, friends and their houseguests so characteristic of "easy" summertime living, call for plentiful cooking. Making a salad to feed twelve to fifteen people requires almost the same amount of time and preparation as making the same recipe for four to six people. Since the majority of salads in this chapter keep for quite a few days, they can be prepared in advance, and dividends include a relaxed host or hostess by the time company arrives and an inspiring refrigerator of terrific leftovers for refreshing lunches or snacks.

Salad making is my passion, and I firmly believe that salads meant as accompaniments must be as memorable as every other serving on the dinner plate. As my quest for preventing a lethargic August palate is never ending, the inspiration for these cooling salads comes from all parts of the globe as well as the backyard where the best flavors of home-grown abound.

Mushrooms à la Grecque

Serve these aromatic mushrooms as an accompaniment to grilled meats, or spoon them into an earthenware crock and serve them with toothpicks for a light summer hors d'oeuvre.

¾ cup olive oil
¼ cup red wine vinegar
2 tablespoons fresh lemon
  juice
2 tablespoons ground
  coriander seeds

1 tablespoon dried
  oregano
Salt and freshly ground
  pepper to taste

BOUQUET GARNI:
1 teaspoon dried
  marjoram
1 teaspoon dried thyme
½ teaspoon crumbled
  dried sage

2 teaspoons fennel seeds
2 bay leaves, broken in
  half
3 garlic cloves, unpeeled,
  slightly crushed

4 pounds small white
  mushrooms, rinsed and
  patted dry

Chopped fresh parsley
  and/or fresh sage
  sprigs for garnish

1. Mix the oil, vinegar, lemon juice, coriander, oregano, salt, and pepper in a large stockpot.

2. Make the bouquet garni by placing all the herbs and the garlic in the center of a double 3-inch square of cheesecloth. Tie it with kitchen string and add to the oil mixture in the pot.

3. Heat the oil mixture to boiling over medium-high heat. Reduce the heat and simmer several minutes. Gradually add the mushrooms to the pot, stirring with a wooden spoon to coat with the hot sauce. Simmer the mushrooms, stirring occasionally, over medium heat for about 20 minutes.

4. Let the mushrooms cool in the pot to room temperature, about 2 hours. Remove and discard the bouquet garni. Transfer the mushrooms and liquid to a serving bowl. Garnish with chopped parsley and/or sage sprigs if desired. Serve at room temperature. They will keep in the refrigerator for at least 1 month.

Makes about 3 quarts.

Vegetables Citronnade

A colorful and crunchy blend of vegetables bathed in a refreshing, light, citrus-spiked mayonnaise.

1 large head cauliflower, broken into 1½-inch flowerets

1 large head broccoli, broken into 1½-inch flowerets, tender stalks cut into ¾-inch pieces

1½ pounds carrots, peeled and sliced diagonally ½ inch thick

2 medium summer squash, sliced ¼ inch thick

2 medium zucchini, sliced ½ inch thick

1½ pounds sugar snap or snow peas, strings removed

1 red bell pepper, cut into thin julienne strips

CITRONNADE MAYONNAISE:

1 large egg yolk

1 large egg

2 tablespoons Dijon mustard

2 cloves garlic, minced

¼ cup fresh lemon juice

1½ cups vegetable oil

Salt and freshly ground pepper to taste

1 tablespoon finely grated lemon zest

½ cup chopped fresh parsley for garnish

1 tablespoon grated orange zest for garnish

1. Steam each vegetable except for the red pepper separately just until crisp-tender. Refresh under cold running water and drain. Combine all the vegetables, including the red pepper, in a large mixing bowl.

2. Prepare the citronnade mayonnaise: Place the egg yolk, egg, mustard, garlic, and lemon juice in a food processor fitted with the steel blade; process just until blended. With the machine running, add the oil in a thin, steady stream through the feed tube to make a thick emulsion. Season with salt and pepper to taste. Add the grated lemon zest and process just to blend.

3. Toss the steamed vegetables with the mayonnaise to coat. Transfer to a large serving bowl and sprinkle the top of the salad with the chopped parsley and orange zest. Refrigerate several hours but no longer than 12 hours before serving.

Makes 15 to 20 servings.

Moroccan Carrots

A wonderful and very popular summer vegetable salad that is quick and easy to make and glistens with exotic flavor. This salad has been a favorite at Que Sera Sarah ever since the store opened.

3 pounds carrots, peeled,
   trimmed, and cut on
   sharp diagonal into
   ⅓-inch slices
1 cup fruity olive oil
¼ cup balsamic vinegar
¾ cup red wine vinegar
¼ cup sweet Hungarian
   paprika

¼ cup ground cumin
5 large cloves garlic,
   coarsely chopped
1 cup finely minced
   fresh parsley
1 tablespoon salt or to
   taste

1. Place the carrots in a large pot and add cold water to cover. Cook over high heat just until the carrots are crisp-tender. Drain immediately. Do not rinse with cool water.

2. While the carrots are cooking, make the dressing: Whisk the oil, balsamic vinegar, and red wine vinegar together in a large mixing bowl. Whisk in the paprika, cumin, and salt.

3. Add the hot carrots to the dressing and stir to coat. Add the garlic and the parsley and toss to combine. Let the salad cool to room temperature, then serve. The salad can be stored in the refrigerator for several days. For the best flavor, let it warm to room temperature before serving.

Makes 10 to 12 servings.

Summer Vegetable Couscous

This Moroccan-style salad looks like intense summer sunshine and lures with hints of exotic flavors. A wonderful luncheon salad by itself or an unusual accompaniment to grilled chicken.

1 quart chicken stock,
    preferably homemade
¼ cup olive oil
1 tablespoon turmeric
1 tablespoon ground
    cinnamon
1 tablespoon ground
    ginger
1 package (17 ounces)
    couscous
½ cup golden raisins
½ cup diced pitted dates
1 large summer squash,
    cut into ¼-inch dice

1 large zucchini, cut into
    ¼-inch dice
4 carrots, peeled and cut
    into ¼-inch dice
1 large red onion,
    chopped
3 ripe medium tomatoes,
    seeded and cut into
    ¼-inch dice
1 cup cooked chick-peas
1 cup slivered almonds,
    lightly toasted

DRESSING:
½ cup olive oil
½ cup fresh lemon juice

Salt to taste

1. Place the chicken stock, oil, turmeric, cinnamon, and ginger in a large saucepan. Heat to a full boil and gradually stir in the couscous. Cook until most of the liquid has been absorbed, about 2 minutes. Remove from the heat and stir in the raisins and dates. Cover the pot tightly and let stand undisturbed for 15 minutes.

2. Meanwhile, combine all the chopped vegetables in a large mixing bowl. Add the chick-peas and almonds and toss to combine. Add the couscous mixture and stir until well combined.

3. Prepare the dressing: Whisk the oil and lemon juice together. Pour the dressing over the salad and toss to coat. Season to taste with salt. Serve the couscous slightly chilled or at room temperature. This salad will keep up to a week stored in the refrigerator.

Makes 15 to 20 servings.

Tabouleh
with Feta

In the early seventies when I was summering with my aunt and uncle on Nantucket, we made at least one batch of tabouleh a week, each more outrageous than the last. The final version I remember was gilded with clusters of green grapes and jumbo shrimp. Fortunately, time has brought with it some well-advised restraint. This recipe is what I believe to be the perfect rendition of this refreshing salad.

2 pounds bulgur wheat
1½ cups fresh lemon
    juice, plus additional
    to taste
6 cups hot water
3 medium cucumbers,
    seeded and chopped
    very small
8 ripe medium tomatoes,
    seeded and chopped
    very small
1 medium red onion,
    minced

2 cloves garlic, minced
3 bunches parsley, finely
    chopped
5 tablespoons minced
    fresh mint
2 cups (8 ounces)
    crumbled feta cheese
1½ cups (or as needed)
    olive oil
Salt and freshly ground
    pepper to taste

1. Place the bulgur in a large mixing bowl and pour over 1½ cups fresh lemon juice and the hot water. Let stand until the bulgur is tender, 30 to 40 minutes. Drain off any excess liquid.

2. Add the cucumbers, tomatoes, onion, garlic, parsley, mint, and feta to the bulgur and toss to combine. Dress with enough of the olive oil and additional lemon juice to make the salad moist but not runny. Season with salt and pepper.

3. Refrigerate the salad for several hours to allow the flavors to blend. Serve cold or at room temperature accompanied with pita bread.

Makes 14 to 16 servings.

Mixed Vegetables
à la Russe

1 medium-large turnip, peeled and cut into ¼-inch dice	2 large egg yolks
	4 cornichons, minced
2 medium boiling potatoes, peeled and cut into ¼-inch dice	2 teaspoons Dijon mustard
	1 tablespoon capers, drained
½ cup small cauliflower flowerets	3 tablespoons fresh lemon juice
5 carrots, peeled and cut into ¼-inch dice	½ cup olive oil
2 cups shelled fresh peas	1 to 1½ cups vegetable oil
1 medium red onion, minced	Salt and freshly ground pepper to taste
1 small red bell pepper, seeded and diced	1 cup chopped fresh parsley

1. Cook the turnip, potatoes, cauliflower, and carrots separately in boiling salted water until crisp-tender. Drain and refresh under cold running water. Combine the cooked vegetables, and the peas, onion, and red pepper in a mixing bowl.

2. Place the egg yolks, cornichons, mustard, capers, and lemon juice in a food processor fitted with the steel blade; process 30 seconds to blend. With the machine running, pour the oils in a thin, steady stream through the feed tube to make a thick emulsion. Season with salt and pepper.

3. Toss the salad with the mayonnaise to bind. Stir in the parsley and refrigerate until ready to serve.

Makes 10 to 12 servings.

Potato Boursin Salad

This is a luscious and rich potato salad that can keep fine company with lobster feasts or the choicest cuts of meat seared over the summer grill.

3½ pounds small Red
Bliss potatoes,
scrubbed but not
peeled
5 large eggs, hard-cooked,
shelled, and coarsely
chopped

4 large ribs celery,
chopped
1 can (6 ounces) pitted
large black olives,
sliced

DRESSING:
2½ packages (5 ounces
each) Boursin cheese
1 cup olive oil

⅓ cup fresh lemon juice
Salt and freshly ground
pepper to taste

1½ cups chopped fresh
parsley

1. Place the potatoes in a large pot and add water to cover.
Heat to boiling, then lower the heat and simmer uncovered just
until fork-tender, 25 minutes. Drain in a colander and let cool
slightly.

2. Cut the warm potatoes into large bite-size chunks. Toss
the potatoes, eggs, celery, and olives together in a large bowl.

3. Prepare the dressing: Crumble the cheese into small pieces
and place it in a food processor fitted with the steel blade. Purée
until smooth. Add the oil and lemon juice and process until
smooth. Season to taste with salt and pepper.

4. Add the dressing to the warm potato mixture and toss
until thoroughly coated. Add the parsley and toss to combine.
Transfer to a serving platter or refrigerate until ready to serve.

Makes 10 to 12 servings.

Perfect Potato Salad

There is a great deal of satisfaction that comes from making
popular foods well. Modesty aside, we make terrific potato salad
at Que Sera, and I believe the secret to our potato salad, or any
good potato salad, lies in tossing the hot potatoes in an aromatic
vinaigrette before proceeding with the rest of the recipe.

6 pounds small Red Bliss
  potatoes, scrubbed but
  not peeled
4 carrots, peeled and cut
  into ¼-inch dice
6 ribs celery, coarsely
  chopped
1 large red onion, minced
1 cup chopped fresh dill
1 cup Basic Herb
  Vinaigrette (see Index)

½ cup dry white wine
1½ cups Hellmann's
  mayonnaise
¾ cup sour cream
Salt and freshly ground
  pepper to taste
Chopped fresh dill for
  garnish

1. Place the potatoes in a large pot and add water to cover. Heat to boiling, then lower the heat and simmer uncovered until fork-tender, 25 minutes. Drain in a colander.

2. Place the carrots, celery, red onion, and dill in a large mixing bowl. Cut the hot potatoes into uneven chunks and combine with the vegetables in the bowl. Toss with the vinaigrette and the white wine.

3. Add the mayonnaise and sour cream and toss well. Season with salt and pepper to taste and refrigerate the salad for a few hours to mellow the flavors. Serve with an additional sprinkling of chopped fresh dill.

Serves 15 to 20.

A sojourn upon the island has been likened to an ocean voyage with the disagreeable features eliminated. There is always a breeze and the pure invigorating salt air and bright sunshine, with the peace and quiet which pervades, are most soothing alike to the tired brain-worker and to those of nervous temperment. Relief from hay fever is assured and malaria is unknown. That the climate is most beneficial for recuperative purposes is the unanimous indorsement of many prominent members of the medical profession.

—Guide to Nantucket 1928

Mr. Power's Potatoes

There is an absolute bevy of blond and red-headed Powers girls that come to my rescue every summer. Their mother is in the catering business in Westport, Connecticut, and all six daughters—from age 14 to 26—possess unbelievable food savvy. I could scarcely imagine a family of so many good cooks when to my amazement I learned that the gregarious father of this clan cooked as well! Here is his recipe for a family favorite.

4 pounds small Red Bliss potatoes, scrubbed but not peeled

2 cups heavy or whipping cream

2 cups well-flavored chicken stock, preferably homemade

1 cup dry white wine

SHERRY VINAIGRETTE:

1 cup sherry vinegar

2 teaspoons dry mustard

1 teaspoon dried thyme

1 cup olive oil

Salt and freshly ground pepper to taste

1 bunch scallions, white bulbs and green stalks, chopped

1 medium red onion, minced

1 cup minced fresh parsley

Salt and freshly ground pepper to taste

1. Place the potatoes in a large pot and add water to cover. Heat to boiling, then lower the heat and simmer uncovered until fork-tender, 25 minutes. Drain in a colander. Using a serrated knife, slice the potatoes about ⅓ inch thick.

2. Cover the warm potato slices with the cream, chicken stock, and wine in a large bowl. Marinate for 15 minutes, then pour off any excess liquid.

3. Prepare the sherry vinaigrette: Whisk the vinegar, mustard, and thyme together in a medium mixing bowl. Whisk in the oil and season to taste with salt and pepper. Pour the vinaigrette over the potatoes and toss to combine.

4. Add the scallions, onion, and parsley to the salad and toss to combine. Taste and adjust the seasonings. Serve the salad warm or at room temperature.

Makes 14 to 16 servings.

Mexican Fiesta

A unanimous choice for the most refreshing of summer salads. It is great as an accompaniment to heartier salads and grilled fare, or by itself as a cooling low-calorie crunch.

2 large zucchini, scrubbed	1 red bell pepper, seeded and diced
2 large summer squash, scrubbed	1 yellow bell pepper, seeded and diced
3 medium cucumbers	1 green bell pepper, seeded and diced
1¼ cups tarragon vinegar, plus additional to taste	½ cup chopped fresh coriander
2 medium red onions, chopped	1½ cups olive oil
8 ripe medium tomatoes, seeded and cut into ¼-inch dice	Salt and freshly ground pepper to taste

1. Trim the zucchini and summer squash, cut lengthwise into long strips, then cut into ¼-inch dice. Peel and seed the cucumbers, then cut into ¼-inch dice. Place the squash and cucumbers in a large mixing bowl. Add 1¼ cups of tarragon vinegar and toss to combine. Let marinate for 45 minutes at room temperature.

2. Meanwhile, combine the onions, tomatoes, bell peppers, and coriander in another large mixing bowl.

3. Drain the squash mixture in a colander. Add to the onion mixture and toss to combine. Dress the salad with the olive oil, salt, and pepper. Taste and add more vinegar if needed. Refrigerate at least 2 hours before serving.

Makes 12 to 16 servings.

Red Cabbage and Roquefort

A simple and quick salad to prepare, yet absolutely spectacular in presentation.

2 medium heads red
    cabbage
1½ cups crumbled
    Roquefort cheese
2 cups chopped fresh
    parsley

½ cup grainy Dijon
    mustard
3½ cups Hellmann's
    mayonnaise

1. Remove the outer leaves from each head of cabbage and reserve. Using a sharp knife, core the cabbages and finely shred them. Place the shredded cabbage in a large mixing bowl. Add 1 cup of the Roquefort and 1 cup of the parsley; toss to combine.

2. Whisk the mustard and mayonnaise together in another mixing bowl. Add to the cabbage mixture and toss to coat thoroughly.

3. Line a large serving bowl with the reserved cabbage leaves. (I like to use a deep blue bowl, which contrasts strikingly with the deep red of the cabbage.) Spoon the cabbage mixture into the leaves and garnish with the remaining Roquefort and parsley. Refrigerate at least 2 hours before serving.

Makes 16 servings.

Carolina Coleslaw

This is the type of great coleslaw that they serve way down in the land of Dixie and induces cravings for a piece or two of crispy fried chicken and a few hush puppies.

1 head red cabbage,
    finely shredded
1 head green cabbage,
    finely shredded
4 carrots, peeled and
    grated
1 large yellow onion,
    chopped
2 green bell peppers,
    seeded and cut into
    julienne strips
1 yellow bell pepper,
    seeded and cut into
    julienne strips

1 red bell pepper, seeded
    and cut into julienne
    strips
2 cups tarragon vinegar
1½ cups vegetable oil
1 cup sugar
1½ tablespoons dry
    mustard
1½ tablespoons celery
    seeds
Salt and freshly ground
    pepper to taste

1. Combine the red and green cabbages, carrots, onion, and bell peppers in a large mixing bowl.

2. Mix the vinegar, oil, sugar, mustard, and celery seeds in a medium saucepan. Heat just to boiling. Reduce the heat and simmer 1 minute. Pour the dressing over the coleslaw and toss well. Season to taste with salt and pepper.

3. Transfer the coleslaw to a serving dish and refrigerate for several hours to allow the flavors to mellow.

Makes 16 to 20 servings.

Lone Star Slaw

A tribute to the spicy palates of the dedicated Texas contingent who summer on Nantucket.

1 large head red cabbage, shredded	1 cup sour cream
5 carrots, peeled and grated	3 tablespoons heavy or whipping cream
1 large green bell pepper, seeded and diced	2 heaping tablespoons Dijon mustard
1 large yellow onion, chopped	1 tablespoon chili powder
12 slices bacon	1½ tablespoons cumin
2 cups Hellmann's mayonnaise	Salt and freshly ground pepper to taste
	¼ cup chopped fresh parsley

1. Toss the cabbage, carrots, green pepper, and onion together in a large mixing bowl.

2. Fry the bacon in a skillet until crisp. Drain on paper towels and crumble into small bits.

3. Add the mayonnaise and sour cream to the bacon fat in the skillet and whisk until smooth. Whisk in the cream, mustard, chili powder, and cumin. Season to taste with salt and pepper.

4. Add half the bacon to the cabbage mixture. Add the dressing and toss well to coat. Transfer to a serving bowl and garnish the salad with the remaining bacon and the parsley. Serve slightly chilled or at room temperature.

Makes 10 to 12 servings.

Green Beans in Dill Walnut Sauce

A vibrant salad when green beans are tender and fresh from a local farm.

3 pounds green beans, trimmed	½ cup walnut halves
1 bunch scallions, white bulbs and green stalks, minced	¼ cup fresh lemon juice
	1½ cups olive oil
1 bunch fresh dill, chopped	Salt and freshly ground pepper to taste
½ cup minced fresh parsley	Cherry tomatoes, quartered (optional)

1. Heat a large pot of water to boiling. Add the green beans and boil until crisp-tender. Drain immediately, then immerse in a large bowl of ice water to prevent further cooking and retain the bright green color.

2. Meanwhile, make the sauce: Place the scallions, dill, parsley, walnuts, and lemon juice in a blender or food processor fitted with the steel blade; process until smooth. With the machine running, pour the olive oil in a thin, steady stream through the feed tube to make a thick green sauce. Add salt and pepper to taste.

3. Drain the beans and dry with a towel. Toss the beans with the dressing in a mixing bowl. Add the cherry tomatoes for color contrast, if desired. Transfer the beans to a flat serving bowl. Serve slightly chilled or at room temperature.

Makes 10 to 12 servings.

White Bean and Goat Cheese Salad

This is the best bean salad I have ever tasted. I'm particularly fond of the way the toasted pine nuts are camouflaged in the beans and then surprise one with an intense little crunch.

1 pound dried small
   white beans, picked
   over, soaked overnight
   in cold water, and
   drained
6 cups chicken stock,
   preferably homemade
3 carrots, peeled and cut
   into ¼-inch dice
2 bay leaves
2 cloves garlic, minced
1½ tablespoons grainy
   Dijon mustard

⅓ cup fresh lemon juice
1¼ cups olive oil
Salt and freshly ground
   pepper to taste
1 medium red onion,
   chopped
12 ounces Montrachet
   goat cheese, crumbled
½ cup pine nuts, toasted
1 bunch parsley, chopped

1. Place the beans, chicken stock, carrots, and bay leaves in a large saucepan. Heat to boiling, skimming off any foam that rises to the surface. Reduce the heat and simmer uncovered just until the beans are tender, 25 to 30 minutes. Remove from the heat and drain.

2. Meanwhile, mix the garlic, mustard, and lemon juice in a small mixing bowl. Whisk in the oil and season to taste with salt and pepper. Toss the warm beans with the dressing.

3. Add the onion, goat cheese, pine nuts, and parsley to the salad and toss to combine well. Serve at room temperature.

Makes 8 to 10 servings.

Indian Cauliflower with Toasted Mustard Seeds

In Indian cuisine this is served to cool the fire of a hot curry. I am so fond of it, however, that I often enjoy it as a salad on its own.

3 heads cauliflower,
   broken into bite-size
   flowerets, steamed just
   until crisp-tender, and
   drained
6 tablespoons unsalted
   butter

⅓ cup golden mustard
   seeds
4 cups plain yogurt
Salt to taste

1. Place the cauliflower in a large mixing bowl and let cool to room temperature.

2. Melt the butter in a small skillet over medium heat. Add the mustard seeds to the butter and immediately cover the skillet. Cook just until you hear the first mustard seeds popping against the cover (similar to popcorn). Remove from the heat but do not uncover until the popping ceases, about 5 minutes.

3. Add the toasted mustard seeds with the butter to the cooled cauliflower and toss to coat. Stir in the yogurt and season to taste with salt. Refrigerate several hours before serving.

Makes 8 to 10 servings.

Asparagus with Sesame Mayonnaise

This crisp Oriental-style salad partners perfectly with cold sliced steak.

3 pounds asparagus
2 cloves garlic, minced
1½ tablespoons chopped fresh ginger
⅓ cup soy sauce
2 tablespoons rice wine vinegar
2 tablespoons brown sugar
1 large egg yolk
1 large egg
1 tablespoon fresh lemon juice
1½ tablespoons Dijon mustard
1¼ cups vegetable oil
¼ cup Oriental sesame oil
⅓ cup sesame seeds, lightly toasted

1. Cut off the tough lower stalks of the asparagus and discard. Cut each stalk diagonally into 2 or 3 pieces; keep the tip pieces separate from the rest, as they need less time to cook. Steam the asparagus tips and stalks separately in steamers placed over boiling water. Steam just until crisp-tender and remove from the heat immediately.

2. Make the sesame mayonnaise: Place the garlic, ginger, soy sauce, vinegar, and brown sugar in a small saucepan. Heat to boiling. Reduce the heat and simmer until reduced by about half.

3. Place the egg yolk, egg, lemon juice, and mustard in a food

processor fitted with the steel blade; process for 10 seconds. With the machine running, pour the vegetable and sesame oils in a thin, steady stream through the feed tube to form a thick emulsion. Add the reduced soy mixture and process until well blended.

4. Toss the asparagus with the sesame mayonnaise and transfer to a serving bowl. Sprinkle the salad with the sesame seeds. Refrigerate at least 2 hours before serving.

Makes 8 servings.

Stuffed Artichokes Vinaigrette

An intriguing way to dress up a steamed artichoke.

4 artichokes, trimmed
8 tablespoons olive oil
3 shallots, minced
1½ cups finely chopped mushrooms
3 tablespoons dry white wine
2 tablespoons Champagne vinegar
1½ tablespoons fresh lemon juice

1 large clove garlic, minced
½ cup finely shredded prosciutto
3 tablespoons freshly grated Parmesan cheese
Salt and freshly ground pepper to taste

1. Sit the artichokes upright on a vegetable steamer placed in a large saucepan. Pour in enough water to come just level with the top of the steamer. Cover the pan and gently simmer the artichokes until tender, 45 minutes to 1 hour. Remove the artichokes and set aside to cool.

2. Heat 2 tablespoons of the oil in a small skillet over medium heat. Add the shallots and sauté just until tender, about 5 minutes. Stir in the mushrooms and sauté 3 minutes longer. Transfer the mixture to a mixing bowl.

3. Add the wine, vinegar, lemon juice, garlic, prosciutto, Parmesan, and remaining 6 tablespoons oil to the mushroom mixture and toss to combine. Season to taste with salt and pepper. Let marinate at room temperature for 30 minutes.

4. Pull out enough center leaves of each artichoke to reach the choke. Scrape out the prickly hairs with a spoon and discard. Spoon the dressing into the artichokes. Serve the stuffed artichokes at room temperature.

Makes 4 servings.

Eggplant and Peppers in Hoisin Marinade

This unusual salad looks like the autumn leaves in New England at their peak of color.

8 tablespoons vegetable oil
4 tablespoons Oriental sesame oil
3 medium eggplants, unpeeled, cut into 3 x ½-inch strips
2 red bell peppers, seeded and cut into ½-inch-wide strips
2 yellow bell peppers, seeded and cut into ½-inch-wide strips
1 green bell pepper, seeded and cut into ½-inch-wide strips
1 can (6 ounces) pitted black olives, drained
1 jar (5 ounces) hoisin sauce
½ cup soy sauce
3 tablespoons honey
Several drops hot chili oil
3 tablespoons chopped fresh coriander

1. Heat 2 tablespoons vegetable oil and 1 tablespoon sesame oil in a large skillet over high heat. Add as many of the eggplant strips as will fit in a single layer and stir-fry just until crisp-tender, about 5 minutes. Repeat with the remaining eggplant and the peppers, adding vegetable oil and sesame oil as needed. Transfer all the vegetables to a large mixing bowl.

2. Add the olives to the salad and toss to combine. Add the hoisin sauce and toss well. Stir in the soy sauce, honey, and chili oil to taste. Transfer to a serving bowl and sprinkle the top of the salad with the coriander. Serve at room temperature or slightly chilled.

Makes 10 to 12 servings.

Mixed Greens with Fennel, Pears, and Parmesan Shards

A harmonious combination of ingredients that makes either a nice first-course salad or an after-dinner salad with pasta or other Italian fare.

2 bunches watercress,
   tough stems removed
3 cups coarsely torn salad
   lettuce
1 small head radicchio,
   leaves separated
1½ cups sliced fresh
   fennel stalks
3 tablespoons pine nuts,
   toasted

2 ripe Bosc pears, peeled,
   cored, and thinly sliced
1 cup shaved Parmesan
   cheese (use vegetable
   peeler)
⅔ cup Lemon Leek
   Dressing (see Index)

Toss the watercress, lettuce, radicchio, and fennel together in a large salad bowl. Scatter the pine nuts, pears, and Parmesan over the greens. Toss the salad with enough dressing to coat. Serve immediately.

Makes 6 servings.

ASPIRING TO BE ITALIAN

Bruschetta

Linguine with White Clam Sauce

Mixed Greens with Fennel, Pears, and Parmesan Shards

Espresso-Walnut Cake

Chilled Orvieto

Vegetables Chinois

A light salad that is always welcome during the really scorching spells of summer heat.

¾ cup dried Chinese
   mushrooms
1 pound snow peas,
   strings removed
3 cups fresh bean sprouts
1 red bell pepper, seeded
   and cut into thin
   julienne strips
1 yellow bell pepper,
   seeded and cut into
   thin julienne strips

2 cans (8 ounces each)
   water chestnuts,
   drained and thinly
   sliced
1 can (8 ounces) sliced
   bamboo shoots,
   drained
1 bunch scallions, white
   bulbs and green stalks,
   sliced diagonally

DRESSING:

2 cloves garlic, minced
3 tablespoons rice wine
   vinegar
¼ cup sweet sherry
1½ tablespoons sugar

2 tablespoons Oriental
   sesame oil
¼ cup vegetable oil
¼ cup soy sauce
Hot chili oil to taste

1. Soak the Chinese mushrooms in boiling water for 20 minutes, drain, pat dry, and slice.

2. Blanch the snow peas in boiling water for 30 seconds. Run under cold water to stop the cooking, drain, and pat dry.

3. Toss all the vegetables together in a large mixing bowl.

4. Prepare the dressing: Whisk the garlic, vinegar, sherry, and sugar together in a small mixing bowl. Whisk in the oils, soy sauce, and chili oil to taste. Pour the dressing over the vegetables and toss to coat. Refrigerate until cold.

Makes 8 to 10 servings.

Caesar Salad Embellished with Sun-Dried Tomatoes

With sun-dried tomtoes the current rage, they seem to pop up almost everywhere. This is one place that I feel they really belong.

1 large head romaine
   lettuce

2 cups fresh spinach
   leaves

SUN-DRIED TOMATO DRESSING:

1 large egg yolk

1 tablespoon grainy Dijon
   mustard

1 tablespoon anchovy
   paste

3 tablespoons balsamic
   vinegar

2½ tablespoons fresh
   lemon juice

2 cloves garlic, minced

8 sun-dried tomatoes
   packed in oil, finely
   chopped

½ cup vegetable oil

1 cup olive oil

2 teaspoons dried thyme

Salt and freshly ground
   pepper to taste

1 cup Croutons (see
   Index)

1 cup freshly grated
   Parmesan cheese

1. Tear the lettuce and spinach into large irregular pieces and toss together in a large salad bowl. Refrigerate until ready to serve.

2. Prepare the dressing: Whisk the egg yolk, mustard, and anchovy paste together in a small mixing bowl until smooth. Gradually whisk in the vinegar and lemon juice, then stir in the garlic and sun-dried tomatoes.

3. Combine the vegetable and olive oils and pour into the dressing in a thin, steady stream, whisking constantly. Whisk in thyme and season to taste with salt and pepper. Let stand at room temperature several hours to allow the flavors to mellow.

4. Toss the salad greens with enough dressing to coat generously. Add the croutons and Parmesan and toss to combine. Serve at once.

Makes 8 servings.

Salad
Stars

From time to time, in the daily course of salad making at Que Sera Sarah, a real salad star is born. While I always try to infuse every salad with its own unique intensity, I find there is no predicting what serendipitous kitchen methodology leads to the creation of a star. The discerning public taste responds equally to the simplicity of a chunky chicken salad, the exoticism of shrimp bathed in raspberries and mint, or the extravagant complicity of plump Italian tortellini dressed with an entire jar of puréed sun-dried tomatoes.

While there are plenty of salads in this chapter with universal appeal, Nantucketers are always particularly fond of salads from the sea. Indeed, a summer spent by the ocean invites culinary exploration as much as it does sportive enjoyment. The pastel colors of crustaceans in varying shades of coral, salmon, apricot, and opalescent pearl seem to appeal to the eye as much as the palate. No summer on Nantucket is ever complete without at least a few fishing expeditions—either casting offshore, braving the high seas, wrestling with the rocks for mussels, or simply vying for a parking space in front of the local fish market.

Whether from land or sea, these are cherishable salads meant to take center stage whenever an impressive meal of cool and elegant fare is in order.

Lobster Salad with Mayonnaise du Midi

Fresh lobster salad in its extravagant simplicity is perfect for those peak summer days when excess seems to be just enough.

3 pounds fresh cooked
   lobster meat (about six
   1¼ pound whole
   lobsters, steamed), cut
   into large chunks

4 inner white ribs celery,
   cut into ½-inch dice
3 shallots, minced

MAYONNAISE:
1 large egg yolk
1 large egg
2½ tablespoons fresh
   lemon juice
1 tablespoon Dijon
   mustard

Finely grated zest of 1 lemon
½ teaspoon saffron threads
½ teaspoon dried thyme
1½ cups best-quality olive oil
Salt and freshly ground
   pepper to taste

1. Combine the lobster, celery, and shallots in a mixing bowl.
2. Prepare the mayonnaise: Place the egg yolk, egg, lemon juice, mustard, lemon zest, saffron, and thyme in a food processor fitted with the steel blade; process for 10 seconds. With the machine running, add the oil in a thin, steady stream through the feed tube to form an emulsion. Season the mayonnaise to taste with salt and pepper.
3. Combine the lobster mixture with enough mayonnaise to bind. Cover and refrigerate at least 1 hour. Serve in generous portions with little else to accompany.

Makes 8 servings.

Insalata di Frutti di Mare

In Venice, restaurant windows frequently display alluring platters of mixed seafood marinating in a glistening bath of olive oil. This is my own local version of this sumptuous Italian classic.

2 pounds jumbo shrimp
(12 to 15 per pound)
peeled, deveined, and
cooked just until
opaque (see box, page
148)
1½ pounds fresh cooked
lobster meat
5 ribs celery, sliced
diagonally ½ inch
thick
1 medium red onion,
sliced into thin rings
1½ cups dry white wine
1½ cups water
1½ pounds sea scallops
2 pounds squid, cleaned
and cut into rings

1¾ cups fruity olive oil
3 cloves garlic, minced
2 teaspoons dried oregano
½ teaspoon dried red
pepper flakes
¼ cup fresh lemon juice
1 cup chopped fresh
parsley
½ cup chopped fresh basil
2 tablespoons Pernod
2 ripe medium tomatoes,
seeded and cut into
¼-inch dice
Salt and freshly ground
pepper to taste

1. Mix the shrimp, lobster, celery, and red onion together in a large bowl.

2. Heat the wine and water in a deep skillet just to simmering. Add the scallops and simmer just until opaque, 1½ to 2 minutes. Remove from the liquid with a slotted spoon, cool, and add to the seafood in the bowl. Add the squid to the poaching liquid and simmer just until tender, about 3 minutes. Remove with a slotted spoon, cool, and add to the seafood. Boil the poaching liquid until it is reduced by half and then remove from the heat.

3. Pour the olive oil into another skillet and heat over medium heat. Stir in the garlic, oregano, and red pepper flakes and simmer for 10 minutes. Stir in the lemon juice, ¾ cup of the reduced poaching liquid, the parsley, basil, and Pernod. Simmer 5 minutes longer. Stir in the tomatoes, season to taste with salt and pepper, and simmer another 5 minutes.

4. Pour the hot dressing over the seafood and toss thoroughly to coat. Transfer the salad to a serving dish and refrigerate for several hours before serving.

Makes 10 to 12 servings.

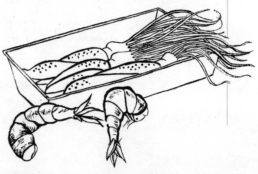

Scallop Ceviche

Ceviche is one of the most cooling of all summer salads and is inspired by the fiery cuisines of Latin America.

3 pounds fresh sea or bay scallops
1 cup fresh lime juice
⅓ cup fresh lemon juice
3 ripe medium tomatoes, seeded and cut into ¼-inch dice
1 yellow bell pepper, seeded and cut into ¼-inch dice
1 red bell pepper, seeded and cut into ¼-inch dice
1 green bell pepper, seeded and cut into ¼-inch dice

2 fresh jalapeño peppers, seeded and minced
1 bunch scallions, white bulbs and green stalks, minced
½ cup minced fresh coriander
¼ cup fruity olive oil
Salt and freshly ground pepper to taste
Lime wedges for garnish

1. Place the scallops in a large mixing bowl and pour over the lime and lemon juices. Add the tomatoes, peppers, and scallions and toss together. Add the coriander, oil, salt, and pepper and toss thoroughly to coat.

2. Transfer the ceviche to a serving bowl and refrigerate covered several hours to allow the lime juice to "cook" the scallops and the flavors to blend. Serve cold on small salad plates, garnished with lime wedges.

Makes 10 to 12 servings.

Smoked Mussels Vinaigrette

A quick and tasty way to dress up smoked mussels for an unusual summer salad or great seaside cocktail fare. As a salad, spoon it into avocado halves or on leafy garden greens. As an hors d'oeuvre, simply supply lots of toothpicks and perhaps a salt-rimmed margarita or two.

1½ pounds smoked
mussels, preferably
freshly smoked from a
reputable smokehouse
5 scallions, white bulbs
and green stalks, sliced
½ red bell pepper, seeded
and diced

½ yellow bell pepper,
seeded and diced
3 tablespoons chopped
fresh coriander
½ cup fresh lime juice
½ cup fruity olive oil
Freshly ground pepper to
taste

1. Toss the mussels, scallions, peppers, and coriander together in a mixing bowl.

2. Whisk the lime juice and olive oil together in a small mixing bowl and pour over the mussels. Toss thoroughly to coat. Sprinkle with pepper to taste. Serve at room temperature.

Makes 8 servings.

Mussels Gribiche

A simple yet richly delicious way to serve chilled mussels.

3 pounds shucked cooked
mussels (about 8 to 10
pounds in the shell)
2 large egg yolks
2 tablespoons balsamic
vinegar
1 tablespoon fresh lemon
juice
2 tablespoons minced
fresh tarragon
3 tablespoons minced
fresh parsley

¾ cup olive oil
¾ cup vegetable oil
8 cornichon pickles,
minced
2 tablespoons capers,
drained
2 hard-cooked eggs,
minced
Salt and freshly ground
pepper to taste
Capers and lemon
wedges for garnish

1. Drain the mussels and place in a large mixing bowl.

2. To make the gribiche sauce, place the egg yolks, vinegar, lemon juice, tarragon, and parsley in a food processor fitted with the steel blade and process for 10 seconds. With the machine running, add the oils in a thin, steady stream through the feed

tube to make an emulsion. Transfer the mayonnaise to a mixing bowl and stir in the cornichons, capers, and eggs. Season to taste with salt and pepper.

3. Add the gribiche sauce to the mussels and toss to coat. Refrigerate several hours before serving. Spoon onto salad plates and garnish with capers and lemon wedges.

Makes 6 to 8 servings.

Scallops with Orange and Chervil Vinaigrette

A refreshing change of pace for those who are squeamish about eating scallops raw in ceviche.

2½ pounds sea scallops	Finely chopped zest of 1
2 cups orange juice	orange
2 cups dry white wine	3 tablespoons chopped
1 bunch scallions, white	fresh chervil
bulbs and green stalks,	1 tablespoon capers,
sliced	drained
⅓ cup Niçoise olives,	1 cup fruity olive oil
pitted and coarsely	Salt and freshly ground
chopped	pepper to taste
3 ripe medium tomatoes,	
seeded and cut into	
¼-inch dice	

1. Place the scallops in a large skillet and pour over the orange juice and wine. Heat to boiling, then reduce heat to low and simmer the scallops just until barely cooked through, 2 to 3 minutes. Using a slotted spoon, transfer the scallops to a mixing bowl. Reduce the remaining liquid in the pan over high heat to ½ cup. Remove from the heat and set aside.

2. Add the scallions, olives, tomatoes, orange zest, chervil, and capers to the scallops; toss to combine.

3. Whisk the reduced poaching liquid and the olive oil together. Season the dressing to taste with salt and freshly ground pepper. Pour over the scallop salad and toss to coat. Serve at once or refrigerate until ready to serve.

Makes 6 servings.

Shrimp in a Bath of Raspberry Vinegar and Mint

The perfect way to infuse irresistible jumbo shrimp with the sparkle of summer.

5 pounds jumbo (12 to 15 per pound) shrimp, peeled, deveined, and cooked until opaque (see box, below)
1 cup Champagne vinegar
1 cup raspberry vinegar

6 tablespoons sugar
3 tablespoons fresh lemon juice
1½ cups chopped fresh mint
1½ cups fruity olive oil
Salt and freshly ground pepper to taste

1. Place the shrimp in a large mixing bowl. Whisk the vinegars and sugar together in a small mixing bowl until the sugar dissolves. Whisk in the lemon juice and mint, then the olive oil. Season with salt and pepper. Pour the dressing over the shrimp and toss well to coat. Marinate in the refrigerator at least 3 hours before serving.

2. Serve the shrimp either as a salad on plates garnished with

COOKING SHRIMP

I like to cook shrimp in a combination of dry white wine and water infused with lemon, herbs, and spices. A ratio of 2 cups wine to 8 cups water works well. I then add 2 or 3 bay leaves, 1 lemon, quartered, 2 teaspoons mustard seeds, and a dash or two of dried red pepper flakes and bring the liquid to a full boil before dropping in the shrimp. I cook the shrimp over high heat just until opaque in the center. Large shrimp generally take 3 to 4 minutes, while small shrimp need only cook 1½ to 2 minutes. The shrimp should be drained immediately, then covered with ice cubes to arrest the cooking and cool them quickly. Drain again and use as called for in the recipes.

sprigs of fresh mint or serve as an hors d'oeuvre on a shallow platter with toothpicks.

Makes 10 to 12 salad servings or 20 to 25 appetizer servings.

Seashells with Shrimp and Sugar Snap Peas

An alliterative and scrumptious combination of ingredients make this coral-hued salad a favorite in the cold pasta category.

3 pounds large (16 to 24 per pound) shrimp, peeled, deveined, and cooked just until opaque (see box, facing page)

2 pounds small pasta shells, cooked al dente, rinsed under cold water, and drained

1 bunch scallions, white bulbs and green stalks, sliced

1 red bell pepper, seeded and cut into fine julienne strips

1½ pounds sugar snap peas, blanched in boiling water for 30 seconds, cooled under cold running water, and drained

DRESSING:

3 tablespoons tomato paste

3 tablespoons fresh lemon juice

½ cup dry vermouth

4 hard-cooked eggs

3 tablespoons chopped fresh tarragon

3 cups Hellmann's mayonnaise

Salt and freshly ground pepper to taste

2 tablespoons Pernod

1. Place 2½ pounds of the shrimp in a large mixing bowl. (Reserve the remaining ½ pound for the dressing.) Add the pasta and peas to the shrimp and toss to combine. Stir in the scallions and red pepper.

2. Prepare the dressing: Place the reserved shrimp, tomato paste, lemon juice, eggs, and tarragon in a food processor fitted with the steel blade; process until smooth. Add the mayonnaise and process again until smooth. Season to taste with salt and pepper and add the Pernod. Process once more just to blend. Pour the dressing over the pasta salad and toss thoroughly to coat. Transfer the salad to a serving bowl. Serve at once or refrigerate covered several hours and serve cold.

Makes 10 to 12 servings.

Paella Salad

This dramatic cold interpretation of classic Spanish paella is a fabulous dish to prepare for guests on hot summer evenings.

2 quarts chicken stock,
    preferably homemade
1 tablespoon curry powder
1 teaspoon saffron threads
1 teaspoon fennel seeds
1 teaspoon dried red
    pepper flakes
6 tablespoons olive oil
1 large red onion, minced
5 cloves garlic, minced
3 cups long-grain rice
3 boneless, skinless whole
    chicken breasts, cut
    into ¾-inch chunks
5 ribs celery, chopped
1 bunch scallions, white
    bulbs and green stalks,
    sliced
2 red bell peppers, seeded
    and cut into ¼-inch dice
1 yellow bell pepper, seeded
    and cut into ¼-inch dice

1 cup pitted black olives, sliced
2 cans (14 ounces each)
    artichoke hearts, drained
    and sliced
1 pound fresh cooked crabmeat
3 pounds large (16 to 24
    per pound) shrimp,
    peeled, deveined, and
    cooked just until
    opaque (see box, page 148)
3 dozen cooked fresh
    mussels, shucked
8 ounces hard sausage,
    thinly sliced
½ cup fresh lemon juice
2 to 2½ cups Hellmann's
    mayonnaise
Salt and freshly ground
    pepper to taste
Lemon slices, red bell
    pepper strips, and
    black olives for garnish

1. Combine the chicken stock, curry powder, saffron, fennel seeds, and red pepper flakes in a medium saucepan and heat just to boiling.

2. Heat the oil in a very large skillet over medium-high heat. Stir in the red onion and garlic and cook, stirring frequently, for 5 minutes. Add the rice and stir to coat with the oil. Cook 2 minutes longer. Gradually stir in the chicken stock mixture. Reduce the heat and simmer covered, stirring occasionally, until half the liquid has been absorbed, 15 to 20 minutes.

3. Stir the chicken into the rice mixture and continue to simmer until all the liquid has been absorbed and the rice is tender, 20 to 25 minutes longer. Remove from the heat and let cool to room temperature, stirring occasionally.

4. When the rice is cooled, transfer it to a large mixing bowl. Add the celery, scallions, peppers, olives, artichoke hearts, crabmeat, shrimp, mussels, and sausage. Toss to combine all the ingredients thoroughly. Stir in the lemon juice and enough mayonnaise to lightly bind. Season to taste with salt and pepper. Transfer the salad to a large shallow serving dish. Garnish with lemon slices, red pepper strips, and whole olives. Refrigerate covered at least 2 hours before serving.

Makes 18 to 20 servings.

Egg and Smoked Salmon Salad

Serve this salad in tomato shells for a light luncheon or on rye or pumpernickel bread for great sandwiches.

12 large eggs,
  hard-cooked, shelled,
  and coarsely chopped
2 ribs celery, chopped
1 small red onion,
  minced
3 tablespoons chopped
  fresh dill

5 ounces smoked salmon,
  cut into ¼-inch dice
1 cup (or as needed)
  Hellmann's mayonnaise
Salt and freshly ground
  pepper to taste

1. Place the eggs, celery, onion, dill, and salmon in a mixing bowl and toss to combine.

2. Stir in enough mayonnaise to bind the salad, being careful not to make it too wet. Season to taste with salt and pepper. Refrigerate for several hours to allow the flavors to blend.

Makes 6 servings.

Tuna Tonnato

In culinary experimentation, redundancy can sometimes achieve a triumph of flavor intensity, as is the case with this salad in which seared chunks of fresh tuna are tossed with a classic Italian tonnato sauce with a canned tuna base. A most elegant interpretation of the forever popular tuna fish salad!

3 pounds fresh tuna, cut
    into ¾-inch chunks
¾ cup fresh lemon juice
½ cup olive oil
2 shallots, minced
Salt and freshly ground
    pepper to taste
1 cucumber, peeled,
    halved lengthwise,
    seeded, and sliced
    diagonally ¼ inch
    thick

2 yellow bell peppers,
    seeded and cut into
    ½-inch squares
5 ripe medium tomatoes,
    seeded and sliced ½
    inch thick
1 medium red onion, cut
    into thin slivers
½ cup chopped fresh dill

TONNATO SAUCE:
2 large egg yolks
1 large egg
5 anchovy fillets, drained
    and chopped
1½ tablespoons capers,
    drained
3 tablespoons fresh lemon
    juice

1½ tablespoons Dijon
    mustard
1 can (12 ounces) white
    meat tuna packed in
    oil (don't drain)
1½ cups olive oil
Salt and freshly ground
    pepper to taste

1. Place the chunks of tuna in a wide shallow bowl. Whisk the lemon juice, oil, shallots, salt, and pepper together in a small mixing bowl and pour over the tuna. Marinate, turning the fish occasionally, for 3 hours in the refrigerator.

2. Combine the cucumber, yellow peppers, tomatoes, onion, and dill in a large mixing bowl. Heat a large skillet over high heat until quite hot. Add the tuna with the marinade and stir-fry just until the tuna is cooked through, 5 to 7 minutes. Add the tuna to the vegetables and toss to combine.

3. Prepare the tonnato sauce: Place the egg yolks, egg, anchovies, capers, lemon juice, mustard, and canned tuna with

its oil in a food processor fitted with the steel blade; process until smooth. With the machine running, slowly pour the oil in a thin, steady stream through the feed tube to make a sauce the consistency of mayonnaise. Season the sauce with salt and pepper to taste. Pour the sauce over the salad ingredients and toss thoroughly to coat. Refrigerate the salad at least 2 hours before serving.

Makes 6 to 8 servings.

Blackened Snapper Vinaigrette

By substituting olive oil for butter in the traditional recipe for blackened snapper, the fish can be served slightly chilled or at room temperature. It's a great way to enjoy this New Orleans specialty when it is just too hot to heat up the cast-iron skillet right before eating.

2 cups olive oil
½ cup fresh lemon juice
2 tablespoons dried thyme
3 tablespoons dried basil
1 tablespoon dried
　oregano
1½ tablespoons coarsely
　ground pepper

2 teaspoons dried red
　pepper flakes
2 teaspoons salt
8 red snapper fillets,
　about 8 ounces each
3 tablespoons shredded
　fresh basil
1 lemon, cut into wedges

1. Heat the oil in a medium skillet and add the lemon juice, thyme, basil, oregano, pepper, red pepper flakes, and salt. Simmer over low heat for 10 minutes, then remove from the heat.

2. Dip the fish fillets, one at a time, in the oil mixture, coating both sides heavily with herbs. Place the fillets on a flat tray and freeze until very cold, 15 to 20 minutes.

3. Heat a large cast-iron skillet over very high heat. Arrange as many fillets as will fit in a single layer in the skillet and quickly sear and blacken both sides, about 4 minutes. Transfer the fillets to a serving platter and refrigerate for several hours. Repeat with any remaining fillets. Serve cold or at room temperature, sprinkled with the basil and garnished with the lemon wedges.

Makes 8 servings.

Steak, Mushroom, and Hearts of Palm with Béarnaise Mayonnaise

Many of the components of a great steak dinner translated into an extravagant and refreshing summer salad.

1 boneless top round
   steak, 3 pounds, 2 to
   2½ inches thick
1 tablespoon dried
   mustard
Salt and freshly ground
   pepper to taste
1 bunch scallions, white
   bulb and green stalks,
   sliced

12 ounces fresh
   mushrooms (as white
   as you can find),
   thinly sliced
2 cans (14 ounces each)
   hearts of palm, drained
   and cut into ½-inch
   slices
½ cup chopped fresh
   parsley

BÉARNAISE MAYONNAISE:
3 shallots, peeled and
   minced
2½ tablespoons dried
   tarragon
½ cup dry white wine
¼ cup tarragon vinegar
2 large egg yolks
2 tablespoons fresh lemon
   juice

1 tablespoon Dijon
   mustard
½ cup olive oil
1 cup vegetable oil
Salt and freshly ground
   pepper to taste
Sliced tomato and fresh
   tarragon or parsley
   sprigs for garnish

1. Preheat the broiler.

2. Rub the steak all over with the dried mustard and sprinkle generously on both sides with salt and pepper. Broil the steak about 6 inches from the heat, turning once, until cooked medium-rare. Let cool several minutes, then cut the steak into thin strips, 2½ to 3 inches long. Combine the steak, scallions, mushrooms, hearts of palm, and parsley in a mixing bowl.

3. Prepare the mayonnaise: Place the shallots, tarragon, wine, and vinegar in a small saucepan and cook over high heat until just 1 tablespoon liquid remains.

4. Place the egg yolks, lemon juice, and mustard in a food

processor fitted with the steel blade; process for 10 seconds. With the machine running, pour the olive and vegetable oils in a thin, steady stream through the feed tube to make a thick emulsion. Add the reduced shallot mixture to the mayonnaise and process to blend. Season the mayonnaise to taste with salt and pepper.

5. Bind the steak salad with the mayonnaise. Refrigerate covered at least several hours but no longer than 12 hours. Garnish with tomato slices and a sprig or two of fresh tarragon or parsley.

Makes 8 servings.

Ham, Cheese, Mushroom, and Walnut Salad

A personal favorite that reminds me of the robust salads I savored in Germany during adolescent bicycle meanderings.

1½ pounds baked ham, thinly sliced
1½ pounds Swiss cheese, thinly sliced
1 pound fresh mushrooms, thinly sliced

3 cups chopped fresh parsley
¼ cup fresh lemon juice
¼ cup olive oil

DRESSING:
1¾ cups chopped walnuts
5 cloves garlic, minced
¼ cup fresh lemon juice
2½ cups olive oil

½ teaspoon cayenne pepper
Salt and freshly ground pepper to taste

1. Cut the ham and cheese into ¼-inch squares and toss together in a large mixing bowl. Add the mushrooms and parsley and toss to combine. Drizzle with the lemon juice and oil and toss once more.

2. Prepare the dressing: Place the walnuts, garlic, and lemon juice in a food processor fitted with the steel blade; pulse just to combine but not purée. Add the oil ½ cup at a time and pulse a

few times after each addition until blended, being careful not to lose the texture of the walnuts. Season the dressing with the cayenne and salt and pepper to taste. Bind the salad with the dressing. Serve at once or refrigerate until ready to serve.

Makes 10 to 12 servings.

Kielbasa Vinaigrette

If I were stranded on a desert isle and allowed only one food, it would probably be kielbasa. A kielbasa supper was always my favorite home-cooked meal when I was growing up. I later devised this salad so I could indulge my passion for cold foods and Polish sausage at the same time.

This salad is very popular with my customers both as a main course and an hors d'oeuvre.

3½ pounds smoked kielbasa sausage
1 jar (4 ounces) chopped pimientos, drained
1 can (6 ounces) large pitted, black olives, sliced

1 bunch scallions, white bulbs and green stalks, sliced
1 cup chopped fresh parsley
1½ cups Basic Herb Vinaigrette (see Index)

1. Put the kielbasa in a large pot and add enough water to just cover the sausage. Heat to boiling over high heat. Reduce the heat and simmer uncovered for 10 minutes. Drain in a colander and let cool just until you can easily slice the sausage without burning your fingers.

2. Using a serrated knife, cut the sausage on a sharp diagonal angle into ½-inch-thick slices. Place the sausage in a large mixing bowl. Add the pimientos, olives, scallions, and parsley and toss to combine. Add the vinaigrette and toss to coat. Serve at room temperature. The salad keeps well in the refrigerator, but it must be warmed to room temperature before serving.

Makes 8 main-course servings or 15 to 20 hors d'oeuvre servings.

Lamb, Eggplant, and Orzo Salad

A Mediterranean-flavored salad that makes great use of leftover lamb in an unusual variation on cold pasta salads.

2 large eggplants, cut into
   ¾-inch chunks
¾ cup olive oil
3 cloves garlic, minced
2 pounds orzo, cooked in
   large pot of boiling
   water until al dente,
   drained, and cooled
   under cold running
   water
2½ pounds rare lamb,
   cut into ¾-inch chunks
1½ cups pitted Greek
   olives, cut in half

1 medium red onion,
   minced
2 yellow bell peppers,
   seeded and cut into
   ½-inch dice
1 cup yellow or red cherry
   tomatoes, quartered
½ cup pine nuts, lightly
   toasted
1 bunch fresh parsley,
   minced
3 tablespoons chopped
   fresh rosemary

LEMON GARLIC DRESSING:
2 large egg yolks
1 large egg
⅓ cup fresh lemon juice
1 tablespoon dried
   oregano
6 cloves garlic, minced

2 teaspoons grated lemon
   zest
2½ cups olive oil
Salt and freshly ground
   pepper to taste

1. Preheat the oven to 375°F.

2. Place the eggplant in a baking pan. Drizzle with the olive oil, add the garlic, and toss to combine. Bake, stirring occasionally, until the eggplant is tender, 30 to 40 minutes. Let cool.

3. Combine the orzo, lamb, olives, onion, yellow peppers, tomatoes, pine nuts, parsley, and rosemary in a large mixing bowl. Add the roasted eggplant and toss all the ingredients together well.

4. Prepare the dressing: Place the egg yolks, egg, lemon juice, oregano, garlic, and lemon zest in a food processor fitted with the steel blade; process for 10 seconds. With the machine running, pour the oil in a thin, steady stream through the feed tube to

make a thick mayonnaise. Season to taste with salt and pepper.

5. Bind the salad with the dressing and transfer to a serving bowl. Garnish with fresh sprigs of rosemary. Serve slightly chilled or at room temperature.

Makes 12 to 15 servings.

Cold Chinese Noodles

Since day one, customers have coveted these noodles. One man from Washington has consumed so many of them over the summers that he is now known by all on Nantucket as the "Big Noodle." This salad is indeed the sort for which midnight cravings are made.

1 boneless, skinless whole chicken breast, poached, cooled, and cut into thin julienne strips (see box, page 163)

5 ounces boiled or baked ham, sliced and cut into thin julienne strips

1 bunch scallions (including green tops), cut into 2-inch lengths, then into julienne strips

½ cup coarsely chopped walnuts

1 pound thin vermicelli, angel hair, or Chinese rice stick noodles, cooked until al dente, drained, and cooled under cold running water

1½ cups vegetable oil

2½ tablespoons Oriental sesame oil

2 tablespoons sesame seeds

3 tablespoons ground coriander seeds

¾ cup soy sauce

1 scant teaspoon (or to taste) hot chili oil

1. Combine the chicken, ham, scallions, and walnuts in a large mixing bowl. Add the pasta.

2. Heat the vegetable and sesame oils and sesame seeds in a small saucepan over medium heat just until the sesame seeds

turn light brown. Remove from the heat. Stir in the coriander and soy sauce; stand back as you do this for the mixture will crackle and sizzle. Stir in the chili oil.

3. Pour the hot dressing over the noodles and toss to coat evenly. The very best way to do this is with your hands. Inevitably at the moment you are up to your elbows in Chinese noodles the phone will ring—it is part of the fun.

4. Transfer the noodles to a serving bowl—again with your hands—and refrigerate until cold, about 3 hours.

Makes 6 to 8 servings or 4 true Chinese-noodle-aficionado servings.

Indonesian Noodles

A more complex, though equally favored, version of the cold Chinese noodles.

2 pounds angel hair or Oriental rice stick noodles, cooked until al dente, drained, and cooled under cold running water

1 bunch scallions white bulbs and green stalks, cut into 2-inch lengths, then into julienne strips

1 pound snow peas, strings removed, blanched in boiling water for 30 seconds, rinsed under cold running water, and then cut lengthwise in half

1 red bell pepper, seeded and cut into thin julienne strips

1 yellow bell pepper, seeded and cut into thin julienne strips

1 can (8 ounces) water chestnuts, drained and thinly sliced

2 cans (8 ounces each) sliced bamboo shoots, drained

1 jar (7¼ ounces) pickled baby corn, drained and cut lengthwise into quarters

½ cup chopped fresh coriander

2½ pounds small (35 to 40 per pound) shrimp, peeled, deveined, and cooked just until opaque (see box, page 148)

¾ cup salted peanuts

¼ cup Oriental sesame oil

¾ cup soy sauce

3½ cups Hellmann's mayonnaise

Hot chili oil to taste

1. Place the drained pasta in a large mixing bowl. Add the julienned vegetables, the water chestnuts, bamboo shoots, baby corn, coriander, shrimp, and peanuts; toss to combine.

2. Whisk the sesame oil, soy sauce, and mayonnaise together in a small mixing bowl. Pour the dressing over the noodles and mix thoroughly with your hands to ensure that the salad is evenly coated. Season with drops of hot chili oil to taste. Refrigerate covered the salad for several hours and serve as a main course.

Makes 10 to 12 servings.

Tortellini with Sun-Dried Tomato Pesto

This is an irresistible way of serving tortellini. My customers have told me that the dish is so good they often can't wait to serve it as the main course and instead spear the tortellini on toothpicks as an hors d'oeuvre.

SUN-DRIED TOMATO PESTO:

½ stick pepperoni (about ¼ pound), cut into small dice

3 tablespoons Dijon mustard

4 cloves garlic, minced

1 tablespoon fennel seeds

1 jar (7 ounces) sun-dried tomatoes packed in oil

1½ cups olive oil

2 tablespoons fresh lemon juice

Salt and freshly ground pepper to taste

SALAD:

2 pounds cheese- or meat-filled tortellini, cooked and drained

2 ripe medium tomatoes, seeded and chopped

1 yellow bell pepper, seeded and diced

1 stick pepperoni, thinly sliced

½ cup chopped fresh parsley

3 tablespoons chopped fresh basil

1. Prepare the pesto: Place the pepperoni, mustard, garlic, fennel seeds, and sun-dried tomatoes with oil in a food processor fitted with the steel blade; process until smooth. With the machine running, pour the olive oil in a thin, steady stream through the feed tube and continue processing until the mixture is smooth. Season with the lemon juice and salt and pepper to taste.

2. Combine the tortellini, tomatoes, yellow pepper, and pepperoni in a large mixing bowl. Add the pesto and toss to coat. Sprinkle with the parsley and basil. Serve warm or at room temperature.

Makes 8 to 10 servings.

Duck and Wild Rice à l'Orange

An expensive combination of the best ingredients, this woodsy salad tastes as fabulous as one would expect.

2 cups wild rice
4 tablespoons (½ stick)
   unsalted butter
4 carrots, peeled and cut
   into ¼-inch dice
1 large red onion, minced
3 cups chicken stock,
   preferably homemade
4 boneless whole duck
   breasts

1 bunch scallions, white
   bulbs and green stalks,
   sliced on slight diagonal
1 cup golden raisins
1½ cups pecan halves
Grated zest of 2 oranges
¾ cup fresh orange juice
¾ cup best-quality olive oil
Salt and freshly ground
   pepper to taste

1. Place the wild rice in a small bowl, add cold water to cover, and let soak for 1 hour. Drain. Heat a 2-quart pot of water to boiling. Add the rice and boil for 5 minutes. Drain again and set aside.

2. Preheat the oven to 375°F.

3. Melt the butter in a large skillet over medium-high heat. Add the carrots and onion and sauté, stirring frequently, for 10 minutes. Add the rice, stir to coat it with the butter, and cook several minutes longer.

4. Transfer the rice mixture to a lasagne-type baking pan, 13 x 11-inches, and pour in the chicken stock. Cover the pan

tightly with aluminum foil and bake until the liquid is absorbed and the rice is tender, 40 to 45 minutes.

5. Meanwhile, place the duck breasts flat on a baking sheet, skin side up, and bake 15 to 20 minutes for rare meat. Remove the duck from the oven and let stand until cool enough to handle. Remove the skin from the meat and return it to the baking sheet. Bake the skins until very crispy, 30 to 40 minutes.

6. Transfer the rice to a large mixing bowl. Cut the duck meat into long, narrow strips and combine it with the rice. Add the scallions, raisins, pecans, and orange zest; toss to combine. Dress the salad with the orange juice and olive oil. Season to taste with salt and pepper.

7. Transfer the salad to a serving bowl. Cut the crisp duck skin into bits and scatter them over the salad. Serve slightly warm or at room temperature.

Makes 8 to 10 servings.

Curried Chicken Salad

Customers at Que Sera are generally divided into two camps of those who favor the chicken and grape salad and those who favor the curried chicken. Then there is a small diplomatic core that often orders a pint of each. The curried chicken recipe is quite simple for a curry. I am convinced that the secret is the addition of the wine in which the raisins are simmered, as it thins the mayonnaise into more of a light curry sauce.

3 pounds boneless, skinless chicken breasts, poached just until tender and cooled to room temperature (see box, facing page)

3 ribs celery, coarsely chopped

2 Granny Smith apples, cored and cut into chunks

¾ cup golden raisins

1 cup dry white wine

2 tablespoons fresh lime juice

2 tablespoons ground ginger

2½ to 3 tablespoons good-quality curry powder

1½ cups Hellmann's mayonnaise

Salt to taste

Sliced Granny Smith apples and curry-colored summer flowers (marigolds, zinnias) for garnish

1. Cut the chicken breasts into ¾- to 1-inch chunks, removing and discarding any tough tendons as you go along. Toss the chicken, celery, and apples together in a large bowl.

2. Place the raisins and wine in a small saucepan. Heat to boiling over medium-high heat. Reduce the heat and simmer for 3 to 4 minutes. Add the raisins and liquid to the chicken and toss to combine.

3. Add the lime juice, ginger, and curry powder and toss again. Bind the salad with the mayonnaise and season to taste with salt.

4. Transfer the salad to a serving bowl and garnish with the apple slices and summer flowers. Refrigerate at least 1 hour before serving.

Makes 6 to 8 servings.

POACHING CHICKEN BREASTS

As reigning queen of chicken salad sales on Nantucket Island in the summertime, I poach zillions and zillions of chicken breasts. The process is much less of a technique and more of a habit that has become second nature to me.

I start by filling a large saucepan with water and spike it with a few splashes of white wine or dry vermouth. I scatter in several onion slices and/or carrot slices, celery leaves, and parsley sprigs over the top, season with a dash of salt and grinding of pepper, then add the chicken breasts. Next I bring the pan to a full boil, and then turn it off, letting the heat of the liquid finish the cooking process. This method seems to keep the breasts especially moist and tender.

When all has cooled, I remove the chicken breasts with a slotted spoon and proceed with the salad making. The poaching liquid can be strained and used for stock in soup recipes.

When I have to poach several batches of chicken breasts over a short period of time, I use the same strained stock over and over again to produce a super rich and wonderfully flavored stock that is great for hearty soup bases and for braising.

Classic Chicken and Grape Salad

Every year about mid-July, I begin to suspect that my entire life revolves around poaching countless ten-pound bags of chicken breasts. Little did I know years ago, when I tried to surprise my uncle on his birthday with a batch of chicken salad as wonderful as that which he raved about at Boston's Ritz Carlton, that so much of my catering reputation and fortune would come to center on that recipe.

While ingredients such as dried thyme, garlic powder, and store-bought mayonnaise reflect the culinary naïveté of my adolescence, the insuing years of food sophistication spent culti-vating window boxes of fragrant fresh herbs and whisking together countless varieties of homemade mayonnaise have yet to yield a more perfectly comforting and soothing chicken salad than this original "Ritz" rendition.

3½ pounds boneless, skinless chicken breasts, poached just until tender and cooled to room temperature (see box, page 163)

5 ribs celery, coarsely chopped

1½ cups seedless green grapes, cut in half

1½ teaspoons dried thyme

1½ teaspoons garlic powder (fresh garlic is overpowering)

Salt and freshly ground pepper to taste

3 cups (or as needed) Hellmann's mayonnaise

1. Cut the chicken breasts into ¾- to 1-inch chunks, remov-ing and discarding any tough tendons as you go along.

2. Toss the chicken, celery, and grapes together in a large bowl. Season with the thyme, garlic powder, salt, and pepper. Bind the salad with the mayonnaise. You want to use a lot of mayonnaise to make the salad very moist and creamy.

3. Transfer the salad to a serving bowl and refrigerate cov-ered at least 1 hour before serving.

Makes 6 to 8 servings.

Chicken and Apricot Salad with Double-Mustard Mayonnaise

Chicken salad seems capable of sustaining an amazing number of incarnations. This autumnal version was created in response to a favorite customer's suggestion.

3 pounds boneless, skinless chicken breasts, poached just until tender and cooled to room temperature (see box, page 163)

1 cup dried apricots, cut into ¼-inch strips

⅓ cup cream sherry

3 ribs celery, coarsely chopped

4 scallions, white bulbs and green stalks, trimmed and sliced on diagonal

½ cup slivered almonds, lightly toasted

3 tablespoons chopped fresh rosemary

DOUBLE-MUSTARD MAYONNAISE:

2 large egg yolks

2 tablespoons fresh lemon juice

2 tablespoons grainy Dijon mustard

¾ cup vegetable oil

⅔ cup olive oil

¼ cup honey mustard

Salt and freshly ground pepper to taste

Fresh rosemary sprigs for garnish

1. Cut the poached chicken breasts into 2 x ¾-inch strips and place them in a large mixing bowl.

2. Place the apricots and sherry in a small saucepan. Heat to boiling. Reduce the heat and simmer for 3 minutes. Add the apricots with the liquid to the chicken.

3. Add the celery, scallions, almonds, and rosemary to the salad and toss to combine.

4. Prepare the mayonnaise: Place the egg yolks, lemon juice, and grainy mustard in a food processor fitted with the steel blade; process for 10 seconds. With the machine running, pour the vegetable and olive oils in a thin, steady stream through the feed tube to make an emulsion. Add the honey mustard and process until smooth. Season to taste with salt and freshly ground pepper. Bind the salad with the mayonnaise.

5. Transfer the salad to a serving bowl and garnish with the rosemary sprigs. Refrigerate covered at least 2 hours before serving.

Makes 6 to 8 servings.

Indian Chicken Salad

This is the most adventuresome chicken salad made at Que Sera Sarah. Lovers of Indian tandoor cooking will appreciate this chilled salad version.

4 pounds boneless, skinless chicken breasts, cut into 1-inch chunks
5 cloves garlic, minced
3 tablespoons chopped fresh ginger
2 tablespoons ground coriander seeds
2 tablespoons fennel seeds
1 tablespoon cumin seeds
1 tablespoon turmeric
1 tablespoon ground cinnamon
1½ teaspoons ground ginger
3 tablespoons tomato paste
3 tablespoons fresh lemon juice
1 can (28 ounces) tomatoes packed in purée
Salt to taste
2 tablespoons fresh coriander leaves for garnish

1. Arrange the chicken in a single layer in a shallow glass or enamel baking dish.

2. Place the garlic, fresh ginger, coriander seeds, fennel, cumin, turmeric, cinnamon, ground ginger, tomato paste, and lemon juice in a food processor fitted with the steel blade; process to a thick paste. Add the tomatoes and process until well

blended. Season to taste with salt. Pour the spice mixture over the chicken. Let marinate covered overnight in the refrigerator, stirring occasionally.

3. Preheat the oven to 450°F.

4. Bake the chicken, stirring frequently, just until it is cooked through, 20 to 25 minutes. Let cool to room temperature.

5. Transfer the salad to a serving bowl and garnish with the fresh coriander. Serve the salad at room temperature or refrigerate for an hour or so.

Makes 8 servings.

Smoked Turkey with Artichoke Hearts

A pretty pastel salad that you can assemble quickly on a hot, hot day when any movement seems overwhelming.

3 pound piece smoked turkey, cut into ¾-inch chunks

1 large red onion, cut into thin slivers

2 cans (14 ounces each) artichoke hearts, packed in water, drained and thinly sliced

4 ribs celery, minced

5 tablespoons fresh lemon juice

7 tablespoons olive oil

1 teaspoon salt

1 teaspoon freshly ground pepper

GREEN-PEPPERCORN TARRAGON MAYONNAISE:

2 large egg yolks

1 large egg

1½ tablespoons Dijon mustard

1½ tablespoons green peppercorns packed in brine, drained

2½ tablespoons minced fresh tarragon

3 tablespoons fresh lemon juice

1¼ cups olive oil

1½ cups vegetable oil

Salt to taste

1. Combine the turkey, onion, artichoke hearts, and celery in a large mixing bowl. Drizzle with the lemon juice and oil and sprinkle with the salt and pepper. Toss to combine. Let marinate at room temperature for 30 minutes.

2. Prepare the mayonnaise: Place the egg yolks, egg, mustard, green peppercorns, tarragon, and lemon juice in a food processor fitted with the steel blade; process for 20 seconds. With the machine running, pour the olive and vegetable oils in a thin, steady stream through the feed tube to make a thick mayonnaise. Season the mayonnaise with salt to taste.

3. Bind the salad with mayonnaise. Refrigerate several hours before serving.

Makes 8 to 10 servings.

Eclectic Dinner Fare

One might suspect a certain lack of worldliness to prevail on a tiny New England island isolated by thirty miles of ocean, but throughout its history the spirit of Nantucketers has never been in the least bit provincial. From the island's prosperous whaling beginnings in the 1700s to the stylish present, the person lured to living or vacationing on Nantucket has always seemed capable of balancing a restless curiosity for the nooks and crannies of the globe with a strong attachment to Nantucket as home.

The joy of creating dinners for such clients is that they immediately understand and appreciate both foreign and native inspirations of a meal. While the rest of America appears to be intently focused on the revival of regional cooking, a wonderful culinary eclecticism thrives on this island. Local Nantucket provisions are always enthusiastically welcomed for preparations that may find their origins in the lagoons of Venice, the olive groves of Greece, the vineyards of Burgundy, the *pousadas* of Portugal, the extremities of Baja, the glitz of New York, or the traditions of New England. The supreme enjoyment of sharing dinner with friends on Nantucket is that the boundaries of one island oasis can expand to include so many imaginative culinary voyages around the world.

Cuban Pork Roast

This is a great feast for a balmy summer evening. The flavorings take their inspiration from a friend's recollections of growing up in Havana and my own personal fascination with Caribbean cuisine. In addition to the recipes for Black Beans and Baked Bananas included here, you may want to serve a side of white rice to make this unusually spiced meal complete.

6 cloves garlic
4 scallions, white bulbs
  and green stalks,
  minced
½ cup pine nuts
1 fresh jalapeño pepper,
  seeded and minced
2 cups minced fresh
  coriander leaves
⅔ cup fruity olive oil
½ cup plus 3 tablespoons
  fresh lime juice
⅓ cup Niçoise or Greek
  olives, pitted and
  minced

Salt and freshly ground
  pepper to taste
1 boneless pork loin roast
  (4 pounds)
½ cup fresh grapefruit
  juice
½ cup fresh orange juice
½ cup hot pepper jelly
  (available at specialty
  food stores)

BLACK BEANS AND BAKED BANANAS:
  (recipes follow), as accompaniments

1. On the day before you plan to serve the pork, prepare the filling and marinade: Place the garlic, scallions, pine nuts, jalapeño pepper, and coriander in a food processor fitted with the steel blade. Process to form a thick paste. With the machine running, pour the olive oil in a thin, steady stream through the feed tube until all is incorporated. Remove to a small bowl and stir in the lime juice, olives, and salt and pepper to taste.

2. If the pork roast is tied, untie it and roll it out flat. Spread two-thirds of the garlic-coriander paste over the meat. Reroll the roast and tie it.

3. Stir the grapefruit, orange, and lime juices into the remaining garlic-coriander paste. Make shallow incisions over the surface of the roast with the tip of a sharp knife. Place the roast in a shallow dish or pan and pour over the marinade. Let marinate in

the refrigerator, turning occasionally, for 24 hours.

4. Preheat the oven to 375°F.

5. Remove the roast from the marinade and place it in a roasting pan. Roast uncovered, basting occasionally with any leftover marinade, for 1¾ hours. Brush the roast all over with the hot pepper jelly and bake 15 minutes more or until cooked to desired doneness.

6. Let the roast rest out of the oven for 10 minutes, then carve into ½-inch-thick slices and serve.

Makes 8 servings.

Black Beans

The seasoning or "sofrito" for these beans has been derived from recipes of many different Caribbean islands. The annatto seeds add authentic flavoring subtleties and impart a bright orange-red color, but are not essential to the success of this dish if they are difficult to locate in your area.

1 pound black beans, soaked overnight in cold water

1½ tablespoons annatto seeds (available in specialty food stores)

⅓ cup olive oil

1 medium onion, diced

2 scallions, white bulbs and green stalks, minced

4 cloves garlic, minced

½ green bell pepper, seeded and diced

½ red bell pepper, seeded and diced

1 fresh jalapeño pepper, seeded and minced

2 tablespoons tomato paste

3 tablespoons red wine vinegar

1 tablespoon dried oregano leaves

1 tablespoon ground cumin

3 tablespoons minced fresh coriander leaves

1 tablespoon salt

2 teaspoons freshly ground pepper

1. Drain the beans and place in a large saucepan or stockpot with water to cover. Heat to boiling over medium-high heat, then

lower the heat and simmer for 1¼ hours. Add more water if necessary to keep the beans moist. Do not drain the cooked beans.

2. Meanwhile, make the sofrito: If you are using the annatto seeds, place them in a small saucepan with the olive oil. Heat over medium heat just until the annatto seeds release their color, 5 to 7 minutes. Strain out the seeds and discard.

3. Heat the flavored oil (or plain olive oil) in a medium skillet over medium-high heat. Add the onion, scallions, garlic, bell peppers, and jalapeño and sauté, stirring frequently, for 7 minutes. Stir in the tomato paste and vinegar, then add the oregano, cumin, coriander, salt, and pepper. Reduce the heat to medium and cook for 5 minutes more. Remove from the heat.

4. Add the sofrito to the cooked beans (there should still be a fair amount of liquid with the beans) and simmer uncovered until the mixture becomes quite thick, 30 minutes. You can serve the beans at once or set aside. (Many cooks like to make black beans in advance as they feel the flavor improves with a little age and reheating.) Reheat the beans covered over low heat.

Makes 8 servings.

Baked Bananas

These provide an interesting sweet balance to the spiciness of the pork and black beans.

4 *ripe bananas, peeled, cut crosswise in half, then halved lengthwise*	1 *tablespoon fresh lime juice*
4 *tablespoons (½ stick) unsalted butter*	⅓ *cup loosely packed brown sugar*
2 *tablespoons dry sherry*	1 *teaspoon ground cinnamon*

1. Preheat the oven to 375°F. Arrange the bananas in a single layer in an 11 x 9-inch glass baking dish.

2. Melt the butter in a small saucepan over medium heat, then stir in the sherry and lime juice. Heat thoroughly, then pour over the bananas. Dot with the brown sugar and cinnamon. Bake in the oven until lightly browned and bubbly, 12 to 15 minutes.

Makes 8 servings.

Filet Mignon with Herbes de Provence and Red Wine Béarnaise

Whille traveling through Provence one fall, I discovered that the local, aromatic herb blend was often used to coat meats in a manner that reminded me of Paul Prudhomme's blackened red-fish. This recipe is my own interpolation, falling somewhere between St. Remy and New Orleans.

6 filet mignon steaks,
   each 2 inches thick
   (6 to 8 ounces each)
Salt and freshly ground
   pepper to taste
4 tablespoons imported
   herbes de Provence
3 shallots, minced
3 tablespoons chopped
   fresh tarragon

3 tablespoons red wine
   vinegar
½ cup dry red wine
2 large egg yolks
¾ cup (1½ sticks)
   unsalted butter,
   melted, then cooled to
   lukewarm
3 tablespoons olive oil

1. One hour before serving, season the steaks generously all over with salt and pepper. Rub a generous 1 teaspoon of the herbes de Provence into each side of the filets. Let sit at room temperature.

2. In the meantime, make the red wine Béarnaise. Combine the shallots, tarragon, vinegar, and wine in a small skillet. Reduce the mixture over medium-high heat until all but 2 tablespoons of liquid remain. Turn off the heat and whisk in the egg yolks, one at a time. Gradually whisk in the melted butter, tablespoon by tablespoon, until all is absorbed and the sauce is thickened. Keep the Béarnaise warm in the top of a double boiler set over simmering water or in a warm spot near the stove. (Be careful not to overheat or the mixture will separate.)

3. Coat a large well-seasoned frying pan with the olive oil. Heat over high heat until very hot. Add the steaks and cook until the bottoms are well browned, 3 to 4 minutes. Turn the steaks and brown the other side for 2 to 3 minutes. Reduce the heat to medium and continue cooking until the meat reaches the desired doneness, 3 minutes more for rare. Transfer the steaks to serving plates and nap each with a generous amount of the red wine Béarnaise.

Makes 6 servings.

Beef Tenderloin au Poivre

W hen entertaining, this pepper-crusted beef tenderloin is much easier to prepare than the classic recipe for individual steak au poivre and much more opulent in presentation. During spells of hot weather, I roast the tenderloin during the cooler morning hours and serve it chilled for dinner accompanied by Tomato Bearnaise Mayonnaise, Remoulade Sauce, or Aioli (see the Index). When serving the tenderloin straight from the oven, I like to dot the rosy pink slices with Herb Garden Butter (recipe follows).

1 beef tenderloin,
   trimmed of fat (3½ to
   4 pounds after
   trimming)
⅓ cup Dijon mustard

4½ teaspoons coarsely
   ground black peppercorns
4½ teaspoons coarsely
   ground white peppercorns

1. Preheat the oven to 425°F.
2. Rub the tenderloin generously all over with the mustard. Combine the peppercorns and press them evenly all over the surface of the meat. Place the meat in a roasting pan and cook for 45 minutes for rare meat, or longer for desired doneness. To serve warm, let stand for 5 minutes, then slice into ½-inch thick slices. Dot each with a dollop of Herb Garden Butter. Serve 2 to 3 slices per person. If serving the tenderloin cold, let the meat cool to room temperature, then wrap it in aluminum foil and refrigerate for several hours. Remove from the refrigerator about 15 minutes before serving and carve into ½-inch-thick slices. Arrange the slices on a platter along with a bowl of the sauce of your choice.
Makes 8 servings.

Herb Garden Butter

1 cup dry red wine
2 shallots, minced
¾ cup (1½ sticks)
   unsalted butter, at
   room temperature

1 tablespoon minced fresh
   tarragon
1 tablespoon minced fresh basil
1 tablespoon minced fresh parsley

1. Combine the red wine and shallots in a small saucepan and reduce over medium-high heat until only 3 tablespoons of the liquid remains.

2. Beat the butter and the herbs together in a mixing bowl until well creamed. Gradually beat in the wine reduction, tablespoon by tablespoon. Refrigerate until 30 minutes before serving. Serve the butter at room temperature.

Makes about ¾ cup.

Rainwater Chili

This recipe was created in honor of a person of boundless and contagious enthusiasm who rescued me many times from the tribulations of life in the food business, yet continues to be my most avid supporter. The friendship that began as a food summit on a widow's walk has survived everything from scandalous culinary confessions to capers with Armenian caviar purveyors in the South of France. Our unique rapport is one of the greatest rewards of my years in this business.

¼ cup olive oil
2 large Spanish onions, chopped
3 to 4 fresh jalapeño peppers, seeded and minced
1 yellow bell pepper, seeded and diced
1 green bell pepper, seeded and diced
5 cloves garlic, minced
¼ cup best-quality chili powder
2 tablespoons ground cumin
2 tablespoons dried oregano
1 tablespoon sweet paprika
1 tablespoon hot paprika
2 teaspoons ground cinnamon

1 teaspoon turmeric
1 teaspoon ground coriander seeds
½ teaspoon ground cardamon
3 tablespoons unsweetened cocoa powder
2 pounds ground beef sirloin
12 ounces hot Italian sausage, removed from casings and crumbled
12 ounces sweet Italian sausage, removed from casings and crumbled
1 can (35 ounces) tomatoes, undrained
½ cup golden tequila
1 bottle (12 ounces) beer
1 cup pitted Niçoise or Greek olives
Salt to taste

1. Heat the oil in a large pot over medium-high heat. Add the onions and cook, stirring occasionally, for 10 minutes.

2. Stir in the jalapeños, bell peppers, and garlic; cook, stirring occasionally, for 5 minutes. And all the seasonings and the cocoa powder and cook, stirring occasionally, 5 minutes longer. Remove from the heat.

3. Brown the sirloin and sausage in a skillet, crumbling the meat with the back of a wooden spoon, over medium-high heat just until the meat is no longer pink. Add the meat to the onion mixture and return the pan to medium heat.

4. Stir in the tomatoes, tequila, beer, and olives. Season to taste with salt. Simmer the chili uncovered over low heat for about 1 hour.

5. Serve the chili hot in deep bowls, accompanied by bowls of sour cream, grated Cheddar cheese, and diced onions, tomatoes, and/or avocado. The chili is even better the next day and makes great nachos.

Makes 6 to 8 servings.

TAPAS TEXAS-STYLE

Great Guacamole
Salsa with Blue Corn Chips
Tex-Mex Turnovers
Baby Chiles Rellenos
Sausage in Brioche
Caviar Tartines
Grilled Soft-Shell Crabs
Miniature Lobster Salad
Club Sandwiches
Rainwater Chili in Pita Pockets
Que Sera Sarah Brownies

Tecate Beer, lots of Tequila, and Limes

Ossobuco

O ssobuco and I go back a long way. The story begins about fifteen years ago with my grandmother. She loved good food and adventurous eating and would always have some recipe or another she wanted us to cook together when I came to visit. Because my grandfather disdained any food that might be labeled "fancy," my grandmother would eagerly await my collaboration to satisfy her more esoteric cravings. Together we shared in gourmet extravaganzas, surreptitiously preparing steak tartare, sweetbreads, chicken fat cupcakes, and calamondin pies. One day we made ossobuco and passed it off on my grandfather as a new Perdue chicken part. It seems as if I've been making osso-buco ever since. This recipe is my thoroughly evolved version of this wonderful Italian dish. A good Italian risotto is the best accompaniment.

¾ cup all-purpose flour
Salt and freshly ground
    pepper to taste
3 pounds veal shank cut
    into 8 pieces, each 1½
    to 2 inches thick
3 tablespoons olive oil
2 tablespoons unsalted
    butter
3 leeks, rinsed, dried,
    and minced

6 carrots, peeled and
    minced
3 plum tomatoes, seeded
    and chopped
5 sun-dried tomatoes
    packed in oil, drained,
    and minced
6 cloves garlic, minced
2 cups beef stock,
    preferably homemade
1 cup dry white wine

GREMOLATA:
Finely grated zest of 1
    lemon

½ cup minced fresh parsley
3 cloves garlic, minced

1. Season the flour with salt and pepper and dredge the veal shanks with the seasoned flour. Heat the oil and butter in a Dutch oven or large ovenproof casserole over medium-high heat. Add the veal shanks in batches and brown on all sides. Remove the browned shanks to a large plate.

2. Preheat the oven to 300°F.

3. Add the leeks and carrots to the pan and cook, stirring occasionally, for about 7 minutes. Stir

in the plum tomatoes, sun-dried tomatoes, and 6 cloves garlic; cook 5 minutes longer.

4. Add the beef stock and wine to the pan. Taste and adjust the seasoning. Return the veal shanks to the pan. Heat to boiling, then remove the pan from the heat. If you want, the dish can be refrigerated overnight at this point and finished the next day.

5. Cover the Dutch oven and place the pan the oven. Cook until the veal is very tender, about 1½ hours.

6. Meanwhile, prepare the gremolata: Combine the lemon zest, parsley, and 3 cloves garlic in a small bowl.

7. Serve the ossobuco in wide shallow bowls or plates and sprinkle each serving with a little of the gremolata.

Makes 6 to 8 servings.

Veal Marengo

For buffet entertaining this dish is a welcome variation on the now familiar *boeuf Bourguignon*.

½ cup all-purpose flour
Salt and freshly ground
   pepper to taste
3 pounds boneless lean
   veal, cut into 2-inch
   cubes
¼ cup olive oil
1 very large onion,
   chopped
1 cup dry white wine
1 cup chicken stock,
   preferably homemade

4 ripe tomatoes, seeded
   and cut into ½-inch pieces
3 cloves garlic, minced
1 tablespoon chopped
   fresh tarragon
1 teaspoon dried thyme
2 tablespoons fine strips
   orange zest
12 ounces fresh small
   button mushrooms
½ cup chopped fresh
   parsley

1. Season the flour with salt and pepper and lightly coat the veal cubes with the seasoned flour. Heat the olive oil in a Dutch oven or heavy casserole over medium-high heat. Add the veal in batches and quickly brown on all sides. Remove the browned veal to a large plate.

2. Add the onion to the pan and sauté over medium heat just until limp, 5 to 7 minutes. Pour in the wine and chicken stock and stir to scrape up any brown bits clinging to the bottom of the pan. Return the veal to the pot and add the tomatoes, garlic, tarragon, thyme, and orange zest. Simmer uncovered, stirring occasionally, until the veal is very tender, for about 1¼ hours.

3. Stir in the mushrooms and simmer 10 to 15 minutes longer. Season to taste with salt and pepper. If the sauce seems too thin at this point, remove the solids with a slotted spoon and keep warm. Reduce the sauce over high heat until thickened to the proper consistency. Return the solids and stir to combine. Sprinkle the stew with the parsley and serve with hot buttered noodles.

Makes 8 servings.

Moussaka

This is a great Mediterranean entrée perfect for summer entertaining, for it is best made ahead and will feed a summer cottage of houseguests quite sumptuously. Take advantage of summer's bountiful plump purple eggplants.

3 large eggplants	1½ tablespoons ground
Salt	cinnamon
2 pounds lean ground	½ tablespoon grated nutmeg
lamb	2 teaspoons dried oregano
¼ to ½ cup olive oil	1 can (14½ ounces)
2 medium onions,	whole tomatoes, undrained
coarsely chopped	1 cup dry red wine
4 cloves garlic, minced	Freshly ground pepper to taste

BÉCHAMEL:

½ cup (1 stick) unsalted	½ teaspoon grated
butter	nutmeg
6 tablespoons all-purpose	Salt and freshly ground
flour	white pepper to taste
4 cups hot milk	3 large eggs, beaten

5 cups grated (about ¾ pound) Kasseri cheese
(or substitute Italian sharp)

1. Using a vegetable peeler, remove the peel from each eggplant in long strips, leaving a few narrow purple stripes of skin. Cut the eggplants crosswise into ½-inch-thick slices. Sprinkle the slices with salt and lay them out on paper towels to absorb the moisture.

2. Place the lamb and 1 tablespoon of the oil in a skillet. Cook, crumbling the meat with a fork, over medium-high heat just until the meat begins to lose its pink color, 3 to 4 minutes.

3. Add the onions and the garlic to the lamb and cook, stirring occasionally, for 10 minutes. Season with the cinnamon, nutmeg, and oregano and cook 1 minute. Stir in the canned tomatoes, wine, and salt and black pepper to taste. Simmer uncovered for 25 to 30 minutes, then remove from the heat.

4. Meanwhile, cook the eggplant: Pat the eggplant slices dry with paper towels. Dribble a little olive oil in a large nonstick skillet and sauté the eggplant in batches until lightly browned on both sides. Add more oil as needed, but be careful not to add too much oil, for the eggplant will absorb it all and become soggy and greasy. Place the cooked eggplant on a large plate.

5. Preheat the oven to 300°F.

6. Prepare the béchamel: Melt the butter in a medium saucepan over medium-high heat. Add the flour and whisk until smooth. Cook, stirring constantly, 1 minute. Gradually whisk in the milk; cook, stirring constantly, until smooth and thickened. Season with the nutmeg and salt and white pepper to taste. Stir ½ cup of the hot sauce into the beaten eggs in a small bowl and then stir the egg mixture into the remaining sauce. Cook several minutes longer, stirring constantly, then remove from the heat.

7. To assemble the moussaka, arrange half the eggplant in a large oval or rectangular casserole, about 17 x 12 inches. Spread all the lamb sauce over the eggplant and sprinkle with half the cheese. Top with the remaining eggplant. Pour the béchamel over all and sprinkle with the remaining cheese.

8. Bake the moussaka for 1 hour. Let cool to room temperature and refrigerate overnight.

9. Let the moussaka warm to room temperature before reheating. Bake in an oven preheated to 350°F until browned and bubbly, about 30 minutes. Serve with a big green salad and crusty rolls. (The moussaka is cooked twice because it tastes better reheated the second day.)

Makes 12 to 14 servings.

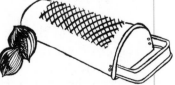

Summer Chicken Sauté

T his is a colorful and light entrée for casual summer entertaining. As with all stir-fry preparations, the work is in the preliminary chopping of ingredients, and the cooking goes very quickly. Serve with it a simple risotto or buttered spinach fettuccine.

4 to 6 tablespoons fruity olive oil

5 whole boneless, skinless chicken breast halves, cut into 2-inch cubes

2 red bell peppers, seeded and cut into 1-inch squares

2 yellow bell peppers, seeded and cut into 1-inch squares

1 large summer squash, cut crosswise into ¼-inch-thick slices, then halved

1 large zucchini, cut crosswise into ¼-inch-thick slices, then halved

½ cup sweet Marsala

2 tablespoons chopped fresh thyme

2 tablespoons chopped fresh rosemary

2 large tomatoes, seeded and finely diced

1 cup heavy or whipping cream

2 to 3 tablespoons fresh lemon juice

Salt and freshly ground pepper to taste

3 tablespoons chopped fresh basil

1. Heat 2 tablespoons of the oil in a wok over medium-high heat. Add as much of the chicken as will comfortably fit in the wok and stir-fry just until barely cooked through, 5 to 6 minutes. Remove with a slotted spoon to a large plate. Repeat with the remaining chicken.

2. Add 1 tablespoon or so more oil to the wok and heat. Add the bell peppers and stir-fry until crisp-tender, 3 to 4 minutes. Remove with a slotted spoon and add to the chicken.

3. Add a bit more oil to the wok and stir-fry the summer squash and zucchini just until crisp-tender, 3 to 4 minutes. Remove with a slotted spoon and toss with the chicken and peppers.

4. Add the Marsala, thyme, rosemary, and tomatoes to the wok. Heat to boiling and cook until the mixture is syrupy. Add the cream and cook until reduced by about half. Season to taste with the lemon juice, salt, and pepper.

5. Return the chicken and vegetables to the wok, stir to coat with the sauce, and heat through. Transfer to a serving platter and sprinkle with the basil.

Makes 8 servings.

Jerry's Chicken Curry

J erry is a wonderfully unique friend and a good, no-nonsense cook. Many strong bonds of friendship have been strengthened around generous meals in his charming old Nantucket home. Over the years, lingering late into the evening over Jerry's legendary candlelight curry dinners has brought much culinary contentment as well as provided many "brilliant" solutions to life's dilemmas. Serve this with rice and favorite curry condiments—cashews, banana chips, diced apples, and mango chutney, toasted coconut, chopped scallions.

½ cup unbleached
  all-purpose flour
Salt and freshly ground
  pepper to taste
3 boneless whole chicken
  breasts, halved
5 tablespoons unsalted
  butter
1 medium onion, minced
2 cloves garlic, minced
2 green bell peppers,
  seeded and diced

3 tablespoons (or more to
  taste) best-quality
  curry powder
1 can (15 ounces) stewed
  tomatoes
1 can (15 ounces) cream
  of coconut
Dash Worcestershire
  sauce
Dash Tabasco sauce
½ cup currants

1. Season the flour with salt and pepper in a shallow bowl. Lightly coat the chicken with the seasoned flour.

2. Heat 3 tablespoons of the butter in a large skillet over medium-high heat. Add the chicken and lightly brown on all sides. Remove the chicken from the skillet.

3. Preheat the oven to 350°F.

4. Add the remaining 2 tablespoons butter to the skillet and melt over medium heat. Add the onions, garlic, and bell peppers;

sauté, stirring frequently, until the vegetables are soft, 5 to 7 minutes. Stir in the curry powder and cook 2 minutes longer.

5. Stir in the tomatoes and coconut cream. Heat to simmering and season with Worcestershire, Tabasco, and salt and pepper to taste. Stir in the currants and remove from heat.

6. Arrange the chicken breasts in casserole and pour the curry sauce over the chicken. Bake covered until the chicken is tender, about 45 minutes.

Makes 4 to 6 servings.

Roasted Chicken

There is nothing more comforting and restorative when suffering from the excesses of rich food and decadent living than a simple roasted chicken. There is, however, a good jigger of Grand Marnier added to the glaze lest the cure provide too sudden a withdrawal from all of life's vices.

1 roasting chicken, about
  7 pounds
1 orange, quartered
1 small onion, quartered

Salt and freshly ground
  pepper to taste
2 teaspoons dried rosemary
½ cup water

GLAZE:
3 tablespoons unsalted
  butter
3 tablespoons grainy
  Dijon mustard
3 tablespoons honey

1 tablespoon apricot jam
3 tablespoons Grand
  Marnier or other fine
  orange liqueur

1. Preheat the oven to 400°F.

2. Rinse the chicken inside and out and pat dry. Squeeze the juice of the orange quarters over the bird, inside and out. Place the orange and onion inside the bird and tie the legs together with kitchen string.

3. Sprinkle salt and pepper all over the outside of the bird, then sprinkle with the rosemary. Place the bird, breast side up, in a roasting pan and pour the water into the pan.

4. Roast the chicken for 20 minutes. Reduce the heat to 350°F and roast for 1 hour.

5. While the bird is roasting, prepare the glaze: Heat the butter, mustard, honey, and jam in a small saucepan until smooth and hot to the touch. Remove from the heat and stir in the Grand Marnier. Spoon the glaze over the chicken and bake until the bird is golden brown and the meat is tender, about 40 minutes longer.

Makes 4 to 6 servings.

Chicken Shoemaker

This was a frequently requested meal from my aunt's Nantucket kitchen. The name is a translation from the Italian, and in Italy the dish is regarded as spicy-hot peasant fare. The easy preparation makes this great for friends with hot pepper palates.

⅓ cup olive oil
3 tablespoons unsalted
*   butter*
10 cloves garlic, very
*   coarsely chopped*
8 to 10 hot cherry
*   peppers, halved but not*
*   seeded (see Note)*

15 chicken thighs, cut
*   crosswise in half*
½ cup dry white wine
1½ tablespoons balsamic
*   vinegar*
Salt to taste

1. Heat the oil and butter in a large skillet over medium-high heat. Add the garlic and hot peppers and sauté for 5 minutes. Add the chicken and sauté until the pieces are very lightly browned on both sides, 7 to 10 minutes. Reduce the heat to low and continue cooking, sitrring frequently, for 25 minutes.

2. Stir in the wine and vinegar. Season to taste with salt. Cook several minutes more to reduce the liquid slightly. Serve with plenty of crusty bread.

Makes 6 servings.

Note: Jars of hot cherry peppers, packed in either brine or oil, are available in most supermarkets.

Apricot-Glazed Rock Cornish Hens

A nice dinner party entrée for end-of-the-summer evenings when there is a bit of an autumn chill in the air.

6 Rock Cornish hens
Salt and freshly ground
    pepper to taste
2 tablespoons chopped
    fresh rosemary
1 cup dried apricot halves
1 cup Rosy Applesauce
    (see Index)

1½ cups dry white wine
¼ cup brown sugar
Finely grated zest of
    1 orange
½ teaspoon ground cloves
Fresh rosemary sprigs for
    garnish

1. Preheat the oven to 350°F.

2. Rinse the hens inside and out under cold running water and pat dry. Season inside and out with salt and pepper. Truss the birds and place them, breast side up, in a roasting pan. Sprinkle the hens all over with the rosemary. Roast the birds 1 hour.

At 'Sconset the morning sport is surf bathing; and when we say surf bathing, we mean surf bathing. To the east there is nothing between 'Sconset and Spain, and to the south nothing between 'Sconset and the West Indies. A wave can get a fairly good running start, and hit 'Sconset beach a tolerably, decisive wallop. Not that it always does, of course. Many a summer day the old Atlantic drowses, glassy to the mother-of pearl horizon, and only tiny breakers lay their lacework on the sand. But when it does take it into its head to kick up a row, the sea cavalry come charging in with white plumes flying, and you can hear its thunder far back on the moors. 'Sconset is so closely a part of the ocean, almost more than of the land, that it is peculiarly susceptible to the ocean's moods, and lovers of the sea find it their favorite resort.

—Guide to Nantucket 1932

3. Meanwhile, prepare the apricot glaze: Quarter the dried apricots and combine with the applesauce and wine in a saucepan. Stir in the brown sugar, orange zest, and cloves. Simmer covered, stirring occasionally, for 30 minutes.

4. Press the glaze through a sieve or food mill, then spoon over the roasting game hens. Roast the birds until tender, 25 to 30 minutes. Serve garnished with fresh rosemary.

Makes 6 servings.

Shrimp Curry

When I have a bit of time to play in the kitchen, I enjoy experimenting with Indian curries. This recipe may not be thoroughly traditional, but I do think it tastes quite wonderful. Serve with basmati rice and plenty of curry condiments.

3 pounds large shrimp
   (16 to 24 per pound),
   peeled and deveined
3 cloves garlic, minced
3 cups unsweetened
   coconut milk (available
   in Indian food markets
   or homemade from
   fresh coconut, see
   Index)
9 tablespoons clarified
   butter (see box,
   page 195)
1 large onion, minced
½ cup shredded
   prosciutto
1 tablespoon fennel seeds
¼ cup (or more to taste)
   best-quality curry
   powder

2 Granny Smith apples,
   cored and cut into
   ½-inch chunks
Finely chopped zest of
   1 lime
½ cup preserved
   kumquats, chopped
¼ cup unbleached
   all-purpose flour
5 tablespoons fresh lime
   juice
Salt to taste
Light cream (see Index),
   as needed
Basmati Rice (recipe
   follows)

1. The day before serving, place the shrimp in a bowl and toss with the minced garlic. Pour in the coconut milk. Cover the bowl and let marinate in the refrigerator overnight.

2. The next day, drain the shrimp, reserving the milk. Heat 6 tablespoons of the clarified butter in a large sauté pan or skillet over medium-high heat. Add the onion and prosciutto and cook, stirring frequently, until the onion is very soft, 10 to 15 minutes.

3. Stir in the fennel seeds and curry powder and cook 1 to 2 minutes. Add the apple, lime zest, and kumquats; cook and stir for another 2 minutes or so. Add the flour and stir well to blend. Gradually whisk in the reserved coconut milk and the lime juice. Simmer the sauce uncovered 25 to 30 minutes and season to taste with salt. If the sauce becomes too thick, thin it with light cream.

4. While the sauce is simmering, sauté the shrimp in the remaining 3 tablespoons clarified butter in a large skillet until pink and just cooked through. Add the shrimp to the sauce and simmer 5 minutes longer. Serve immediately with basmati rice.

Makes 6 to 8 servings.

Basmati Rice

2 cups basmati rice
3 tablespoons clarified
    butter (see box,
    page 195)
1 small onion, minced

1 teaspoon crushed
    cardamom seeds
1 teaspoon saffron
    threads
3 cups water

1. Sort through the rice with your fingers, picking out and discarding any foreign objects. Soak the rice in water to cover for 30 minutes, changing the water twice. Rinse well and drain.

2. Melt the butter in a medium saucepan over medium-high heat. Add the onion, cardamom, and saffron; sauté for 5 minutes.

3. Add the rice to the pot and stir to coat with the butter and spices. Add 2 cups of the water, cover the pan, and heat to boiling. Reduce the heat, add the remaining 1 cup water, and simmer covered until all the liquid has been absorbed and the rice is tender, about 20 minutes. Serve hot.

Makes 8 servings.

Spicy Codfish Cakes Remoulade

This is my New England adaptation of Maryland's famed crabcakes. It is a fabulous use for inexpensive and readily available codfish. While these codfish cakes make a wonderful, homey supper, they are so delicious and habit forming that you may even be tempted to serve them to company.

3 pounds codfish fillets, poached in water just until tender, and drained
1 small red onion, minced
4 scallions, white bulbs and green stalks, chopped
2 ribs celery, minced
2 red bell peppers, seeded and diced
½ cup minced fresh parsley
8 cups fresh bread crumbs
3 tablespoons Dijon mustard
1 teaspoon dried thyme
1½ teaspoons cayenne pepper
½ teaspoon Worcestershire sauce

4 large eggs
1 cup Hellmann's mayonnaise
Salt and freshly ground pepper to taste
1 cup unbleached all-purpose flour, seasoned lightly with salt and pepper
½ cup light cream (see Index)
3 tablespoons unsalted butter, or more as needed
Remoulade Sauce (see Index)
Lemon wedges and fresh parsley sprigs for garnish

1. Flake the codfish in a large mixing bowl using a wooden spoon. Add the onion, scallions, celery, peppers, and parsley and toss to combine.

2. Add 3 cups of the bread crumbs, the mustard, thyme, cayenne, and Worcestershire sauce. Toss to combine thoroughly.

3. Beat 2 of the eggs into the codfish mixture until well blended. Fold in the mayonnaise and season the mixture with salt and pepper.

4. Place the seasoned flour in a small bowl. Beat the remaining eggs with the light cream in a second bowl. Place the

remaining bread crumbs in a third bowl (or as much as will fit, replenishing as needed).

5. Use your hands to form the codfish mixture into patties 3 inches in diameter. Dip each patty lightly but thoroughly in the flour mixture, then in the egg mixture, and finally in the bread crumbs, being sure they are coated all over. Place the patties as they are formed on a flat tray in a single layer. You should have about 16 codfish cakes.

6. Melt 3 tablespoons of butter in a large frying pan over medium heat. Add as many codfish cakes as will comfortably fit in the pan and fry, turning once, until golden brown on both sides, about 4 to 5 minutes per side. Keep the codfish cakes warm in a low oven while cooking the rest. Add more butter to the pan as needed. Serve the codfish cakes with a generous dollop of the remoulade. Garnish with lemon wedges and sprigs of parsley.

Makes 8 servings.

Scallops with Sauternes and Leek Cream

Sauternes heightens the natural sweetness of bay scallops.

5 tablespoons unsalted butter	2½ cups heavy or whipping cream
4 leeks, rinsed, dried, and minced	Salt and freshly ground pepper to taste
1 tablespoon very fine strips orange zest	1½ pounds fresh bay scallops
1½ cups Sauternes	

1. Melt the butter in a medium skillet over medium-high heat. Add the leeks and sauté, stirring constantly, 5 minutes. Stir in the orange zest and pour in the Sauternes. Raise the heat and bring to a rapid boil, then lower the heat and cover the mixture with a sheet of waxed paper. Simmer until just a few tablespoons liquid remain, 20 minutes.

2. Remove and discard the waxed paper. Pour in the cream and cook until reduced by about half. Season to taste with salt and pepper.

3. Preheat the oven to 450°F.

4. Divide the scallops among 6 individual 5- to 6-inch oval ramekins. Spoon a generous amount of the sauce over the scallops in each dish. Bake just until the scallops are cooked through and the sauce is bubbling, 7 to 10 minutes. Serve at once.

Makes 6 servings.

Swordfish Portugaise

Swordfish aficionados who swear to the pure tastes of grilling this meaty fish, might wince at the thought of baking it indoors smothered in a tomato sauce. I recommend trying this method once the grill has been stored away for the winter as I find that the slightly sweet, sherry-laced sauce is a wonderful complement to the swordfish in this authentic Portuguese dish.

3 pounds swordfish steaks
Salt and freshly ground
   pepper to taste
¼ cup fresh lemon juice
3 tablespoons olive oil
1 large yellow onion,
   chopped
4 cloves garlic, minced
3 ripe large tomatoes,
   seeded and cut into
   ¼-inch dice

½ cup tomato paste
1 tablespoon brown sugar
½ cup dry sherry
¾ cup dry white wine
½ cup chopped fresh
   parsley or fresh
   coriander leaves
1 lemon, thinly sliced

1. Arrange the swordfish in a single layer in a lightly oiled shallow baking dish. Sprinkle with salt and pepper and rub all over with the lemon juice.

2. Heat the oil in a medium saucepan over medium-high heat. Add the onion and garlic and cook, stirring frequently, for 10 minutes. Stir in the tomatoes, tomato paste, brown sugar, sherry, and wine. Simmer uncovered for 15 minutes. Stir in the parsley and season to taste with salt and pepper.

3. Preheat the oven to 375°F.

4. Pour the sauce over the fish in the baking dish and scatter the lemon slices over the top. Cover the dish tightly with aluminum foil. Bake just until the fish is cooked through, 25 to 30 minutes.

Makes 6 servings.

Poached Salmon

This is Mrs. Nathaniel Benchley's favorite summer dinner dish. Each time a platter with the fish's head peering decoratively outward is sent off to her Nantucket home, I cannot help but wonder where her son Peter really got the story idea for *Jaws!*

1 whole salmon, 7 to 8 pounds, cleaned

POACHING STOCK:

15 cups water	2 carrots, sliced
1 bottle (750 ml) dry white wine	2 tablespoons dried thyme
1 cup dry red wine	2 tablespoons fennel seeds
3 medium onions, sliced	6 sprigs fresh parsley
3 cloves garlic, halved	2 bay leaves
2 cups coarsely chopped celery tops	1 tablespoon salt
	1 tablespoon freshly ground pepper

Aspic and Garnishings for Poached Salmon (recipe follows)	Tomato Béarnaise Mayonnaise (see Index)

THINKING PINK

Chilled Mussels with Tomato-Cognac Sauce

Whole Poached Salmon with Tomato Béarnaise
Mayonnaise
Purée of Fresh Beets with Horseradish
Fresh Peas with Prosciutto
Potato Boursin Salad

Deep-Dish Rhubarb Pie

California Blush Wine

1. Rinse the salmon under cold running water and pat dry.

2. Prepare the poaching stock: Place all the ingredients in a large pot and heat to a full boil. Reduce the heat and simmer the stock for 30 minutes. Strain the stock through a sieve into a fish poacher; press hard on the vegetables with the back of a wooden spoon to extract the flavorful juices.

3. Place the fish on the poaching rack, cover, and poach the fish over the simmering stock for 10 minutes per inch of thickness.

4. Remove the fish from the pan and let cool. Reserve the liquid if you wish to coat the fish with aspic. Peel the skin from the fish, leaving the head and tail intact. Transfer to a serving platter and refrigerate until cold.

5. Coat the chilled fish with aspic and scale decorations if desired. Serve with the Béarnaise mayonnaise.

Makes 10 to 12 servings.

Aspic and Garnishing for Poached Salmon

3 cups salmon poaching
   liquid
2 egg whites
1 egg shell, broken into
   medium pieces
4½ teaspoons unflavored
   gelatin softened in ½
   cup cold water
1 tablespoon Pernod

Zest of 1 lemon, cut into
   2 x 2-inch strips
Zest of 1 lime, cut into
   2 x 2-inch strips
Zest of 1 orange, cut into
   2 x 2-inch strips
Fresh tarragon or dill
   sprigs

1. Clarify the salmon poaching liquid: Pour the liquid into a medium saucepan and heat over medium heat. Whisk the egg whites until they hold soft peaks and add them to the poaching liquid along with the broken egg shell. Bring to a boil, stirring occasionally. The egg white foam will rise to the top and float. Remove the pan from the heat and let it stand to allow the froth to settle to the bottom, 10 minutes. Repeat the boiling and settling process two more times.

2. Strain the liquid through a fine sieve lined with a double

thickness of dampened cheesecloth. Measure 2 cups of the clarified liquid into a clean saucepan and stir in the softened gelatin. Bring the liquid to a simmer just to dissolve the gelatin, and remove from the heat. Stir in the Pernod and refrigerate to chill the aspic, about 5 minutes.

3. When the aspic begins to thicken, spoon a thin layer over the top of the poached salmon. Using a small crescent-shaped cookie cutter, cut crescents from the citrus zests. Place these crescents decoratively over the aspic layer to resemble fish scales. Place a row of tarragon or dill sprigs down the center of the fish to look like feathery seaweed. Making sure the remaining aspic is still lightly jelled, spoon another layer over the decorations. If the aspic starts to melt and become runny, return both it and the fish to the refrigerator to set. Complete the garnishing by spooning a third layer of aspic over the fish. Refrigerate for at least 1 hour to set completely and keep chilled until serving time.

Soft-Shell Crabs with Smoked Salmon and Bacon Butter

I adore soft shell crabs. During their short summer season I invent endless ways to eat them—a crispy aside to scrambled eggs in the morning, tucked into an extravagant club sandwich at noon, on a toast point with evening cocktails. But of all the ways to enjoy this East Coast delicacy, this recipe is my very favorite.

2 shallots, minced
3 tablespoons dry white wine
1 tablespoon fresh lemon juice
¾ cup (1½ sticks) unsalted butter, cold
¼ pound smoked salmon, minced fine
8 slices bacon, cooked crisp and crumbled into small pieces

Freshly ground pepper to taste
8 soft-shell crabs, dressed
½ cup unbleached all-purpose flour seasoned with 1 teaspoon salt and 1 teaspoon freshly ground pepper
4 tablespoons clarified butter (see box, facing page)

1. Place the shallots, wine, and lemon juice in a small, non-aluminum skillet. Reduce the liquid over medium-high heat until all but 1 tablespoon remains. Reduce the heat to low and gradually whisk in the butter, tablespoon by tablespoon, until all is absorbed and the sauce is thickened. Stir in the smoked salmon and bacon. Season to taste with pepper. Remove from the heat and set aside in a warm place.

2. Dredge the crabs lightly in the flour. Melt the clarified butter in a large skillet over medium-high heat. Place the crabs topside down in the skillet and sauté until lightly browned, about 3 minutes. Turn and cook the other side until browned, 2 to 3 minutes longer.

3. Place 2 crabs on each dinner plate and spoon the smoked salmon and bacon butter generously over them. Serve at once.

Makes 4 servings.

CLARIFIED BUTTER

The reason for clarifying butter is to remove the milk solids that will burn and ruin the flavor of a dish when butter is heated over high temperatures. Clarification permits you to cook over high heat and still retain a wonderful buttery flavor.

Clarified butter keeps well in the refrigerator, so I find it worthwhile to clarify 1 pound at a time. Cut the butter into tablespoons and melt in a small saucepan over medium heat. Remove the pan from the heat and let stand for 10 minutes. Skim the white foam off the top with a slotted spoon and discard. Pour the clear yellow liquid through a fine sieve, lined with a double thickness of cheesecloth. When you get close to the bottom, avoid pouring the milky white solids that have sunk there by carefully spooning off any remaining clear butter. Discard the rest. One pound of butter yields about 1½ cups clarified butter.

Spring Seafood Pasta

When returning to the beach house for the first time in the spring, one craves something that tastes of the shore and ocean. I think this creamy scallop and smoked salmon sauce is the perfect end to a day of spring cleaning and a great welcoming dinner for old summer friends.

2 cups heavy or whipping
   cream
4 tablespoons vodka
Grated zest of 1 lemon
4 ounces cream cheese, at
   room temperature, cut
   into small bits
4 ounces smoked salmon,
   cut into thin julienne
   strips
4 tablespoons (½ stick)
   unsalted butter
½ cup finely chopped red
   onion

3 medium plum
   tomatoes, seeded and
   chopped
3 tablespoons chopped
   fresh dill
1 tablespoon chopped
   fresh tarragon
1 pound bay scallops
Salt and freshly ground
   pepper to taste
1 pound linguine or
   fettuccine, cooked and
   drained

1. Combine the cream, 3 tablespoons of the vodka, and the lemon zest in a medium saucepan. Heat to boiling and continue to cook until reduced by half. Stir in the cream cheese and smoked salmon and set aside.

2. Melt the butter in a small sauté pan or skillet over medium-high heat. Add the onion and tomatoes and cook, stirring occasionally, for 10 minutes. Stir in the dill and tarragon and cook 2 minutes longer.

3. Add the tomato mixture, bay scallops, salt and pepper to the cream mixture. Heat over medium heat until the sauce is hot and the scallops are just cooked through. Swirl in the remaining 1 tablespoon vodka and toss the sauce with the cooked pasta. Serve at once.

Makes 4 to 6 servings.

Lasagne with Red Clam Sauce

This is a good summery lasagne to make when a casual dinner for a crowd of hungry people is in order.

1 pound lasagne noodles,
   preferably homemade
3 large eggs
4 cups ricotta cheese
1 cup freshly grated
   Parmesan cheese
½ cup chopped fresh
   parsley

¼ cup chopped fresh basil
Salt and freshly ground
   pepper to taste
6 cups Red Clam Sauce
   (see Index)
1½ pounds smoked or
   regular mozzarella,
   thinly sliced

1. Heat a large pot of water to boiling. Add the lasagne noodles and cook until they are almost done but still a little chewy. (They will cook more as they bake.) Drain and rinse under cold running water.

2. Whisk the eggs and ricotta cheese together until smooth. Stir in the Parmesan, parsley, and basil. Season to taste with salt and pepper.

3. Preheat the oven to 375°F. Lightly oil a 15 x 10-inch baking pan.

4. Layer half the noodles in the prepared pan. Cover with half the clam sauce and half the ricotta filling. Arrange half the mozzarella over the ricotta. Layer the remaining noodles on top, then the remaining ricotta, clam sauce, and mozzarella.

5. Bake the lasagne until lightly browned and bubbly, 40 to 45 minutes. Let cool for 10 minutes before cutting and serving.

Makes 12 servings.

Spaghetti alla Carbonara

I am quite partial to this popular pasta dish, which I can never resist eating when in Italy and lured by the ubiquitous outdoor trattorias of the grand piazzas. I have often found that home versions skimp on the essential ingredients. This is my perfected version of the recipe created in remembrance of Trastevere days.

1 pound Italian pancetta
 or good-quality sliced
 bacon
1 medium onion, cut into
 thin crescent slivers
8 ounces fresh
 mushrooms, sliced
¼ cup dry white wine
5 large eggs, at room
 temperature

¾ cup heavy or whipping
 cream
¾ cup coarsely grated
 Parmesan cheese
Salt and freshly ground
 pepper to taste
1 pound imported
 spaghetti
½ cup chopped fresh
 parsley

1. Fry the bacon in a large skillet over medium-high heat until quite crisp. Remove from the pan, drain on paper towels, and crumble into coarse irregular pieces. Reserve 3 tablespoons of the bacon fat in the skillet.

2. Add the onion to the reserved bacon fat and cook, stirring frequently, over medium-high heat for 7 minutes. Add the mushrooms and wine and cook for 5 minutes.

3. Heat a large pot of water to boiling to cook the pasta.

4. Whisk the eggs and cream together in a mixing bowl until well blended. Stir in the Parmesan and season to taste with salt and pepper.

5. Cook the pasta in the boiling water until tender but still firm to the bite. Drain and return to the warm cooking pot. Immediately add the egg mixture, crumbled bacon, and onion mixture and toss thoroughly. Stir in the parsley. Serve at once with additional freshly grated Parmesan.

Makes 4 to 6 servings.

Penne with Tomatoes and Asparagus

This is one of my very favorite pasta recipes. I love the combination of the slowly simmered tomatoes with the crisp-tender asparagus. You can make it with fettuccine or other pasta, but I like the way the penne mirrors the shape of the asparagus.

6 tablespoons extra-virgin
 olive oil
4 cloves garlic, minced
2 carrots, peeled and
 minced
1 red bell pepper, seeded
 and minced
1 leek, rinsed, dried, and
 minced
2 ripe large tomatoes,
 seeded and diced
1½ cans (28 ounces each)
 whole tomatoes,
 drained
½ cup dry red wine
3 tablespoons chopped
 fresh fennel tops

1 tablespoon chopped
 fresh tarragon
4 tablespoons chopped
 fresh basil
Salt and freshly ground
 pepper to taste
1½ pound penne
1½ pounds fresh thin
 asparagus
2 large egg yolks
1 large egg
1 cup heavy or whipping
 cream
2 cups freshly grated
 Parmesan cheese

1. Heat 4 tablespoons of the olive oil in a large saucepan over medium-high heat. Add the garlic, carrots, bell pepper, and leek; sauté, stirring occasionally, for 10 minutes. Stir in the fresh tomatoes and cook 2 minutes.

2. Add the drained tomatoes to the sauce and mash with the back of a wooden spoon. Add the wine, fennel, tarragon, and half the basil. Season the sauce with salt and pepper to taste. Simmer uncovered, stirring occasionally, over low heat for 45 minutes.

3. Heat a large pot of water to boiling. Add the pasta and cook until tender but still firm to the bite.

4. Meanwhile, slice the tender parts of the asparagus stalks on a slight diagonal into 2-inch pieces. Heat the remaining 2 tablespoons oil in a sauté pan or skillet over high heat. Add the asparagus and stir-fry until just barely tender. Set aside.

5. When the pasta is almost ready, whisk the egg yolks, egg, and cream together in a small bowl. Add the asparagus and remaining basil to the tomato sauce and heat through.

6. Drain the pasta and toss with the tomato sauce. Quickly stir in the egg mixture and 1 cup of the Parmesan. Toss well and serve at once. Pass the remaining Parmesan.

Makes 6 servings.

Tagliolini con Caviale

This melodious-sounding Italian creation (pasta with caviar) is one of my most requested recipes and my favorite dish to serve when in a romantic mood.

2 tablespoons unsalted butter	¼ cup vodka
3 tablespoons olive oil	1½ cups heavy or whipping cream
2 cloves garlic, minced	¾ cup freshly grated Parmesan cheese
1 small red onion, minced	Salt and freshly ground pepper to taste
Zest of 1 lemon, cut into very fine strips	1 pound dried tagliolini, linguine, or fettuccine
1¼ cups Fish Stock (see Index), or bottled clam juice	4 ounces golden caviar

1. Heat the butter and oil in a medium skillet over medium-high heat. Add the garlic and onion and sauté, stirring frequently, for 5 minutes. Add the lemon zest, fish stock, and vodka and simmer until reduced by about half, about 15 minutes.

2. Heat a large pot of water to boiling to cook the pasta.

3. Stir the cream into the sauce and continue to simmer until thickened to the consistency of a light béchamel sauce, about 15 minutes. Stir in the cheese and heat until it melts. Season the sauce to taste with salt and pepper. Keep warm over low heat while you cook the pasta.

4. Add the pasta to the boiling water and cook until tender but still firm to the bite. Drain well.

5. Toss the warm pasta with the sauce to coat well. Divide the pasta among 4 plates. Top each serving with a heaping spoonful of caviar. Serve at once.

Makes 4 servings.

Private
Grilling

Grilling in the great outdoors is not something I do in the daily course of events at Que Sera Sarah. Rather, it is what I do during the ever scarce moments that I am not cooking for the shop or catering an island extravaganza. While I know that normal people view the all-American barbecue as an inherent part of summer living and entertaining, I personally see it as a private source of summer serenity.

When a rare interlude of uncommitted time appears in the midst of summer frenzy and I discover that I still have an appetite and friend or two who will forgive me for having been far more interested in blue corn chips, rare strains of radicchio, and escargot roe than their personal lives, I grill.

So in a weak moment of culinary confession, induced by inhaling the concentrated fumes of arcane hardwoods and vines, I am disclosing these treasured grilling recipes which have never been cooked for the public palate.

Grilled Lobster with Champagne

There is something at once extravagant and primitive about grilling lobster by the beach. The fiery red lobster shells when singed with the flames of the grill permeate the air with the most wonderful essence of ocean and seashore imaginable. I recommend preparing this dish under the full moon—the most conducive to wild feasting.

1 bottle (750 ml) dry Champagne	Salt and freshly ground pepper to taste
Leafy tops of 3 ribs celery	4 live lobsters (1½ to 2 pounds each)
3 shallots, minced	
¾ cup (1½ sticks) unsalted butter, slightly softened	4 tablespoons olive oil

1. Prepare charcoal or wood chips for grilling.

2. Place the Champagne, celery leaves, and shallots in a medium saucepan; cook over medium-high heat until just 1 cup liquid remains, about 20 minutes. Remove the celery leaves and discard. Slowly whisk in the butter, 1 tablespoon at a time, over very low heat to emulsify with the Champagne. When all the butter has been incorporated, season the mixture with salt and pepper to taste. Keep warm while grilling the lobster.

3. Kill the lobsters by inserting a sharp knife crosswise where the head meets the shell to sever the spinal cord. Turn each lobster on its back and butterfly the meaty tail. Remove the claws and crack to facilitate cooking on the grill. (If any of this makes you queasy, have your fishmonger kill and split the lobsters; just make sure it is done as close to cooking time as possible.)

4. Brush the lobsters, flesh and shells, all over with oil. Place the lobsters, flesh-side down and the claws alongside, a few inches from red-hot coals. Grill just until the flesh turns opaque, 6 to 8 minutes. Turn the lobsters over and grill just a few minutes more. Check the claws for doneness as they may take slightly longer than the tails.

5. Serve the lobsters butterflied with some of the Champagne-butter sauce spooned over the flesh. Place the claws alongside the lobsters. Serve the remaining Champagne-butter sauce in little dipping bowls.

Makes 4 servings.

Grilled Soft-Shell Crabs

One day I wondered why no one ever grilled soft-shells and decided to experiment. The results were sensational!

Juice of 4 limes
2 tablespoons golden
   tequila
1 clove garlic, minced
1 fresh jalapeño pepper,
   seeded and minced
¼ cup chopped fresh
   coriander
½ cup olive oil
Salt and freshly ground
   pepper to taste
8 soft-shell crabs, dressed

1. Three hours before you plan to grill the crabs, whisk the lime juice, tequila, garlic, jalapeño pepper, and coriander together in a small bowl. Gradually whisk in the oil, then season to taste with salt and pepper. Place the crabs in a single layer in a shallow bowl. Pour the marinade over the crabs. Cover the bowl and let marinate in the refrigerator for 3 hours.

2. Prepare charcoal or wood chips for grilling.

3. When the coals are quite hot, remove the crabs from the marinade and place them 3 to 4 inches from the heat. Grill just until cooked through, 2 to 3 minutes each side. Transfer the crabs to a serving platter and drizzle with some of the marinade. Serve at once.

Makes 4 servings.

Swordfish Union Street

This recipe for my aunt's Nantucket grilled swordfish is my first memory of the very best thing I thought I had ever eaten. During my days as mother's helper on Union Street, I learned from her the secret of coating the fish with mayonnaise to keep it very moist on the grill.

To this day, grilled swordfish steaks remain the taste of

Nantucket for me. One of my favorite summer meals is grilled swordfish steaks, Summer Squash Casserole (see Index), sliced Nantucket tomatoes, and a salad of farm lettuce.

2 lemons
3 to 3½ pounds very
    fresh swordfish steaks,
    1½ to 2 inches thick
Salt and freshly ground
    pepper to taste
6 tablespoons
    mayonnaise, preferably
    homemade (if not, use
    Hellmann's)

6 tablespoons (¾ stick)
    unsalted butter, cut
    into tablespoons and at
    room temperature
3 tablespoons chopped
    fresh parsley

1. Prepare charcoal or wood chips for grilling.

2. Cut one of the lemons in half and rub the juice all over the swordfish steaks. Sprinkle the steaks on both sides with salt and pepper, then smear both sides of the steaks with the mayonnaise.

3. When the coals are hot, grill the swordfish a few inches from the heat until just cooked through, about 6 minutes each side. Remove the swordfish from the grill and spread the butter over the tops of each steak. Sprinkle with parsley and serve with the remaining lemon cut into wedges.

Makes 6 servings.

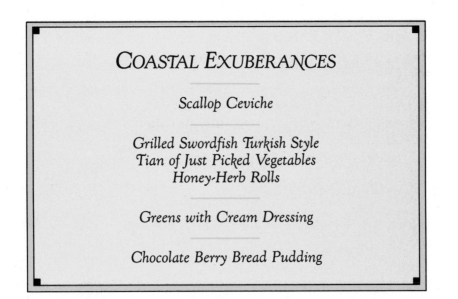

COASTAL EXUBERANCES

Scallop Ceviche

Grilled Swordfish Turkish Style
Tian of Just Picked Vegetables
Honey-Herb Rolls

Greens with Cream Dressing

Chocolate Berry Bread Pudding

Grilled Swordfish Turkish Style

This is a simple but superb method of preparing swordfish that my sister Holly discovered on one of her many ventures through Turkey.

3 pounds fresh swordfish, cut into 1-inch chunks
¾ cup fresh lemon juice
½ cup fruity olive oil
2 cloves garlic, finely minced
1 medium red onion, cut into thin rings

Salt and freshly ground pepper to taste
36 bay leaves
2 yellow bell peppers, seeded and cut into ¾-inch pieces

1. Prepare charcoal or wood chips for grilling.
2. Place the swordfish in a shallow bowl. Whisk the lemon juice and oil together in a small bowl, then stir in the garlic and onion. Season to taste with salt and pepper. Pour the marinade over the swordfish. Cover the bowl and let marinate, tossing occasionally, in the refrigerator for 6 hours.
3. Cover the bay leaves with boiling water in a small bowl; let stand for 10 minutes to soften. Drain thoroughly.
4. Thread the swordfish chunks alternately with the bay leaves on 6 metal skewers. Every third piece or so, thread a bell pepper chunk on the skewer. Drape some of the onion slices from the fish marinade randomly in a figure-8 fashion over the fish kabobs.
5. Grill the swordfish skewers a few inches from medium-hot coals, basting occasionally with the marinade and turning the skewers every 5 minutes or so, until just cooked through, about 15 minutes.

Makes 6 servings.

Tuna Steaks with Wasabi Butter

Meaty red tuna steaks can stand up to the strong Oriental flavors of a sesame marinade. The wasabi butter transfers the Japanese influence of the raw to the cooked.

¼ cup Oriental sesame oil
½ cup vegetable oil
¼ cup rice wine vinegar
2 tablespoons sweet vermouth
1 tablespoon brown sugar
¼ cup soy sauce

2 tablespoons chopped fresh ginger
3 cloves garlic, minced
3 to 3½ pounds tuna steaks, about 1½ inches thick

WASABI BUTTER:
½ cup (1 stick) unsalted butter
1½ teaspoons green wasabi paste (or more to taste if you like it very hot; wasabi paste is available at specialty food stores)

3 tablespoons chopped fresh coriander

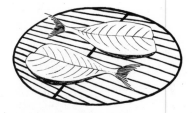

1. At least 4 hours before you plan to grill the tuna, whisk the sesame oil, vegetable oil, vinegar, vermouth, brown sugar, and soy sauce together in a small bowl. Stir in the ginger and garlic. Pour the marinade over the tuna steaks in a shallow bowl. Cover and let marinate in the refrigerator at least 4 hours, turning the fish occasionally.

2. Meanwhile, prepare the wasabi butter: Beat the butter and wasabi paste together in a small bowl until creamy. Beat in the coriander until well blended. Store in a cool place, but let warm to room temperature before serving.

3. Prepare charcoal or wood chips for grilling.

4. When the coals are hot, remove the tuna steaks from the marinade and grill a few inches from the heat just until cooked through, 5 to 6 minutes each side. As the tuna cooks, baste it with some of the marinade to keep it moist. When the tuna is cooked, cut it into serving portions and top each serving with a heaping tablespoon of the wasabi butter.

Makes 6 servings.

Bluefish Antibes

For the past few Octobers I have been fortunate enough to spend time recuperating from my hectic summers on Nantucket lazing on the still tepid beaches of the French Riviera. I have a favorite little beach set in a cove in Antibes, which is complete with a seaside restaurant that prepares fabulous grilled local fish for lunch everyday. Longing for the R & R of the Riviera, I decided to apply the same technique to Nantucket's most common local fish—with excellent results!

3 pounds bluefish fillets	1½ tablespoons chopped
5 tablespoons extra-virgin	fresh lavender leaves
olive oil	2 teaspoons fennel seeds,
Salt and freshly ground	lightly crushed
pepper to taste	1 teaspoon ground cumin
2 tablespoons chopped	Lemon wedges
fresh rosemary	

1. Place the bluefish fillets in a shallow bowl. Brush all over with the oil and sprinkle lightly with salt and pepper.
2. Combine the rosemary, lavender, fennel, and cumin; sprinkle over the top of the fish fillets. Let marinate at room temperature for 30 minutes.
3. Prepare charcoal or wood chips for grilling.
4. When the coals are ready, grill the fish, skin-side down, a few inches from the heat for about 5 minutes. With a large spatula, flip the fillets over and grill just several minutes longer until the fish is done. Serve immediately with lemon wedges.
Makes 6 servings.

Seared Chicken Breasts with Cranberry Pecan Butter

The exquisite tenderness and moistness achieved by searing chicken breasts quickly over a hot fire is unrivaled. The brilliant pink butter adds great flavor and flair to the final presentation.

CRANBERRY PECAN BUTTER:

2 cups fresh cranberries	¾ cup (1½ sticks) unsalted
½ cup fresh orange juice	butter, at room temperature
½ cup sugar	½ cup finely chopped
Grated zest of 1 orange	toasted pecans

½ cup fruity olive oil	Salt and freshly ground
1 cup fresh orange juice	pepper to taste
2 tablespoons chopped	6 boneless, skinless whole
fresh rosemary	chicken breasts

1. Prepare the cranberry pecan butter: Combine the cranberries, the ½ cup of orange juice, the sugar, and orange zest in a small saucepan. Heat to boiling over medium-high heat. Reduce the heat and simmer, stirring occasionally, for 15 minutes. Let the cranberries cool to room temperature.

2. Purée the cooled cranberries in a blender or food processor fitted with the steel blade. Cream the butter in a medium bowl, then beat in the purée. Beat the pecans into the mixture. Store the butter in the refrigerator, but bring to room temperature when ready to serve.

3. Whisk together the olive oil and 1 cup orange juice. Stir in the rosemary and season with salt and pepper. Place the chicken breasts in a shallow dish and pour over the marinade. Let marinate at room temperature for 1 hour.

4. Prepare charcoal or wood chips for grilling.

5. Remove the chicken breasts from the marinade and grill them a few inches above the hot coals, basting continually with the leftover marinade, 3 to 4 minutes per side. Top each chicken breast with a generous rounded scoop of the cranberry pecan butter and serve.

Makes 6 servings.

Chicken Tapenade

This grilling recipe takes a little poetic license with the basic tapenade concept and stretches it into an unusual marinade for chicken. The result is very different from most barbecued chicken recipes and is probably the most succulent chicken I have ever tasted.

4 whole chicken breasts, halved

2 cloves garlic, minced

1 red onion, minced

6 anchovy fillets, minced

½ cup olivada (black olive paste, available at specialty food stores)

⅓ cup Cognac

⅓ cup olive oil

1½ cups dry red wine

Salt and freshly ground pepper to taste

½ cup chopped fresh basil

1. Place the chicken breasts in a shallow bowl. Combine the garlic, onion, anchovies, and olivada in a mixing bowl. Whisk in the Cognac and oil. Stir in the wine and season to taste with salt and pepper. Pour the marinade over the chicken and sprinkle with the basil. Let the chicken marinate for 3 hours.

2. Prepare charcoal or wood chips for grilling.

3. When the coals are ready, grill the chicken bone-side down, a few inches from the heat, basting occasionally with the marinade, about 15 minutes. Turn and continue grilling just until the chicken is cooked through but still very moist and tender, about 15 minutes more. Serve at once.

Makes 6 to 8 servings.

THE BIG ANNUAL SUMMER COCKTAIL PARTY

Scallop Puffs Que Sera
Miniature Tex-Mex Turnovers
Cornmeal Blinis with Favorite Caviars
Brie in Brioche
Country Pâté with Beer and Fennel • Mustard and Cornichons
Vegetable Crudité • Basil Parmesan Mayonnaise and Roasted Red Pepper Dip
Great Guacamole • Blue Corn Chips
Smoked Mussels Vinaigrette
Platter of Chicken Tapenade
(served at room temperature)

Open Bar

Duck Breasts with Grilled Radicchio and Honey Glazed Pears

A spectacular grilled dinner that heralds autumn in both flavor and color. The symphony of flavors calls for celebrating with a bottle of Burgundy or California Cabernet Sauvignon.

1 cup dry red wine
¼ cup plus 2 tablespoons
   port
3 tablespoons balsamic
   vinegar
½ cup fresh orange juice
½ cup olive oil
Zest of 1 orange, finely
   grated
1 carrot, peeled and
   sliced into thin rounds
½ cup minced fennel bulb
3 tablespoons minced
   fennel tops

2 shallots, minced
2 cloves garlic, minced
2 tablespoons minced
   fresh rosemary
Salt and freshly ground
   pepper to taste
6 boneless duck breasts
   (from 3 ducks)
6 heads radicchio, halved
3 firm pears, peeled,
   cored, and halved
3 tablespoons honey

1. Whisk together the wine, the ¼ cup of port, vinegar, orange juice, and olive oil in a small bowl. Add the orange zest, carrot, fennel and fennel tops, shallots, garlic, and rosemary. Season with salt and pepper. Place the duck breasts and radicchio flat in a large, shallow dish. Pour the marinade over all and marinate at room temperature, turning the duck breasts and radicchio occasionally, for 2 hours.

2. Prepare charcoal or wood chips for grilling.

3. Remove the radicchio from the marinade and thread onto metal skewers. Grill about 4 inches from the hot coals until wilted and lightly charred on the outside, about 5 minutes per side. Grill the duck breasts skin-side down, basting occasionally with leftover marinade, for 6 minutes. Turn and continue grilling just until the duck breasts are pink in the center, 2 to 3 minutes longer. Place the pear halves flat on the grill and brush with the 2 tablespoons port and the honey. Grill, turning once, for 3 to 4 minutes.

4. Carve the duck breasts into thin diagonal slices and fan onto a serving plate, surrounded by the radicchio and pears.

Makes 6 servings.

Lamb with Mint Salsa Verde

The lushness of a meaty pink leg of lamb may come as a hearty surprise in the heat of a midsummer's night, but a shimmering bath of mint sauce placates the palate.

1 leg of lamb (6 to 7 pounds), boned and butterflied	½ cup fruity olive oil
	1 medium red onion, minced
	3 cloves garlic, minced
1½ cups Zinfandel	Salt and freshly ground
½ cup raspberry vinegar	pepper to taste

MINT SALSA VERDE:

2 bunches fresh parsley, chopped	6 tablespoons fresh lemon juice
	1 cup fruity olive oil
4 scallions, white bulbs and green stalks, chopped	2 hard-cooked eggs, peeled and minced
1 cup fresh mint leaves	2 tablespoons capers, drained
4 anchovy fillets, minced	Salt and freshly ground
3 cloves garlic, minced	pepper to taste

1. The morning of the day you plan to serve the lamb, place the butterflied leg of lamb in a large, shallow bowl. Whisk the Zinfandel, vinegar, and oil together in a mixing bowl. Stir in the onion and garlic and season to taste with salt and pepper. Pour the marinade over the lamb. Cover and let marinate, turning the lamb frequently, in the refrigerator at least 6 hours.

2. Meanwhile, prepare the mint salsa verde: Place the parsley, scallions, and mint in a food processor fitted with the steel blade; process to make a smooth green paste. Add the anchovies, garlic, and lemon juice and process again until smooth. With the machine running, pour the oil in a thin, steady stream through the feed tube to make a glistening green sauce. Transfer the sauce to a bowl and stir in the eggs and capers. Season to taste with salt and pepper. Store in the refrigerator but let warm to room temperature before serving.

3. Prepare charcoal or wood chips for grilling.

4. When the coals are hot, remove the lamb from marinade and place it on the grill about 4 inches from the heat. Grill, basting frequently with the marinade, about 20 minutes each side for medium rare. Cut the lamb into thin slices, spoon the mint salsa over, and serve.

Makes 10 to 12 servings.

Rosemary Lamb Chops Provençal

In the South of France anchovies are sometimes used to impart a subtle saltiness, rather than fishiness, to the flavor of meat. This is an exquisitely simple way to cook lamb chops.

3 cloves garlic, peeled
3 anchovy fillets
2 tablespoons fresh
   rosemary leaves
¼ cup fresh parsley leaves
½ teaspoon dried thyme
½ teaspoon salt

1 teaspoon freshly ground
   pepper
3 tablespoons olive oil
2 tablespoons dry red wine
8 thick lamb loin chops,
   fat trimmed
8 fresh rosemary sprigs

1. Place the garlic, anchovies, rosemary leaves, parsley, thyme, salt, pepper, oil, and wine in a food processor fitted with the steel blade; process until smooth.

2. Using a small sharp knife, make several shallow incisions in both sides of each lamb chop. Rub the marinade generously over both sides of the lamb chops and press it into the incisions. Place the chops on a platter and let marinate at room temperature for 1 to 1½ hours.

3. Prepare charcoal for grilling.

4. Wrap the "tail" of each lamb chop around the chop to form a circle of sorts. Wrap a fresh rosemary sprig around each chop and secure the "tail" and sprig in place by tying with kitchen string.

5. Grill the chops about 4 to 5 inches from the hot coals. They should be cooked 5 to 6 minutes each side for medium-rare meat. Serve 2 chops per person and accompany with Oil-Roasted Farm Vegetables (see Index) or Ratatouille (see Index).

Makes 4 servings.

Grilled Steak with Many Mustards

Crunchy golden mustard seeds add a crisp crust to the steak, while the mustard-Cognac Béarnaise is a great variation on the classic. A dreamy grilling recipe for the lover of both mustard and steak.

3 tablespoons whole mustard seeds	1 tablespoon freshly ground pepper
2 teaspoons dry mustard	3 to 4 pounds sirloin or strip steaks, 1½-inches thick
1 tablespoon coarse salt (kosher)	

MUSTARD-COGNAC BEARNAISE:

2 shallots, minced	1 teaspoon grainy mustard
1½ tablespoons dried tarragon	Pinch cayenne pepper
¼ cup Cognac	½ cup plus 2 tablespoons (1¼ sticks) unsalted butter, melted and hot
½ cup tarragon vinegar	
4 large egg yolks	
1 tablespoon fresh lemon juice	Salt and freshly ground pepper to taste
1 tablespoon Dijon mustard	

2 tablespoons Dijon mustard	½ cup dry white wine

1. Place the mustard seeds, dry mustard, coarse salt, and pepper in a mortar. Using a pestle, grind the mixture coarsely together. Rub both sides of the steaks generously with the mustard seasoning. Let stand for 30 minutes.

2. Prepare charcoal or wood chips for grilling.

3. Meanwhile, prepare the mustard-Cognac Béarnaise: Place the shallots, tarragon, Cognac, and vinegar in a small pan. Cook over medium-high heat until almost all of the liquid has evaporated. Set aside.

4. Place the egg yolks, lemon juice, mustards, and cayenne in a blender; process for 10 seconds. With the machine running, pour the hot butter through the top; process until all is blended

and the sauce is thickened. Add the shallot reduction and blend. Season with salt and pepper to taste.

5. When the coals are hot, grill the steaks a few inches from the heat for about 5 minutes each side for rare to medium-rare meat. While the steaks are grilling, whisk the 2 tablespoons Dijon mustard and white wine together; baste the steaks with this mixture as they grill. When the steaks are done, cut into serving portions and top each serving with a generous spoonful of the Béarnaise.

Makes 6 servings.

Grilled Hamburgers au Poivre

A sumptuous version of this all-American classic. The barely cooked tomato-leek sauce adds a refreshing contrast to the peppery beef.

2 pounds best-quality
   ground sirloin
4 shallots, minced
1½ tablespoons capers,
   drained and chopped
5 tablespoons dry red wine
1½ teaspoons salt
5 tablespoons plus 1
   teaspoon grainy Dijon
   mustard

5 tablespoons plus 1
   teaspoon coarsely
   ground mixed
   peppercorns (black,
   green, pink, and
   white)

TOMATO-LEEK SAUCE:
4 tablespoons (½ stick)
   unsalted butter
2 leeks, rinsed, dried,
   quartered, and minced
5 ripe large plum
   tomatoes, seeded and
   diced

3 tablespoons Cognac
2½ tablespoons minced
   fresh tarragon
3 tablespoons heavy or
   whipping cream
Salt to taste

1. Mix the sirloin, shallots, capers, wine and salt together in a large bowl until well combined. Divide the meat mixture into 8 equal parts and shape each part into a hamburger patty.

2. Spread each side of the patties with 1 teaspoon of the mustard (2 teaspoons per patty), then press 1 teaspoon of the ground peppercorns lightly into each side of the patties (again 2 teaspoons per hamburger). Let stand at room temperature for 30 minutes.

3. Prepare charcoal or wood chips for grilling.

4. Meanwhile, prepare the tomato-leek sauce: Melt the butter in a saucepan over medium-high heat. Add the leeks and cook for 5 minutes. Stir in the tomatoes and cook 5 minutes longer. Stir in the Cognac, tarragon, cream, and salt to taste. Reduce the heat and simmer for 5 minutes and keep warm until ready to serve.

5. When the coals are hot, grill the hamburgers to desired doneness. Serve on a bed of the tomato-leek sauce or, if pre-ferred, serve with the sauce alongside.

Makes 8 hamburgers.

Grilled Pork Tenderloin with Port, Plums, and Apricots

Great September dinner fare when the heat of the grill is as welcome for warmth as for the smoky flavor it imparts to food.

1 boneless pork loin, about 4 pounds, cut in half lengthwise	3 shallots, minced
	3 cloves garlic, halved
	½ cup dried apricots
4 tablespoons olive oil	8 fresh prune plums, cut in half and pitted
Coarse (kosher) salt	
1½ cups port	2 tablespoons chopped fresh rosemary
1 cup fresh orange juice	
3 tablespoons honey	Salt and freshly ground pepper to taste
3 tablespoons cider vinegar	

1. Rub the 2 pieces of pork loin all over with the oil and coarse salt. Place in a 5- to 6-inch-deep bowl or pan.

2. Place the remaining ingredients in a saucepan and heat to simmering. Simmer for 5 minutes, then pour the warm marinade over the pork. Let cool to room temperature. Cover the bowl and

let marinate, turning the pork occasionally, in the refrigerator at least 4 hours.

3. Prepare charcoal or wood chips for grilling.

4. When the coals are hot, remove the pork from the marinade and sear a few inches from the heat on all sides until nicely browned. Adjust the grill rack so that the pork is about 4 to 5 inches from the coals. Cover the grill and cook the pork, turning occasionally, to desired doneness, 35 to 45 minutes.

5. Boil the marinade in a saucepan for just 1 to 2 minutes. Cut the pork into ½-inch-thick slices and spoon the warm marinade over the slices.

Makes 6 to 8 servings.

Grilled Sausage Extravaganza

Sausage is one of the easiest and tastiest foods to sizzle over a grill. The accompaniments of grilled polenta and red onion all splashed with sweet red pepper butter turns this simple dish into a fabulous feast.

POLENTA:
4 cups water
1 teaspoon salt
1 cup yellow cornmeal
2 tablespoons unsalted
  butter

3 tablespoons chopped
  fresh basil
5 tablespoons freshly
  grated Parmesan cheese

SWEET PEPPER BUTTER:
3 red bell peppers,
  roasted, peeled, seeded,
  and coarsely chopped
6 tablespoons unsalted
  butter, at room
  temperature

½ teaspoon dried red
  pepper flakes
3 tablespoons chopped
  fresh basil
Salt and freshly ground
  pepper to taste

2 medium red onions, cut
  into thick rings
Olive oil

3 pounds smoked kielbasa
  sausage

1. The day before serving, prepare the polenta: Heat the water to boiling in a medium saucepan. Add the salt and gradually stir in the cornmeal with a wooden spoon. Cook over low heat until quite thick, 40 to 45 minutes, stirring occasionally and pressing out any lumps. Remove from the heat and stir in the butter, basil, and Parmesan. Transfer the polenta to a 9 x 5 x 3-inch loaf pan and refrigerate overnight to firm.

2. Prepare charcoal or wood chips for grilling.

3. Meanwhile, prepare the sweet pepper butter: Place the bell peppers and butter together in a food processor fitted with the steel blade and process until very smooth. Add the red pepper flakes and basil and blend thoroughly. Season to taste with salt and pepper. Transfer to a decorative crock and keep at room temperature.

4. When the coals are hot, cut the polenta into ½-inch-thick slices and brush both sides of each slice with olive oil. Brush the onion slices on both sides with oil as well. Cut the kielbasa into manageable grilling lengths. Place all on the grill and cook, turning as needed, until each is nicely browned on both sides. Arrange the kielbasa, polenta, and onions on a large platter. Pass the sweet pepper butter.

Makes 6 servings.

Sweet
Splurges

You never know what is enough unless you know what is more than enough.
—WILLIAM BLAKE

Personally, I am convinced that summer is the most indulgent time of all the year. While there are certainly the excesses of Thanksgiving and Christmas, or the consolations of copious amounts of comfort food in the frigid depths of winter, no season sustains an aura of continual and refreshing celebration more than summer.

It seems unfortunate that we often associate lethargy and lack of appetite with the scorch of summer. The flip side to this torrid season is the heat-inspired pursuit of temptations and healthy hedonism. As the temperature soars so does an uninhibited desire for sun-permeated outdoor activity and the consumption of perfect foods bulging with brilliant color and concentrated flavor. We really do want to have it all in the summertime! When we can't resist afternoons lazing at the beach followed by siestas, sun-stroke tennis matches, wind-surf mania, or yet another wild cocktail party, why should we pass up the tart glistening with a small fortune of raspberries or the cheesecake as comforting to the inner self as aloe to our surface sunburns?

Indeed, there is no simpler sense of gratification (or even mildly rewarding perversion) than to savor extravagantly rich confections on squelching August afternoons. An accompanying sip of steaming double espresso is all that is needed to raise the body temperature to a perfect mesh with the surrounding environs.

Espresso-Walnut Cake

Nothing heightens the intensity of chocolate more than a good jigger of espresso. This cake is assembled in the style of a European torte and it has an interior so moist and dense that it has been known to give confirmed chocolate fanatics a glimpse of heaven. It is the favorite chocolate dessert at the Que Sera Sarah.

CAKE:

1 cup granulated sugar
¼ cup water
1 tablespoon instant espresso powder
6 ounces semisweet chocolate bits
2 teaspoons vanilla extract

½ cup (1 stick) unsalted butter, at room temperature
8 large eggs, separated
1¼ cups walnuts
1 slice fresh white bread, crusts removed
Pinch salt

FROSTING:

6 ounces semisweet chocolate bits
⅓ cup water
1 tablespoon instant espresso powder
1 cup (2 sticks) unsalted butter, at room temperature

3 large egg yolks
¾ cup sifted confectioners' sugar
Ground walnuts, for garnish
Chocolate-covered coffee beans, for garnish

1. Preheat the oven to 350°F. Butter two 9-inch round cake pans and line the bottoms with 8-inch parchment paper circles. Butter the paper and dust with flour, shaking out any excess.

2. Prepare the cake: Place the sugar, water, and espresso in a small saucepan. Bring to a boil over medium heat, stirring constantly with a wire whisk. Add the chocolate and the vanilla and heat, whisking constantly, just until the chocolate melts and the mixture is smooth. Remove from the heat and let cool.

3. Cream the butter in a large mixing bowl until light and fluffy. Beat in the egg yolks, one at a time, beating well after each addition. Gradually beat in the cooled chocolate mixture.

4. Place the walnuts and bread in a food processor fitted with the steel blade; process until ground. Stir the walnut mixture into the chocolate mixture.

5. Beat the egg whites with the salt in a mixing bowl until stiff, but not dry. Gently fold the egg whites into the chocolate mixture. Divide the batter evenly between the 2 pans.

6. Bake the cakes until the edges have pulled slightly away from the pans, 25 to 30 minutes. Cool in the pans for 15 minutes, then invert onto a wire rack to cool completely.

7. Prepare the frosting: Place the chocolate, water, and espresso in a small saucepan. Cook over low heat, stirring constantly, just until the chocolate is melted and the mixture is smooth. Refrigerate until slightly chilled.

8. Beat the butter in a large mixing bowl until light and fluffy. Beat in the egg yolks, one at a time, beating well after each addition. Gradually beat in the chilled chocolate mixture, then the confectioners' sugar, continuing to beat until the mixture is of a thick, spreading consistency.

9. Place 1 cake on a serving platter and frost the top. Top with the second cake and spread the top and sides with frosting. Place any remaining frosting in a pastry bag fitted with a decorative tip and pipe the frosting over the top of the cake. Garnish with ground walnuts and candy coffee beans, if desired. Serve the cake slightly chilled.

Makes 8 to 10 servings.

There are pleasant drives to all parts of the island, with a never-ending variety of exquisite marine views or stretches of unfenced moorlands covered with wild flowers and overgrown with bayberry and huckleberry bushes, wild roses and sweet fern, with here and there a small pond around which and nestling among the many graceful grasses grow the beautiful pink marsh-mallows, butter-cups, and violets. Many of the beauty spots lie hidden among the hills, away from the main thoroughfares and to see which it will be necessary to turn off into the old deep rutted roads which form a network over the moors or wander along the bluffs where an occasional patch of Broom or Scotch Heather blooming in all its native beauty may be found. Artists and botonists will find a wealth of material in store.

—Guide to Nantucket 1928

Honeymoon Torte

This rich nut torte recipe is another family favorite handed down from my Polish grandmother. The result is as romantic looking and tasting as its name. The chocolate and maple flavoring in the frosting have a wonderful affinity, not unlike that of honeymooners. . . .

12 large eggs, separated
1 cup granulated sugar
3½ cups ground walnuts
6 graham crackers,
    crushed to fine powder

3 tablespoons sifted
    all-purpose flour
1 teaspoon baking powder
2 teaspoons vanilla
    extract

FROSTING:
1 cup (2 sticks) unsalted
    butter, at room
    temperature
2 cups sifted
    confectioners' sugar
2 ounces unsweetened
    chocolate, melted

2 tablespoons strong
    brewed coffee
1 teaspoon maple extract
2 large eggs

1. Preheat the oven to 325°F. Butter and flour three 8-inch round cake pans.

2. Place the egg yolks and ¾ of the sugar in a large mixing bowl. Using an electric mixer, beat at high speed until the mixture is very light and fluffy, 8 to 10 minutes.

3. Mix the walnuts, graham crackers, flour, and baking powder together in a small bowl. Add to the egg yolk mixture and stir until well blended. Stir in the vanilla.

4. With clean beaters and in a clean bowl, beat the egg whites and the remaining ¼ cup sugar just until stiff peaks begin to form. Gently fold the egg whites into the nut mixture. Divide the cake batter evenly among the prepared pans.

5. Bake until the cakes pull away from the edges of the pans and the centers spring back when touched lightly in the middles, 20 to 25 minutes.

6. Cool the cakes in the pans for 30 minutes then invert onto wire racks to cool completely.

7. Meanwhile, prepare the frosting: Beat the butter and the confectioners' sugar in a mixing bowl until smooth, then beat in the melted chocolate, coffee, and maple extract. Beat in the eggs,

one at a time, beating well after each addition. Refrigerate the frosting until set but still spreadable.

8. Place 1 cake layer on a serving plate and spread the top with frosting. Top with the second layer and frost. Top with the third layer and frost the top and sides. Pipe any remaining frosting through a pastry bag fitted with a decorative tip on the top of the torte. Store the torte in the refrigerator. Let warm to room temperature 20 minutes before serving.

Makes 12 servings.

French Nut Icebox Cake

If asked to nominate a single sweet as my idea of the ultimate dessert, this icebox cake would be my choice. It is a sophisticated, rich cake that manages to be creamy, crunchy, and intensely nutty all at the same time. The unusual recipe has been handed down from my Polish grandmother and it is always served on special occasions in my family.

1 cup (2 sticks) unsalted
   butter, at room
   temperature
1¼ cups confectioners'
   sugar
3 large eggs
3 large eggs, separated
8 ounces pecans, finely
   ground

2 packages (3 ounces
   each) ladyfingers
12 chewy almond
   macaroons, 2 inches in
   diameter, from a good
   bakery
Whipped cream
   (optional)

1. Cream the butter and the sugar in a large mixing bowl until very smooth. Beat in the whole eggs, one at a time, beating well after each addition.

2. Beat the 3 egg yolks in a small bowl until lemon colored. Add to the butter mixture and beat until blended. Stir in the pecans.

3. Beat the egg whites in another mixing bowl until stiff, but not dry. Gently fold the egg whites into the batter just until blended.

4. Line a 9½-inch springform pan with waxed paper, folding the overhanging edges over the rim of the pan. Line the bottom and sides of the pan with split ladyfingers.

5. Pour half the batter into the pan. Place 6 of the macaroons gently on top. Pour in the remaining batter and top with the remaining macaroons.

6. Cover the top of the cake with a layer of waxed paper and place a plate on top to lightly weight it. Refrigerate the cake for 24 hours.

7. Unmold the cake from the springform pan and cut into thin wedges. Serve whipped cream, if desired.

Makes 12 to 16 servings.

Chocolate Macadamia Cake with Goslings Rum Crème Anglaise

A flourless cake dense with chocolate and ground macadamia nuts. Goslings is a favorite summer sipping rum that adds a nice tropical touch to the crème anglaise.

CAKE:
- ¾ cup unsalted macadamia nuts
- 12 ounces semisweet chocolate bits
- 2 ounces unsweetened chocolate
- ½ cup (1 stick) unsalted butter
- 1 cup heavy or whipping cream
- 5 large eggs
- ½ cup granulated sugar
- 1 teaspoon vanilla extract

RUM CRÈME ANGLAISE:
- 1½ cups light cream (see Index)
- 6 tablespoons brown sugar
- 6 large egg yolks
- 6 tablespoons Goslings or other dark rum

1. Preheat the oven to 325°F. Butter a 9-inch round cake pan and line the bottom with an 8½-inch parchment paper circle. Butter the paper and lightly flour the pan.

2. Toast the macadamias on a baking sheet just until lightly browned, 7 to 10 minutes.

3. Heat the semisweet chocolate, unsweetened chocolate, butter, and cream in a saucepan over medium-low heat, just until the chocolate melts and the mixture is smooth. Remove from the heat.

4. Place the eggs in a large heatproof mixing bowl and beat in the sugar and vanilla. Set the bowl in a pan of simmering water on the stove. Beat the egg mixture with a hand-held mixer just until it is warm to the touch. Remove the bowl from the water and continue beating on high speed until tripled in volume, 7 to 10 minutes.

5. Process the macadamia nuts in a food processor fitted with the steel blade until finely ground, then fold into the chocolate mixture. Gently fold the egg mixture into the chocolate mixture just until blended. Pour the batter into the prepared pan. Place the pan in a larger pan and fill the larger pan with water to come half-way up the sides of the cake pan.

6. Bake the cake until a toothpick inserted in the center comes out clean, 40 to 45 minutes. Remove the cake from the oven and waterbath. Let cool completely in the pan, then invert onto a serving plate.

7. Prepare the crème anglaise: Heat the cream and brown sugar in a small saucepan just until the sugar dissolves. Remove from the heat. Whisk the egg yolks in a mixing bowl until blended. Gradually beat in one-third of the warm cream mixture. Whisk the egg yolks back into the cream mixture and return to the stove. Cook over low heat, stirring constantly, until thickened to the consistency of a light custard. Remove from the heat.

8. Transfer the egg mixture to a clean bowl. Stir in the rum and set the bowl in a larger bowl filled with ice water. Cool the crème completely. Refrigerate until ready to serve.

9. To serve the cake, pool a few spoonfuls of the crème anglaise on each dessert plate. Place a small wedge of the chocolate cake in the center. Garnish with a tropical-looking flower and serve.

Makes 8 to 10 servings.

Chocolate Bombe

I believe the name says it all with this dessert!

2 packages (3 ounces
  each) ladyfingers
½ cup Grand Marnier,
  dark rum, or crème de
  cacao
3 packages (12 ounces
  each) semisweet
  chocolate bits

2 cups (1 pound)
  unsalted butter, at
  room temperature
4 cups sifted
  confectioners' sugar
16 large egg yolks
1½ tablespoons vanilla
  extract

GLAZE:
1 package (12 ounces)
  semisweet chocolate
  bits

2 tablespoons unsalted
  butter

1. Line a 2-quart mixing bowl with plastic wrap. Brush the pre-split sides of each ladyfinger with the liqueur. Line the bowl with the ladyfingers, reserving the extras for the top.

2. Melt the chocolate, stirring constantly, in the top of a double boiler over simmering water until smooth. Beat the butter, sugar, and egg yolks in a large mixing bowl at high speed until fluffy. At low speed, gradually beat in the melted chocolate and the vanilla extract.

3. Pour the chocolate mixture into the ladyfinger-lined bowl. Cover the top completely with the reserved ladyfingers. Refrigerate the bombe overnight to set.

4. The following day, invert the bombe onto a serving plate. Prepare the glaze: Melt the chocolate and butter in a small saucepan, stirring constantly, over low heat until smooth. Spread the glaze completely over the bombe. Serve the bombe slightly chilled in thin wedges.

Makes 20 to 24 servings.

Viennese Hazelnut Torte with Coffee Buttercream

A beautifully dramatic, delicious, and quintessential example of the fine art of European-style confection. The crunchy
nuttiness of the cake layers are a perfect contrast to the silky
smooth coffee buttercream.

CAKE:

¼ cup best-quality
   unsweetened cocoa
   powder
4½ cups hazelnuts,
   skinned, lightly
   toasted, and finely
   ground

12 large eggs, separated
2 cups granulated sugar
Pinch of salt

COFFEE BUTTERCREAM:

3 heaping tablespoons
   instant espresso powder
⅓ cup boiling water
6 large egg yolks
½ cup granulated sugar
2 cups (1 pound)
   unsalted butter, at
   room temperature

¼ cup dark sweet rum
¾ cup sifted
   confectioners' sugar

Additional rum for
   sprinkling on cakes

Chocolate-covered coffee
   beans, for garnish

1. Preheat the oven to 350°F. Butter three 9-inch round cake
pans and line the bottoms with 8-inch parchment paper circles.
Butter the paper and lightly dust each pan with flour.

2. Process the cocoa and hazelnuts in a food processor fitted
with the steel blade until combined.

3. Using an electric mixer, beat the egg yolks in a mixing bowl
at high speed until thick and pale yellow, 3 to 4 minutes.
Gradually beat in the sugar; continue beating until the mixture is
very thick, 4 to 5 minutes.

4. Beat the egg whites with the salt in a large mixing bowl
until stiff but not dry.

5. Fold half the cocoa mixture into the egg yolk mixture. Lighten by gently folding in one-third of the egg whites. Fold in the remaining cocoa mixture, then gently fold in the remaining egg whites just until incorporated. Divide the batter evenly among the 3 pans.

6. Bake the cakes until the sides pull away from the pans and the centers spring back when lightly touched, 40 to 45 minutes. Let the cakes cool in the pans for 15 minutes, then invert onto wire racks to cool completely.

7. Prepare the buttercream: Dissolve the espresso in the boiling water. Whisk the egg yolks, granulated sugar, and espresso together in the top of a double boiler. Set over simmering water and cook the egg yolk mixture, whisking constantly, until it is the consistency of a medium custard, 10 to 15 minutes. Remove the pan from the water and cool to room temperature.

8. Beat the butter in a mixing bowl until creamy. Gradually beat in the coffee custard mixture and the rum. Beat in the confectioners' sugar. If the buttercream seems too runny, refrigerate it to thicken to spreading consistency.

9. Moisten each cake layer with a liberal sprinkling of rum. Spread the top and sides of each cake with a thin layer of the buttercream, stacking the layers on top of each other. Even the sides and top of the cake with more buttercream. Place any remaining buttercream in a pastry bag fitted with a decorative tip. Pipe rosettes of buttercream over the top of the torte. Decorate with the candy coffee beans. Refrigerate the torte until 15 minutes before you are ready to serve.

Makes 12 servings.

My Vision of Cheesecake

I adore cheesecakes that are dense and creamy, but I abhor them with graham cracker crumb crusts. This recipe, which I've perfected over the years, has a pastry crust with a subtle hint of citrus and a sinfully rich filling. The cheesecake can be made even more outrageous by topping it lavishly with ripe summer berries.

CRUST:

1½ cups unbleached
   all-purpose flour
⅓ cup sugar
1 teaspoon grated lemon
   zest
1 teaspoon grated orange
   zest

¾ cup (1½ sticks)
   unsalted butter, cold,
   cut into small pieces
1 large egg yolk
½ teaspoon vanilla
   extract

FILLING:

2½ pounds cream cheese,
   at room temperature
1½ cups sugar
3 tablespoons all-purpose
   flour
5 large eggs
2 large egg yolks

1 tablespoon grated
   orange zest
2 teaspoons grated lemon
   zest
1 teaspoon vanilla extract
¼ cup heavy or whipping
   cream

Ripe berries, whole or puréed (optional)

1. Prepare the crust: Place the flour, sugar, lemon and orange zests, and butter in a food processor fitted with the steel blade; process until the mixture resembles coarse meal. Add the egg yolk and vanilla and process just until the mixture starts to form a ball. Gather the dough, wrap it in plastic wrap, and refrigerate 1 hour.

2. Preheat the oven to 400°F. Butter the bottom and sides of a 9½-inch springform pan.

3. Using your fingers, press one-third of the pastry in an even layer on the bottom of the pan. Bake 10 minutes, then remove to a cool spot to cool completely.

4. Increase the heat to 475°F.

5. Prepare the filling: Beat the cream cheese and sugar in a large mixing bowl until very soft and creamy. Beat in the flour, then beat in the eggs and egg yolks, one at a time, beating well after each addition. Mix in the lemon and orange zests, vanilla, and cream.

6. Press the remaining pastry evenly around the sides of the pan. Pour the cheesecake filling into the pan.

7. Bake 10 minutes. Reduce the oven heat to 275°F and bake until the cheesecake is firm when pressed lightly in the center,

about 1 hour. Turn the oven off and let the cheesecake cool for several hours or overnight in the oven.

8. Remove the cheesecake from the side of the springform pan and refrigerate until cold. Top with lush summer berries, if desired.

Makes 12 servings.

Apricot Cheesecake

I love both the intense color and flavor of this cheesecake variation. During the summer I like to top it with a purée of fresh strawberries or raspberries for dramatic contrast. In the fall I often make a topping of simmered and sweetened cranberries.

1 cup dried apricots	1½ pounds cream cheese,
1 cup gingersnap crumbs	at room temperature
3 tablespoons unsalted	¾ cup sugar
butter, melted	4 large eggs
Grated zest of 1 orange	½ cup sour cream

1. Simmer the apricots in water to cover for 30 minutes, then drain.

2. Preheat the oven to 350°F. Butter an 8- or 9-inch springform pan.

3. Toss the gingersnap crumbs with the melted butter in a small mixing bowl. Press the crumbs over the bottom and 1 inch up the side of the prepared pan. Set aside.

4. Purée the apricots with the orange zest in a food processor fitted with the steel blade.

5. Beat the cream cheese and sugar in a large mixing bowl until very smooth and creamy. Beat in the eggs, one at a time, beating well after each addition. Using a rubber spatula, gently fold in the sour cream and apricot purée until completely blended. Pour the batter into the springform pan.

6. Bake until the center is firm when touched lightly, 50 to 60 minutes. Cool the cake on a wire rack, then refrigerate until thoroughly chilled. Top with a fruit topping, if desired, and serve.

Makes 10 to 12 servings.

Little Sarah's Shortcake

Little Sarah is one of the trusty crew of teenage girls that help me in the kitchen during Nantucket's high season frenzy. She is blond, freckled, delightfully giggly, and a real whiz in the baking department. This is the recipe for the terrific shortcake she churned out for a recent Fourth of July celebration.

2¼ cups unbleached
  all-purpose flour
½ cup plus 1 tablespoon
  sugar
1½ teaspoons baking
  powder
¾ teaspoon baking soda
½ teaspoon salt
6 tablespoons (¾ stick)
  unsalted butter, cold,
  cut into small pieces
⅔ cup buttermilk

1 large egg yolk
½ teaspoon vanilla extract
⅛ teaspoon almond
  extract
3 tablespoons heavy or
  whipping cream
⅓ cup sliced almonds
Fresh berries, and/or
  sliced peaches or
  nectarines, and
  whipped cream, for
  serving

1. Preheat the oven to 425°F. Line a baking sheet with parchment paper.

2. Place the flour, ½ cup sugar, the baking powder, baking soda, and salt in a food processor fitted with the steel blade; process briefly to combine. Add the butter and process just until the mixture is crumbly.

3. Whisk the buttermilk, egg yolk, and vanilla and almond extracts together in a small bowl. With the food processor running, pour the buttermilk mixture through the feed tube and process until the dough is somewhat sticky but still manageable. Transfer the dough to a floured sheet of waxed paper.

4. With lightly floured fingertips, gently pat the dough to an even ¾-inch thickness. Be careful not to handle the dough too much. Cut out six 3-inch circles, using a floured fluted cutter. Place the dough circles on the baking sheet.

5. Brush the tops of the cakes with the cream and arrange the almonds on top to look like the petals of a flower. Sprinkle with the remaining 1 tablespoon sugar.

6. Bake the shortcakes until lightly golden brown, 12 to 15 minutes. Cool, then split in half with a serrated knife. Fill with berries, sliced peaches or nectarines, and whipped cream.

Makes 6 shortcakes.

Blueberry-Raspberry Galette

As a young girl, I made this dessert with the blueberries and raspberries that grew wild on my grandfather's island in Maine. The recipe is still a favorite because there is something wonderfully light and summery about the combination of the barely cooked blueberries with the fresh raspberries.

CRUST:
1 cup unbleached
   all-purpose flour
1½ tablespoons sugar
6 tablespoons (¾ stick)
   unsalted butter, cold,
   cut into small pieces
½ teaspoon salt

1 teaspoon finely grated
   lemon zest
1 large egg yolk
1 tablespoon fresh lemon
   juice
1 tablespoon ice water

FILLING:
2½ cups fresh blueberries,
   preferably small wild
   ones
¼ cup sugar
2 teaspoons ground
   cinnamon

4 tablespoons (½ stick)
   unsalted butter, melted
1 tablespoon fresh lemon
   juice

1 cup fresh raspberries   Whipped cream (optional)

1. Prepare the crust: Place the flour, sugar, butter, salt, and lemon zest in a food processor fitted with the steel blade; process just until the mixture resembles coarse meal. Add the egg yolk. With the machine running, add the lemon juice and water through the feed tube and process just until the dough starts to hold together and form a ball. Gather the dough, wrap it in plastic wrap, and refrigerate at least 2 hours.

2. Roll out the dough into a 14-inch circle on a lightly floured surface. Line a 12-inch tart pan with a removable bottom with the dough; trim and crimp the edges. Freeze the shell for 30 minutes.

3. Preheat the oven to 425°F.

4. Prepare the filling: Toss the blueberries, sugar, cinnamon, butter, and lemon juice together. Spoon the filling evenly into the tart shell.

5. Bake the tart for 12 minutes. Reduce the heat to 350°F and bake until the berries are slightly soft, about 10 minutes. Let the tart cool completely.

6. Decorate the tart with 2 circles of fresh raspberries around the edge. Cut into wedges and serve with a dollop of whipped cream, if desired.

Makes 8 servings.

Double Raspberry Tart

This tart epitomizes the best of summer. It is extravagant in its use of raspberries both in the creamy filling and clustered all over the top. The combination of colors—berry red, cloud pink, and pale green—always make me imagine that I am surrounded by a gorgeous roll of chintz fabric.

CRUST:

1¼ cups unbleached all-purpose flour

2 tablespoons sugar

½ cup (1 stick) unsalted butter, cold, cut broken into small pieces

2 teaspoons grated lemon zest

1 large egg yolk

1 to 2 tablespoons ice water

RASPBERRY CREAM:

2 cups fresh raspberries

1 tablespoon fresh lemon juice

½ cup sugar

6 tablespoons (¾ stick) unsalted butter

5 large egg yolks

1½ cups fresh raspberries

2 kiwis, peeled and sliced into thin rounds

½ cup apricot jam

¼ cup orange-flavored liqueur

1. Prepare the crust: Place the flour, sugar, butter, and lemon zest in a food processor fitted with the steel blade; process just until the mixture resembles coarse meal. Add the egg yolk and

pulse just to combine. With the machine running, add the water through the feed tube a few drops at a time, just until the dough begins to hold together. Gather the dough into a ball, wrap it in plastic wrap, and refrigerate for at least 2 hours.

2. Meanwhile, prepare the raspberry cream: Purée the raspberries, lemon juice, and sugar together in the food processor. Strain the mixture through a fine sieve to remove the seeds. Place the purée in the top of a double boiler set over simmering water. Add the butter and stir until completely melted. Whisk in the egg yolks and continue to cook over low heat, stirring constantly, until the mixture thickens to a light custard consistency. Remove from the heat and chill covered in the refrigerator at least 2 hours.

3. Roll out the dough on a lightly floured surface to a 12-inch circle. Line a 10-inch tart pan with a removable bottom with the dough; trim and crimp the edges. Freeze the shell for 30 minutes.

4. Preheat the oven to 375°F. Line the tart shell with aluminum foil and fill with lead pie weights or dried beans.

5. Bake the shell until light golden brown, about 20 to 25 minutes. Remove the foil and weights; cool the shell completely.

6. To assemble the pie, spread the raspberry cream evenly over the tart shell. Arrange concentric circles of the raspberries, interspersed with the kiwi, over the top.

7. Combine the apricot jam and orange liqueur in a small saucepan and heat over low heat just until the jam is melted and smooth. Brush all over the fruit to glaze. Serve the tart at once or refrigerate until ready to serve.

Makes 8 servings.

Deep-Dish Rhubarb Pie

My love for the color pink is absolutely inexhaustible. This pretty pie, oozing with cassis-infused spring rhubarb, is pink at its most palatable. I only lament that rhubarb has such a short growing season.

CRUST:

2½ cups unbleached
   all-purpose flour
5 tablespoons sugar
1 tablespoon ground
   cinnamon
Pinch salt
6 tablespoons unsalted butter,
   cold, cut into bits

6 tablespoons unsalted
   margarine, cold, cut
   into bits
4 to 5 tablespoons ice
   water

FILLING:

10 cups diced rhubarb
1½ cups cassis liqueur
Finely chopped zest of 2
   oranges

1¾ cups sugar
⅓ cup cornstarch
1 large egg
1 tablespoon water

1. One day before you plan to serve the pie, prepare the crust: Process the flour, sugar, cinnamon, salt, butter, and margarine in a food processor fitted with the steel blade just until the mixture resembles coarse meal. With the machine running, pour the ice water through the feed tube and process just until the dough starts to form a ball. Gather the dough, wrap it in plastic wrap, and refrigerate.

2. Start the filling: Toss the rhubarb with the cassis and orange zest in a large mixing bowl. Cover the bowl with plastic wrap and let marinate at room temperature overnight.

3. Drain the liquid from the rhubarb into a small saucepan. Stir in the sugar and cornstarch. Cook, whisking constantly, over medium-high heat until thickened. Pour the sauce over the rhubarb and stir until well combined.

4. Preheat the oven to 350°F.

5. Roll out half the dough into a 12-inch circle on a lightly floured surface. Line a 10-inch pie dish with the dough; trim and crimp the edges decoratively. Mound the filling in the pie shell.

6. Roll out the remaining dough ⅛ inch thick. Cut the dough into ⅓-inch-wide strips and arrange the strips over the top of the pie in a lattice pattern. Gather the scraps and roll out ⅛ inch thick. Cut out a heart shape and place on the center of the pie.

7. Beat the egg and water together in a small bowl. Brush the egg wash over the dough. Place the dish on a baking sheet to catch any overflowing juices. Bake the pie until the crust is golden brown and the filling is bubbling, 50 to 60 minutes. Serve warm or at room temperature.

Makes 8 servings.

Lemon Chiffon Pie

A cloudlike pie that is both light and opulent.

CRUST:
½ cup (1 stick) unsalted butter, cold, cut into small pieces
4 tablespoons unsalted margarine, cold, cut into small pieces
2 cups unbleached all-purpose flour
Pinch salt
2 to 3 tablespoons ice water

FILLING:
4 large eggs, separated
6 tablespoons fresh lemon juice
¾ cup sugar
Finely grated zest of 1 lemon
1 scant tablespoon unflavored gelatin
⅓ cup cold water

TOPPING:
1 cup heavy or whipping cream
¼ cup sugar
2 teaspoons grated orange zest
½ cup ground lightly toasted almonds

1. Early in the morning or one day before you plan to serve the pie, prepare the crust: Place the butter, margarine, flour, and salt in a food processor fitted with the steel blade; process just until the mixture resembles coarse meal. With the machine running, add the ice water through the feed tube and process just until the mixture starts to form a ball. Gather the dough, wrap it in plastic wrap, and refrigerate at least 2 hours.

2. Roll out the dough into an 11-inch circle on a lightly floured surface. Line a 9-inch pie dish with the dough; trim and crimp the edges decoratively. Freeze the pie shell for 30 minutes.

3. Preheat the oven to 375°F.

4. Line the pie shell with aluminum foil and fill with pie weights or dried beans. Bake the shell until light golden brown, 20 to 25 minutes. Remove the foil and weights; cool the shell completely.

5. Prepare the filling: Beat the egg yolks, lemon juice, ½ cup of the sugar, and all but 1 teaspoon of the lemon zest in the top of a double boiler. Cook, stirring constantly, over simmering water until the mixture is the consistency of a thick custard. Remove from the heat and transfer to a medium bowl. Soften the gelatin in the cold water and stir into the lemon custard until dissolved. Let cool.

6. Beat the egg whites in a mixing bowl until stiff but not dry, then beat in the remaining ¼ cup sugar. Gently fold the egg whites into the custard. Pour the filling into the baked pie shell and refrigerate at least 2 hours.

7. When ready to serve, prepare the topping: Whip the cream, sugar, and orange zest until stiff. Transfer to a pastry bag fitted with a decorative tip and pipe the cream decoratively over the pie.

8. Dust the top of the pie with the ground toasted almonds and the reserved 1 teaspoon lemon zest. Serve at once.

Makes 8 servings.

Apple Cream-Cheese Tarts

The inspiration for these tarts comes from German fruit kuchens. However, I think the accent on the pure vanilla flavor make these tarts especially unique. Use any crisp apple or feel free to innovate with other seasonal fruits and liqueurs. I particularly like purple plums with cassis and peaches with amaretto.

CRUST:

1¼ cups unbleached
   all-purpose flour
½ cup (1 stick) unsalted
   butter, cold, cut into
   small pieces

⅓ cup sugar
2 teaspoons vanilla
   extract

APPLES:

2 large apples, peeled,
   cored, and cut into
   very thin wedges
1 tablespoon fresh lemon
   juice

2 tablespoons brandy
3 tablespoons sugar
2 teaspoons ground
   cinnamon

CREAM-CHEESE FILLING:
8 ounces cream cheese   2 teaspoons vanilla
½ cup sugar   extract
1 large egg

1. Prepare the crust: Place the flour, butter, and sugar in a food processor fitted with the steel blade; process until the mixture resembles coarse meal. Add the vanilla and process just until the mixture starts to hold together. Gather the dough into a ball, wrap in plastic wrap, and refrigerate 30 minutes.

2. Meanwhile, prepare the apples: Toss the apples, lemon juice, brandy, sugar, and cinnamon together in a mixing bowl. Let stand at least 20 minutes.

3. Prepare the cream-cheese filling: Break the cream cheese into small pieces and place in the food processor fitted with the steel blade. Add the sugar, egg, and vanilla and process until smooth.

4. Preheat the oven to 350°F.

5. Divide the chilled dough into 5 equal pieces. Using your fingers, press each piece of dough into a 4½-inch tart pan with a removable bottom to completely line the bottom and sides.

6. Spoon the filling into the tart shells, then arrange the apple slices overlapping in a circle on the filling in each tart shell. Pour any juices in the bowl over the tops of the tarts.

7. Place the tarts on a baking sheet and bake until the tarts are light golden brown, 35 to 45 minutes. Let cool completely, then remove the tarts from the pans. Serve at room temperature.

Makes 5 individual tarts.

Applesauce Cake with Caramel Glaze

While I dislike the very thought of carrot cake, I find that applesauce cake is an ostensibly "healthful" cake in a whole other league. This cake is the perfect treat for one of those "try-to-remember" September days when all the tourists have gone home and you can finally appreciate your summer home.

¾ cup (1½ sticks)
  unsalted butter, at
  room temperature
1½ cups (packed) brown
  sugar
2 large eggs
2½ cups Rosy
  Applesauce (see Index)
  or unsweetened
  best-quality applesauce

3 cups unbleached
  all-purpose flour
1 tablespoon baking soda
1½ tablespoons ground
  cinnamon
1 teaspoon grated nutmeg
½ teaspoon ground cloves
1¼ cups pitted dates, chopped
½ cup Calvados
1 cup coarsely chopped walnuts

GLAZE:
2 cups (packed) brown
  sugar
½ cup (1 stick) unsalted
  butter

½ cup milk

1. Preheat the oven to 350°F. Butter a 10-inch bundt or tube pan.

2. Using an electric mixer, cream the butter and sugar in a large mixing bowl until light and fluffy. Add the eggs and applesauce and beat until blended.

3. Sift the flour, baking soda, cinnamon, nutmeg, and ground cloves together and gradually stir into the butter mixture.

4. Heat the dates and Calvados in a small saucepan to boiling; boil 1 minute. Add to the cake batter. Add the walnuts and stir until combined. Pour the batter into the prepared pan.

5. Bake until a knife inserted in the center of the cake comes out clean, 50 to 60 minutes. Cool the cake in the pan for 30 minutes, then invert onto a cake rack to cool completely.

6. Meanwhile, prepare the glaze: Combine the sugar, butter, and milk in a heavy saucepan. Heat, stirring constantly, over high heat to boiling. Boil without stirring until it registers 234°F on a candy thermometer. Let cool to room temperature. Transfer the mixture to a mixing bowl and beat until fluffy. Drizzle the glaze lavishly over the cooled cake.

Makes 12 servings.

Que Sera Sarah Brownies

Over the summers these superb brownies have achieved a sort of cult status with my customers. Many have tried in vain to duplicate them at home and others offer season-to-season guesses as to the alleged secret ingredient. The combination of sheer exasperation over failed attempts to copy them and winter withdrawal brings me several desperate phone calls a year for brownie care packages.

While all of this chocolate intrigue has been entertaining, I am at last ready to reveal my formula. Although my recipe is actually a close adaptation of Maida Heatter's widely published Palm Beach Brownies, there is a catch: the secret of the Que Sera Sarah rendition does not rest so much on mystery ingredients, but on cooking technique. To achieve the incomparable combination of wafer thin crust and dense fudge-like interior of my shop brownies, you must bake the recipe in a *convection oven* and then patiently refrigerate the brownies for several hours before devouring them. I regret to inform those chocolate lovers without state-of-the-art kitchens that the same results just cannot be achieved with a regular oven. I do suggest, however, that these brownies might be worth the investment!

8 ounces unsweetened chocolate
1 cup (2 sticks) unsalted butter
5 large eggs
1 tablespoon vanilla extract
2 teaspoons almond extract

3 tablespoons instant coffee powder
3¾ cups sugar
1⅔ cups unbleached all-purpose flour
1 cup coarsely chopped walnuts

1. Preheat a convection oven to 350°F. Line an 11 x 9-inch pan with aluminum foil leaving a little overhang around the edges of the pan. Butter the foil.

2. Melt the chocolate and butter in a small saucepan over low heat, watching carefully and stirring occasionally, just until smooth.

3. Using an electric mixer, beat the eggs, vanilla and almond extracts, coffee, and sugar in a large mixing bowl at the highest speed for about 10 minutes. The mixture should increase in volume and look like softened coffee ice cream. Mix in the melted

chocolate and butter on low speed just until blended. Add the flour and nuts and stir just until mixed. Turn the brownie mixture into the prepared pan.

4. Bake the brownies in the center of the convection oven just until a hard crust forms on the top and the edges are very slightly browned, 18 to 20 minutes. The batter underneath the crust will be runny and undercooked by normal baking standards. Let the brownies cool to room temperature.

5. Refrigerate the brownies at least 6 hours or overnight. Using the foil, lift the brownies from the pan. Cut into 20 to 25 squares.

Makes 20 to 25 brownies.

White Chocolate Brownies

Another rich brownie recipe, this one for lovers of white chocolate.

1 cup (2 sticks) unsalted butter	4 large eggs
10 ounces white chocolate, broken into small pieces	1 tablespoon vanilla extract
	2 cups unbleached all-purpose flour
1¼ cups sugar	½ teaspoon salt
	1 cup coarsely chopped pecans

1. Preheat the oven to 325°F. Line an 11 x 9-inch pan with aluminum foil leaving a little overhang around the edges of the pan and butter the foil.

2. Heat the butter and chocolate, stirring frequently, in a large saucepan over low heat until melted and smooth. Remove from the heat.

3. Using a wooden spoon, stir the sugar into the melted chocolate, then stir in the eggs and vanilla. (The mixture will look curdled.) Add the flour, salt, and chopped pecans and quickly stir just until mixed. Pour the batter into the pan.

4. Bake the brownies until the top is lightly golden but the center is still somewhat soft when pressed lightly, 30 to 35 minutes. Let cool to room temperature.

5. Refrigerate the brownies at least 3 hours. Using the foil, lift the brownies from the pan. Cut into 20 to 25 squares.

Makes 20 to 25 brownies.

My Grandmother's Oatmeal Cookies

I am passionate about these cookies. They are hearty, old-fashioned cookies that contain many of the special qualities of my favorite grandmother, who taught me so much about growing up, as well as a vast amount about eating well. The cookies are quite generous in size; in fact, nibbling on one throughout the day can make the very notion of breakfast and lunch disappear. I have been known to live solely on these cookies throughout my hectic summer season.

2⅔ cups unsalted
   margarine
3½ cups (packed) brown
   sugar
3 large eggs
3 tablespoons honey
1 tablespoon vanilla
   extract
1½ teaspoons salt

4 cups unbleached
   all-purpose flour
4 pounds old-fashioned
   rolled oats (there are a
   lot of oats in these
   cookies!)
8 ounces dark raisins
8 ounces coarsely chopped
   walnuts

1. Preheat the oven to 350°F. Line baking sheets with parchment paper.

2. Cream the margarine and sugar in a very large bowl until smooth. Beat in the eggs, honey, vanilla, and salt until smooth and creamy.

3. Using a large wooden spoon or your hands, work in the flour and oats until well combined. Add the raisins and walnuts and mix until evenly distributed.

4. Shape the dough into large 3-inch balls and press into 5- to 6-inch flat cookies on the baking sheets.

5. Bake the cookies 15 minutes or to desired doneness. (Some people like slightly underdone cookies and others like very well-browned cookies. We debate this every time we make these.) Let cool on wire racks.

Makes 24 cookies.

Graham Cracker Chewies

This is a favorite recipe of my mother's. These are a moist and chewy alternative to brownies and are great packed for picnics or tailgate parties.

CRUST:

1⅓ cups graham cracker crumbs

1 tablespoon sugar

½ cup (1 stick) unsalted butter, at room temperature

2 tablespoons all-purpose flour

TOPPING:

1½ cups (packed) brown sugar

½ cup chopped pecans

⅓ cup graham cracker crumbs

½ teaspoon salt

¼ teaspoon baking powder

1 teaspoon vanilla extract

2 large eggs, beaten

1. Preheat the oven to 350°F.
2. Prepare the crust: Mix the graham cracker crumbs, sugar, butter, and flour in a mixing bowl until moist and crumbly. Press the mixture firmly and evenly in the bottom of a 9-inch-square baking pan. Bake until lightly browned, about 20 minutes.
3. Prepare the topping: Stir all the ingredients together until blended. Spread the topping over the baked crust and bake for 20 minutes. Let cool completely, then cut into 16 squares.

Makes 16 bars.

Lace Cookies

This is one of the very first recipes I learned to cook on Nantucket as a young girl. The cookies are delicate, crisp, and addictive. Serve them with goblets of afternoon iced tea or savor them with a late night demitasse of lemon-scented espresso. Be sure to choose a dry day for baking and store in an airtight tin to avoid soggy or limp cookies.

½ cup (1 stick) unsalted
 butter, at room
 temperature
1 cup sugar
1 large egg
1 teaspoon vanilla extract

Pinch salt
1 cup quick-cooking oats
2 tablespoons unbleached
 all-purpose flour
¼ teaspoon baking
 powder

1. Preheat the oven to 325°F. Line baking sheets with aluminum foil and butter the foil well.

2. Using an electric mixer, cream the butter and sugar in a medium bowl until smooth. Add the egg and the vanilla and beat until well blended.

3. Combine the oats, flour, and baking powder in a small bowl. Gradually beat the oat mixture into the butter mixture.

4. Roll the cookie dough with the palms of your hands into balls the size of a nickel. Place the balls a good 2 inches apart on the baking sheets.

5. Bake the cookies until they have spread out and look like lace and the outer edges are quite brown, 8 to 10 minutes. Remove the cookies from the oven and let cool on the baking sheets a minute or so, then transfer to wire racks to cool completely.

Makes about 40 cookies

French Lace Cookies à l'Orange

Another delicate lace cookie, this one with an enticing hint of orange.

1 cup unbleached
 all-purpose flour
1 cup finely chopped
 pecans
⅓ cup light corn syrup
2 tablespoons frozen
 orange juice
 concentrate, thawed

2 teaspoons grated orange
 zest
½ cup (1 stick) unsalted
 butter
⅔ cup (packed) brown
 sugar

1. Preheat the oven to 375°F. Line baking sheets with aluminum foil and butter the foil.

2. Sift the flour into a small bowl and toss with the pecans.

3. Place the remaining ingredients in a saucepan and heat to boiling over medium heat. Using a wooden spoon, gradually stir in the flour mixture. Drop the batter by level teaspoons 2 inches apart on the prepared baking sheets.

4. Bake until the edges of the cookies are golden brown and the centers are cooked, 6 to 8 minutes. Cool on the cookie sheets a minute or so, then transfer to wire racks with a metal spatula to cool completely. Store between layers of waxed paper in an airtight container.

Makes about 48 cookies.

Date Squares

A favorite healthy and old-fashioned recipe that has been handed down from my mother's side of the family.

FILLING:
8 ounces pitted dates   1 cup orange juice

CRUST:
2 cups rolled oats   1 teaspoon baking soda
1 cup unbleached   ¾ cup (1½ sticks)
   all-purpose flour   unsalted butter, melted
1 cup (packed) brown
   sugar

1. Combine the dates and orange juice in a small saucepan and simmer, stirring occasionally, until thick, 30 minutes.

2. Preheat the oven to 350°F. Butter a 9-inch-square baking pan.

3. Meanwhile, make the crust: Stir the oats, flour, brown sugar, and baking soda together in a mixing bowl. Add the melted butter and stir until moist and crumbly.

4. Press half the oat mixture evenly in the bottom of the prepared pan. Spread the date mixture on top and sprinkle with the remaining oat mixture.

5. Bake the date squares until nicely browned, 40 to 45 minutes. Let cool completely then cut into 16 squares.

Makes 16 squares.

COCONUT MILK

Although packaged unsweetened coconut milk is becoming more widely available, many cooks still prefer to make their own. There are subtle variations of technique, but the following is the method I prefer.

Choose a coconut in which you can hear the inner liquid when the nut is shaken. Pierce the three black eyes at the top of the nut with a hammer and large nail and drain and discard the liquid. Bake the coconut on a tray in a preheated 350°F oven for 20 minutes, or until the outer shell has cracked in several places. Cool the coconut, then finish cracking the shell with a couple of good whacks of a hammer. Remove the shell, then peel the thin brown skin from the coconut meat with a sharp paring knife. Grate the white flesh with a hand grater or in a food processor. You should have about 2½ cups grated coconut.

Combine 1½ cups milk with 1 cup water and bring just to a boil. Pour the liquid over the coconut and let stand for at least 1 hour. Strain the coconut through a fine sieve lined with a double thickness of dampened cheesecloth. Place the coconut in a cloth towel and wring it to extract as much of the coconut essence as possible. Discard the solids. You should now have about 3 cups fresh coconut milk. Store, covered, in the refrigerator for 3 to 5 days and use as called for in the recipes.

Coconut Cream for Summer Fruits

This smooth custard adds a delicious tropical flair to summer fruit desserts. I particularly like it spooned over a mixture of cantaloupe, pineapple, strawberries, and blackberries that have been marinated in a little lime juice.

6 large egg yolks
½ cup sugar
2 cups coconut milk (see
  box, page 247)

½ teaspoon coconut extract or
  2 tablespoons coconut liqueur
Toasted shredded coconut
  for garnish

1. In the top of a double boiler, but off the heat, beat the egg yolks and sugar together until mixture is pale yellow and thick.

2. Bring the coconut milk just to a boil in a small saucepan, then whisk it very slowly into the egg mixture. Place over simmering water and cook, stirring constantly, until the mixture thickens to a light custard, about 10 minutes. Remove from heat and stir in the coconut extract.

3. Cool the cream to room temperature, stirring occasionally. Refrigerate until cold. Spoon liberally over bowls of your favorite mixed fresh fruits and garnish with toasted coconut.

Makes about 2 cups

Coffee
Pot de Crème

A luscious yet simple-to-make dessert for the coffee lover.

3 cups heavy or whipping
  cream
½ cup sugar
1½ tablespoons instant
  coffee powder

1 teaspoon vanilla extract
5 large egg yolks
Whipped cream
Chocolate-covered coffee
  beans

1. Preheat the oven to 325°F.

2. Mix the cream, sugar, and coffee in a medium saucepan. Cook, stirring occasionally, over medium heat until the sugar is dissolved and the mixture is quite hot to the touch. Remove from the heat and stir in the vanilla.

3. Beat the egg yolks in a mixing bowl until thick and lemony. Gradually whisk in the hot cream. Strain the mixture through a sieve into a measuring cup with a pouring lip. Pour the mixture into eight ½-cup pot-de-crème cups.

4. Place the cups in a pan and fill the pan with water to come halfway up the sides of the cups. Bake until the custard is firm to the touch when pressed gently in the center, 25 to 30 minutes. Remove the cups from the water bath and let cool to room temperature.

5. Refrigerate the pots de crème for several hours. Serve with a dollop of whipped cream and a candy coffee bean on top.

Makes 8 servings.

White Chocolate and Pear Mousse

This shimmering pearl-colored mousse is sublime in flavor combination and texture.

PEAR PURÉE:

3 tablespoons unsalted
   butter
3 ripe pears, cored,
   peeled, and sliced

⅓ cup granualted sugar
2 tablespoons Poire
   Williams or other pear
   brandy

MOUSSE:

10 ounces best-quality
   white chocolate, broken
   into small pieces
4 tablespoons (½ stick)
   unsalted butter
6 large eggs, separated
1 cup sifted confectioners'
   sugar

⅓ cup Poire Williams or
   other pear brandy
2 cups heavy or whipping
   cream
Fresh mint sprigs, for
   garnish

1. Prepare the pear purée: Melt the butter in a medium skillet over medium heat. Add the pear slices and sauté until somewhat mushy, about 15 minutes. Stir in the sugar and simmer until the pears begin to caramelize, about 10 minutes longer. Remove the pears from the heat and place in a food processor

fitted with the steel blade. Add the Poire Williams and purée until smooth. Set aside.

2. Prepare the mousse: Melt the white chocolate and butter together in a small saucepan over low heat, stirring constantly until smooth. Set aside.

3. Combine the egg yolks, sugar, and Poire Williams in the top of a double boiler. Beat with a hand-held mixer until the mixture falls into ribbons when the beaters are lifted. Place the pan over simmering water and continue whisking until quite thick, 4 to 5 minutes.

4. Transfer the egg mixture to a large mixing bowl. Add the melted white chocolate, stirring until smooth. Let cool to room temperature.

5. In a chilled bowl, beat the cream until quite stiff. In a separate bowl with clean beaters, beat the egg whites until stiff, but not dry. Gently fold the egg whites into the chocolate mixture, then gently fold in the whipped cream.

6. Divide one-third of the mousse among 8 to 10 large wine goblets. Top each serving with a layer of the pear purée. Spoon another one-third of the mousse into the goblets, and top with the remaining pear purée. Fill the goblets with the remaining mousse. Chill in the refrigerator until set, at least 2 to 3 hours. Serve chilled, garnished with fresh mint sprigs.

Makes 8 to 10 servings.

Chocolate Berry Bread Pudding

With the current revival of old-fashioned desserts, bread puddings have become quite acceptable at even the poshest dinners. Still, I wanted to concoct a bread pudding that would be dazzling and refined rather than homey. The result is this show-stopping combination of a dense chocolate bread with tart raspberries and strawberries saturated with the richest and creamiest of custards. Comfort redefined!

CHOCOLATE BREAD:

½ cup (1 stick) unsalted butter

2½ squares (1 ounce each) unsweetened chocolate

2 cups unbleached, all-purpose flour

2 teaspoons baking powder

Pinch salt

2 large eggs

¾ cup sugar

1 teaspoon vanilla extract

⅔ cup sour cream

BERRIES:

2 cups fresh or frozen (unsweetened) raspberries

1½ cups quartered fresh strawberries (about 1 pint whole berries)

3 tablespoons cassis liqueur

CUSTARD:

4 large eggs

¾ cup sugar

¼ cup unbleached all-purpose flour

2 cups heavy or whipping cream

1 tablespoon unsalted butter for assembling the pudding

1 tablespoon sugar for assembling the pudding

1. Prepare the chocolate bread: Early in the day or the day before serving, preheat the oven to 350°F. Heavily butter a 9 x 3-inch loaf pan.

2. Melt the butter and chocolate in a small saucepan over low heat. Set aside to cool.

3. Sift together the flour, baking powder, and salt in a small bowl. Set aside.

4. Beat the eggs and sugar together in a large bowl until light and fluffy. Beat in the vanilla, then the cooled chocolate mixture. With a wooden spoon, stir in half of the flour mixture. Stir in the sour cream, then the remaining flour. Continue stirring until the batter is smooth. Pour the batter into the loaf pan and bake until a toothpick inserted in the middle of the loaf comes out clean, 50 to 55 minutes. Cool the bread for 10 minutes, then remove it to a rack and let cool completely.

5. Prepare the berries by combining them in a medium bowl, then tossing them with the cassis. Set aside.

6. Prepare the custard: Whisk the eggs, sugar, and flour together in a medium bowl. Add the cream in a thin, steady stream, whisking constantly, until well blended and smooth.

7. Assemble the pudding: Preheat the oven to 350°F. Butter a 1½-quart soufflé dish and sprinkle with sugar.

8. Slice the chocolate bread into half-inch-thick slices and lay them out flat on a baking sheet. Toast the bread in the oven for 15 minutes, then turn and toast the other side 10 minutes more. Set aside to cool. Do not turn off the oven.

9. Place one-third of the toasted bread slices in the soufflé dish. Top with half the berries; spoon one-third of the custard over the berries. Use half the remaining bread to make a second bread layer. Top with the remaining berries and half the custard. Make a final layer with the remaining bread and top it with the remaining custard.

10. Bake the bread pudding in the oven until the custard has set and the top is lightly browned, 1½ hours. Serve slightly warm or at room temperature.

Makes 6 to 8 servings.

Purple Plum Crunch

A great use for the late August abundance of Italian prune plums, which I find better cooked than eaten out-of-hand. The concept of apple crisp soars to new heights in this recipe.

3 pounds Italian prune
    plums, pitted and
    quartered
1½ cups (packed) brown
    sugar
6 tablespoons cassis
    liqueur
1 cup unbleached
    all-purpose flour
¾ cup old-fashioned
    rolled oats

½ cup chopped walnuts
1 tablespoon ground
    cinnamon
Pinch salt
¾ cup (1½ sticks)
    unsalted butter, cold,
    cut into small pieces
1 large egg, lightly beaten
Whipped cream or
    vanilla ice cream, for
    serving

1. Preheat the oven to 375°F.
2. Combine the plums, ½ cup of the sugar, and the cassis

together in a mixing bowl. Turn into a 12 x 8-inch shallow baking dish.

3. Combine the flour, oats, walnuts, remaining 1 cup sugar, the cinnamon, and salt in another mixing bowl. Cut in the butter with a pastry blender until the mixture resembles coarse meal. Add the egg and mix until moist and crumbly. Sprinkle the topping evenly over the plums.

4. Bake the plum crunch until the plums are bubbling and the top is nicely browned, 40 to 45 minutes. Serve warm or at room temperature with a dollop of whipped cream or a scoop of vanilla ice cream, if desired.

Makes 8 to 10 servings.

Apple Crisp

A dessert that says September and always brings back memories of Mother's home cooking.

14 McIntosh apples (about 2½ to 3 pounds), peeled, cored, and cut into ½-inch slices
⅓ cup granulated sugar
1 tablespoon ground cinnamon
½ teaspoon grated nutmeg
2 tablespoons fresh lemon juice
3 tablespoons Calvados

TOPPING:
¾ cup (1½ sticks) unsalted margarine
2 cups unbleached all-purpose flour
¾ cup (packed) brown sugar
1 cup old-fashioned rolled oats
1 tablespoon ground cinnamon
Pinch salt
¾ cup coarsely chopped skinned, toasted hazelnuts
1 large egg, lightly beaten

Vanilla ice cream (optional)

1. Preheat the oven to 350°F.

2. Combine the apples, sugar, cinnamon, nutmeg, lemon juice, and Calvados in a large mixing bowl. Let stand at room temperature.

3. Prepare the topping: Place the margarine, flour, brown sugar, oats, cinnamon, and salt in another mixing bowl and mix with your hands until crumbly. Add the hazelnuts and egg and mix just until evenly moistened.

4. Spoon the apple mixture into a 15 x 10-inch baking dish. Crumble the topping evenly over the apples. Bake until the topping is golden brown and the apples are bubbling and tender, about 45 minutes. Serve warm or at room temperature with vanilla ice cream, if desired.

Makes 8 to 10 servings.

Cottage Comforts

The notion of retreating to a cottage far away from the pressures of routine workaday life always conjures up an uninhibited hunger for those types of food which I consider supremely comforting. I dream of leisurely breakfasts filled with the wafting aromas of childhood delights such as crispy bacon and flapjacks, golden yellow farm eggs, bowls of wild berries, and rustic baskets of homey baked goods. The concepts of dietary discipline, meal schedules, and daily vitamin quotas cease to exist as a nostalgic lure to cuddling the self with soothing treats creeps in.

The tattered but cozy wicker chair that always catches the first rays of morning sun begs for a basket of warm, berry-speckled muffins alongside. The crunch of a buttery croissant harmonizes beautifully with the distant drone of the crashing surf. An energizing bowl of homemade granola provides just the boost to make the mid-morning tennis match seem effortless. Indulging in a sly little cornstick or two in the laze of the afternoon reveals such simple access to the complicated concept of contentment. Sinking into the soft interior of freshly baked bread is as pacifying as a shady siesta in the hammock.

While there are few guidelines to happy cottage life, comfort should always be primary and I can conceive of no better culinary metaphor than these heart-warming recipes.

Sterling's Croissants

Sterling and I first met when I was just about to become the proprietress of Que Sera Sarah. A gifted art student, she more or less came with my building as bohemian-artist-in-residence.

Sterling the artist filled her tableaus with bowls of cobalt blue mussel shells, wedges of pink cake, and platters of pompano, while Sterling the baker created ethereal croissants. Both mediums have gained her a most appreciative Nantucket following. The croissants are the best I have ever tasted either in France or this country. In order to prepare them, you will need a large butcher block or marble surface.

5 cups unbleached all-purpose flour	3 cups water
2 cups instant nonfat dried milk	2 cups cake flour
1 cup sugar	1 cup pastry flour (see Note)
2 packages (¼ ounce each) active dry yeast	2 cups (4 sticks) unsalted butter, cold
1 teaspoon salt	Favorite Croissant Filling (recipes follow)

EGG WASH
2 large eggs   2 tablespoons water

1. Combine 4 cups of the all-purpose flour, the dried milk, sugar, yeast, and salt in a large mixing bowl or the bowl of a heavy-duty mixer. With a wooden spoon or the dough-hook attachment, mix until well combined. Add the water and mix quickly, scraping down the bowl with a rubber spatula, just until combined. Add the remaining 1 cup of all-purpose flour, the cake and pastry flours, and mix again just until combined. Turn the dough out onto a flat baking sheet (it will be rather wet and sticky), cover with plastic wrap, and refrigerate for 6 to 8 hours.

2. Scrape the dough off the tray onto a large clean butcher block or marble rolling surface that has been dusted lightly with flour. Pat the dough gently into a 15 x 10-inch rectangle and flatten it slightly with a rolling pin. Slice the butter as quickly and thinly as possible and lay it evenly all over the dough.

3. Roll out the butter-covered dough until the butter is blended in. Dust lightly with flour as needed to prevent sticking. You will have a rectangle, about 2 to 3 times its original size.

4. Fold the dough over itself in thirds, just as you would a business letter. With an open end facing you, roll out the dough again. This is the first turn. Fold the dough again into thirds and turn it clockwise one-quarter turn. Roll out the dough. This is the second turn. Repeat this process two more times for 4 turns altogether. (This gives the dough the layers needed to make light pastry.) When the dough has been rolled out for the fourth time, shape the croissants. (If you do not wish to bake the full amount, divide the dough in half, fold one half into thirds, wrap it tightly in plastic wrap, and freeze for up to 2 months. When ready to use, thaw and continue with the recipe.)

5. Roll out the dough into a very large rectangle ¼ inch thick. Cut the dough into triangles about 7 x 7 x 5½ inches. Fill as desired (see the recipes that follow for amounts) or leave plain. Roll up each triangle beginning with the smaller edge. Place them 2 to 3 inches apart on baking sheets lined with parchment paper.

6. Beat the eggs and water together in a small bowl. Brush the croissants lightly with egg wash and cover with a lightly dampened cloth. Let rise in a warm spot until doubled in bulk and springy to the touch, 45 minutes.

7. Preheat the oven to 400°F.

8. Brush the croissants once more with egg wash and bake until light golden brown all over, 20 minutes. Cool for 5 minutes and serve warm or at room temperature.

Makes 25 to 30 croissants.

Note: Three cups of a cake and pastry flour blend may be substituted for the individual ingredients listed here.

Favorite Croissant Fillings

CREAM CHEESE AND POPPY SEED:
8 ounces cream cheese   3 tablespoons poppy seeds
⅓ cup confectioners'
   sugar

Place cream cheese and confectioners' sugar in a food processor fitted with the steel blade. Process together until smooth, scraping down the sides of the workbowl with a spatula as necessary. Add the poppy seeds and process until thoroughly incorporated. Spread a generous 1 tablespoon across the wider edge of each croissant before rolling it up.

ORANGE ALMOND:

8 ounces almond paste
3 tablespoons unsalted
butter, softened
Finely grated zest of
1 orange

Sliced almonds, optional,
for garnish

Beat together the almond paste and butter with a hand mixer until well blended. Add the orange zest and beat to incorporate. Spread the filling in a thin snake-like line across the wider edge of each croissant before rolling it up. Top each formed croissant with a scattering of sliced almonds, if desired.

HAM AND HONEY MUSTARD:

¼ pound prosciutto or
Wesphalian ham,
thinly sliced

½ cup honey mustard

Spread a generous coating of mustard over the surface of each croissant to within ¼ inch of the edges. Top with 1 slice of ham, then roll it up.

Bran Muffins

Everyone loves a good moist bran muffin. I have friends who have spent years searching for the best bran muffin recipe. This recipe may not be the best in the whole world, but it comes fairly close.

1 cup (2 sticks) unsalted
butter, at room
temperature
1 cup (packed) brown
sugar
½ cup honey
3 large eggs
2½ cups unbleached
all-purpose flour
1 heaping tablespoon
baking soda

1 teaspoon ground
cinnamon
½ teaspoon salt
2½ cups unsweetened
bran cereal
2½ cups buttermilk
8 ounces chopped dates
½ cup coarsely chopped
walnuts (optional)

1. Preheat the oven to 375°F. Place paper liners in 24 muffin cups.

2. Cream the butter and sugar in a large mixing bowl until well blended. Add the honey and beat until smooth. Add the eggs, one at a time, beating well after each addition.

3. Sift the flour, baking soda, cinnamon, and salt into another bowl. Add the bran and toss to combine. Add the flour mixture alternately with the buttermilk to the batter, gently beating after each addition just until mixed. Stir in the dates and walnuts, if using.

4. Spoon the batter into the cups, filling each cup almost to the top. Bake until puffed and lightly crusted, about 25 minutes. Serve warm or at room temperature with butter.

Makes 24 muffins.

Cranberry Harvest Muffins

A rich, dense, and fruity muffin that is a nourishing little boost on frosty mornings and elegant enough for special holiday entertaining.

3 cups unbleached
  all-purpose flour
1 tablespoon baking
  powder
½ teaspoon baking soda
½ teaspoon salt
1 tablespoon ground
  cinnamon
2 teaspoons ground
  ginger
1¼ cups milk
2 large eggs

1 cup (2 sticks) unsalted
  butter, melted
1½ cups coarsely chopped
  fresh cranberries
½ cup diced Calimyrna
  figs
¾ cup coarsely chopped,
  toasted and skinned
  hazelnuts
¾ cup (packed) brown
  sugar
¾ cup granulated sugar

1. Preheat the oven to 375°F. Place paper liners in 20 muffins cups.

2. Sift the flour, baking powder, baking soda, salt, cinnamon, and ginger together in a large mixing bowl. Make a well in the

center of the mixture and add the milk, eggs, and melted butter. Stir quickly just to combine. Add the cranberries, figs, hazelnuts, and both sugars and stir just to distribute the fruits, nuts, and sugar evenly throughout the batter.

3. Spoon the batter into the cups, filling each cup almost to the top. Bake until puffed and golden brown, 20 to 25 minutes.

Makes 20 muffins.

BREAKFAST AMIDST PALE PEONIES

Pink Bellinis
Unbeatable Scrambled Eggs
Avocado on Toast
Sliced Smoked Salmon
Tri-Berry Muffins

Iced Espresso

Tri-Berry Muffins

The secret to these muffins was discovered far too early one morning after a wild night on the town. Sterling and I had drowsily mixed a big bowl of the batter and then realized—in the nick of time—that we had forgotten to add the sugar. We decided that the only viable solution was to stir in the sugar as quickly as possible and hope for the best. Once the muffins were baked we were thrilled to discover that our serendipitous technique produced muffins with an irresistibly crunchy and crackled top. Now the catch is remembering to add the sugar last.

All of one berry or fruit can be used in these muffins, but the tri-berry combination is a favorite.

3 cups unbleached
   all-purpose flour
1 tablespoon baking
   powder
½ teaspoon baking soda
½ teaspoon salt
4½ teaspoons ground
   cinnamon
1¼ cups milk

2 large eggs
1 cup (2 sticks) unsalted
   butter or unsalted
   margarine, melted
1 cup blueberries
½ cup diced strawberries
½ cup raspberries
1½ cups sugar

1. Preheat the oven to 375°F. Place paper liners in 20 muffin cups.

2. Stir the flour, baking powder, baking soda, salt, and cinnamon together in a large bowl. Make a well in the center of the flour mixture. Add the milk, eggs, and butter to the well and stir quickly just to combine. Add the berries and sugar and stir quickly again just to combine.

3. Spoon the batter into the cups, filling each cup almost to the top. Bake until brown and crusty, about 20 minutes.

Makes 20 muffins.

Pumpkin Muffins with Crystallized Ginger

A moist and dense, autumn-hued muffin that delights the ever-increasing contingent of ginger lovers. This recipe makes quite a few muffins, but they do freeze well.

1 can (15 ounces)
   unsweetened pumpkin
   purée
2 cups (packed) brown
   sugar
1 cup (2 sticks) unsalted
   margarine, melted
4 large eggs
½ cup apple cider
3½ cups unbleached
   all-purpose flour
2 teaspoons baking soda

2 teaspoons baking
   powder
1 teaspoon salt
4½ teaspoons ground
   cinnamon
4½ teaspoons ground
   ginger
1 teaspoon grated nutmeg
½ teaspoon ground cloves
1 cup finely chopped
   crystallized ginger

1. Preheat the oven to 350°F. Place paper liners in 28 muffin cups.

2. Stir the pumpkin, sugar, and margarine together in a large mixing bowl. Add the eggs and beat until the mixture is smooth. Stir in the cider.

3. Sift the flour, baking soda, baking powder, salt, cinnamon, ground ginger, nutmeg, and cloves into another bowl. Gradually stir the flour mixture into the pumpkin mixture until thoroughly mixed. Fold in the crystallized ginger until evenly distributed.

4. Spoon the batter into the cups, filling each cup almost to the top. Bake until puffed and golden, 20 to 25 minutes. Serve warm with butter.

Makes 26 to 28 muffins.

Crunchy Cornsticks with Chiles and Cheddar

These cornsticks are filled with flavors Texans adore. However, if you prefer a milder and more traditional cornstick, you can simply omit the chile pepper, chili powder, and cumin. The creamed corn makes these cornsticks extra rich and the grated Cheddar adds a golden crunch.

Melted lard or bacon fat
  for the molds
1 cup yellow cornmeal
1 cup plus 2 tablespoons
  unbleached all-purpose
  flour
2 teaspoons baking
  powder
1 teaspoon baking soda
2 teaspoons cumin
1 teaspoon best-quality
  chili powder
1 teaspoon salt
1 can (17 ounces)
  creamed corn
1 cup buttermilk

4 tablespoons (½ stick)
  unsalted butter, melted
2 large eggs
1¼ cups grated sharp
  Cheddar cheese
1 fresh long red chile,
  seeded and minced, or
  1 can (4 ounces)
  minced green chiles

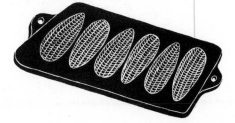

1. Preheat the oven to 350°F. Lightly coat cornstick molds with the melted lard or bacon fat.

2. Stir the cornmeal, flour, baking powder, baking soda, cumin, chili powder, and salt together in a mixing bowl.

3. Whisk the corn, buttermilk, butter, and eggs together in a large mixing bowl. Add the cornmeal mixture to the corn mixture and stir just until combined. Add the Cheddar and chile and fold just until they are evenly distributed.

4. Spoon the batter into the prepared molds, filling each two-thirds full. Bake until the cornsticks are crusty golden brown, 10 to 12 minutes. Let cool slightly then turn out onto a wire rack to cool completely. If necessary, repeat with the remaining batter, lightly coating the molds with melted fat after each batch.

Makes 28 cornsticks.

Currant and Caraway Scones

A winning combination that is great for nibbling any time of the day.

4½ cups unbleached all-purpose flour	1¼ cups heavy or whipping cream
2 teaspoons baking powder	1 cup currants
1 teaspoon baking soda	¼ cup sweet Marsala
3 tablespoons sugar	1 tablespoon caraway seeds
1 cup (2 sticks) unsalted butter, cold, cut into small pieces	1 large egg
	1 tablespoon water

1. Stir the flour, baking powder, baking soda, and sugar together in a large mixing bowl. Cut the butter into the flour mixture with a pastry blender until it resembles coarse meal. Add the cream and mix with your hands until the dough comes together.

2. Place the currants and Marsala in a small pan and heat to boiling. Reduce the heat and simmer for 2 minutes. Remove from the heat and cool 10 minutes. Mix the currants with liquid and the caraway seeds into the dough. Wrap the dough in plastic wrap and refrigerate at least 1 hour.

3. Preheat the oven to 350°F. Line baking sheets with parchment paper.

4. Divide the scone dough in half. Roll out each half ¾ inch thick on a floured surface. Cut into hearts, using a 2- to 3-inch heart-shaped cutter. Place the hearts 1 inch apart on the baking sheets. Mix the egg and water in a small bowl. Brush the egg wash over the top of each scone.

5. Bake the scones until light golden brown, about 15 minutes. Serve warm or at room temperature with whipped butter.

Makes about 36 scones.

Marbled Apricot Bread

The swirl of cream cheese in this moist tea bread adds a special flair. The bread keeps well in the refrigerator and is wonderful to have on hand for houseguests.

1 cup dried apricots, cut into thin strips
½ cup golden raisins
4 tablespoons (½ stick) unsalted butter, at room temperature
½ cup (packed) brown sugar
½ cup granulated sugar

1 large egg
2 cups unbleached all-purpose flour
2 teaspoons baking powder
½ teaspoon baking soda
½ teaspoon salt
¾ cup orange juice
½ cup chopped walnuts

CREAM CHEESE FILLING:
6 ounces cream cheese
⅓ cup granulated sugar
1 large egg
1 tablespoon grated orange zest

1. Combine the apricots and raisins in a small bowl. Add boiling water to cover and let stand for 30 minutes. Drain.

2. Preheat the oven to 350°F. Grease a 9 x 5-inch loaf pan and lightly dust with flour.

3. Beat the butter, brown sugar, and granulated sugar in a medium mixing bowl until creamy. Beat in the egg.

4. Sift the flour, baking powder, baking soda, and salt together in a medium bowl. Add the flour mixture alternately with the orange juice to the butter mixture to make a fairly thick batter. Stir in the apricots, raisins, and walnuts.

5. Prepare the filling: Place all the ingredients in a food processor fitted with the steel blade; process until smooth.

6. Pour two-thirds of the batter into the prepared pan. Top with all the filling, then top with the remaining batter. Lightly swirl with a knife.

7. Bake until the bread is golden brown and firm to the touch, 55 to 60 minutes. Let cool in the pan 10 minutes, then turn out onto a wire rack to cool completely. Store, wrapped in foil or plastic wrap, in the refrigerator. Cut into thick slices to serve.

Makes 1 loaf.

Portuguese Beer Bread

Nantucket's Portuguese heritage has encouraged a keen curiosity about Portuguese food. While Portuguese white bread is daily fare, even today, on the island, I particularly like the malty heartiness of this crusty Portuguese beer bread. Enjoy it on a blustery autumn day while gazing at the ocean—perhaps in the direction of Portugal.

2 packages (¼ ounce each) active dry yeast
2 tablespoons dark molasses
2 cups strong beer or imported dark beer, warmed to 105°F to 115°F

1½ cups whole-wheat flour
2 teaspoons salt
¼ cup fruity olive oil
4½ to 5 cups unbleached all-purpose flour

1. Place the yeast and molasses in a large mixing bowl. Add the warm beer and let the mixture stand until doubled in bulk and quite spongy, 10 to 15 minutes.

2. Using a wooden spoon, stir in the whole-wheat flour, salt, and olive oil. Gradually work in the all-purpose flour, 1 cup at a time, to make a stiff but elastic dough. Turn out onto a lightly floured surface and knead the dough until smooth and elastic, 5 to 10 minutes.

3. Lightly coat a large bowl with olive oil. Place the dough in the bowl and turn once to coat with oil. Cover the bowl with plastic wrap. Let rise in a warm place until doubled in bulk, about 1½ hours.

4. Punch the dough down, shape into a ball, and let rise again until doubled in bulk, about 1 hour.

5. Punch the dough down again and turn it out onto a lightly floured work surface. Divide the dough into 6 equal pieces. Roll each part into a rope, 12 to 14 inches long. Braid 3 ropes together and coil the braid into a circle. Repeat with the remaining 3 ropes.

6. Place the braided circles on lightly greased baking sheets and cover with dampened towels. Let rise again until doubled in bulk, about 45 minutes.

7. Meanwhile, preheat the oven to 475°F. When the oven is hot, place a large baking pan of boiling water in the bottom of the oven to create steam while the bread bakes.

8. When the bread has risen, mist it all over with water and place it in the hot oven. Bake, misting the bread 3 times during the first 15 minutes, until the bread is crusty and golden brown, 25 to 30 minutes. Serve warm with a frothy mug of beer and a steaming bowl of Kale Soup (see Index).

Makes 2 braided loaves.

Saffron and Pistachio Bread

Serve this rustic, sunny yellow bread with an assortment of ripened cheeses.

1½ packages (¼ ounce each) active dry yeast
2 teaspoons sugar
2 teaspoons saffron threads
2½ cups warm water (105°F to 115°F)
2 teaspoons salt
2 large eggs

½ cup freshly grated Parmesan cheese
¼ cup shelled pistachio nuts
6 to 6½ cups unbleached all-purpose flour
1 tablespoon water
2 tablespoons fruity olive oil
1 tablespoon coarsely chopped fresh rosemary

1. Combine the yeast, sugar, and 1½ teaspoons of the saffron in a large mixing bowl. Pour in the warm water and let stand for 5 minutes.

2. Stir in the salt, 1 egg, the cheese, and pistachios. Stir in the flour, ½ cup at a time, until the dough is somewhat stiff. Turn the dough out onto a floured surface and knead until smooth and elastic, about 10 minutes.

3. Lightly coat a large bowl with olive oil. Place the dough in the bowl and turn once to coat with oil. Cover the bowl with plastic wrap or a dampened towel and let the dough rise in a warm place until doubled in bulk, about 1¼ hours.

4. Punch the dough down and turn out onto a floured surface. Roll the dough into a thick rope, then shape into a large ring with a center opening about 5 inches in diameter. Place the ring on a baking sheet lined with parchment paper. Beat the remaining egg with 1 tablespoon water and brush it all over the top and sides of the bread. Sprinkle the top of the loaf with the remaining ½ teaspoon saffron and the rosemary. Let rise covered in a warm spot for another 30 to 40 minutes.

5. Preheat the oven to 350°F.

6. Bake the bread until light golden brown and it sounds hollow when tapped on the bottom, 50 to 60 minutes. Let the bread cool completely on a wire rack before serving.

Makes 1 large ring (at least 12 servings).

Honey-Herb Rolls

Sterling began making these rolls one summer, and we fell instantly in love with their rustic look and fabulous sweet-and-savory flavor combination. They are tasty rolls for a summer dinner bread basket, and the leftovers make great sandwich beginnings.

7 to 8 cups unbleached
   all-purpose flour
1½ packages (¼ ounce
   each) active dry yeast

1 tablespoon salt
1 cup honey
3 cups warm water
   (105°F to 115°F)

HERB MIX:
¼ cup olive oil
1 large red onion, minced
3 cloves garlic, minced
1 bunch parsley, minced

1 bunch dill, minced
3 tablespoons fines
   herbes

EGG WASH:
2 large eggs   2 tablespoons water

1. Combine 4 cups of the flour, the yeast, and salt in a large mixing bowl. Using a wooden spoon, stir in the honey and warm water until smooth. Gradually stir in the remaining flour to make a soft dough. Knead the dough on a floured surface until smooth and satiny, about 10 minutes. Transfer the dough to a clean bowl. Cover and let rise until doubled in bulk, about 2 hours.

2. Meanwhile, prepare the herb mix: Heat the oil in a small skillet over medium-high heat. Add the onion and garlic and sauté, stirring occasionally, for 10 minutes. Add the parsley, dill, and *fines herbes* and sauté several minutes. Remove from the heat.

3. Punch the dough down and cut into 24 equal pieces. Place a little bit of the herb mixture in the center of each piece of dough and shape into round roll on a lightly floured surface. Make sure the herb mixture is completely enclosed. Place the rolls about 2 inches apart on baking sheets lined with parchment paper. Brush some of the herb mixture over the outside of the rolls. Let the rolls rise covered in a warm spot until doubled in bulk, about 45 minutes.

4. Preheat the oven to 350°F.

5. Mix the eggs with the water in a small bowl. Brush each roll with the egg wash. Bake until the rolls are light golden brown, 15 to 20 minutes. Serve warm or cooled.

Makes 24 three-inch rolls.

Avocado on Toast

When our family used to visit my grandparents in Florida, my grandmother would invite each one of her grandchildren in turn to share in his or her favorite breakfast. My special request was always my grandmother's invention of avocado on toast. To this day, it would still be what I would order if I had the indulgent luxury of savoring breakfast in bed.

1 *perfectly ripe large*   *Salt and freshly ground*
   Florida avocado   *pepper to taste*
4 *slices rye bread, lightly*
   toasted and buttered

Quarter, pit, and peel the avocado. Place 1 avocado quarter on each slice of rye toast and mash the avocado lightly with a fork. Sprinkle with salt and pepper to taste. Serve at once. (You can further embellish the avocado with crisp, crumbled bacon or a scattering of finely minced smoked salmon.)

Makes 2 servings.

Foggy Morning Flapjacks

Thick fogs and misty mornings are an inevitable part of coastal living. These oversize hearty pancakes provide wonderful consolation during those damp and gloomy spells without sunshine. Top with seasonal fruits or your favorite homemade preserves.

⅔ cup old-fashioned rolled oats
1⅓ cups whole-wheat flour
⅔ cup unbleached all-purpose flour
⅔ cup yellow cornmeal
4 teaspoons baking powder
2 teaspoons baking soda

2 teaspoons salt
¾ cup (1½ sticks) unsalted butter, cold, cut into bits
4 cups buttermilk
4 large eggs
⅓ cup maple syrup
Melted butter for the griddle

BRUNCH UNDER THE EIDERDOWN

Foggy Morning Flapjacks
with
Whipped Butter and Beach Plum Jam
Sautéed Sausages

Rich Hot Chocolate

The Sunday New York Times

1. Process the oats in a blender or food processor fitted with the steel blade to a coarse powder. Mix the oats, whole-wheat flour, unbleached flour, cornmeal, baking powder, baking soda, and salt together in a large mixing bowl.

2. Using a pastry blender or your hands, work the butter into the dry ingredients until well blended.

3. Whisk the buttermilk, eggs, and maple syrup together in another bowl. Add to the flour mixture and stir until well blended. Let the batter stand for 5 minutes.

4. Heat a large griddle over medium heat. When hot, brush the surface with some of the melted butter.

5. Drop large spoonfuls of the batter onto the griddle to make pancakes 4 to 5 inches in diameter. When bubbles form on the top and the bottoms are light brown, flip them over and continue to cook until cooked through, about 2 minutes. Serve at once or keep them warm in a 275°F oven until all of the pancakes are cooked. (Leftover batter may be stored in the refrigerator in a covered plastic container for 2 to 3 days or frozen for up to 2 months.)

Makes 8 to 10 servings or about 24 pancakes.

Homemade Granola

When the granola craze first struck in the late sixties, my mother started to make her own, and it was better than any granola that I had ever tasted. I still believe it to be the best. I always have a huge bowl of freshly toasted granola in the store, and it sells well at any time of year. In the summer it is wonderful mixed with plain yogurt and fresh berries. In the chillier months a hearty bowl mixed with milk is a delicious and fortifying start to the day. Don't think that you have to be a "nuts-and-berries" health freak to enjoy this; the blend of ingredients makes this granola truly indulgent.

9 cups old-fashioned
   rolled oats
4 cups shredded coconut
1½ cups whole hazelnuts
1½ cups slivered or sliced
   almonds

¾ cup honey
1½ cups vegetable oil
1 cup golden raisins
1 cup dark raisins
½ cup chopped dates
   (optional)

1. Preheat the oven to 375°F.

2. Toss the oats, coconut, hazelnuts, and almonds together in a 13 x 9-inch baking pan.

3. Whisk the honey and oil together in a small bowl. Pour over the oat mixture and stir with a wooden spoon until all the oats and nuts are coated.

4. Bake, stirring occasionally with the wooden spoon, until the mixture turns a nice even golden brown, 35 to 45 minutes.

5. Remove the granola from the oven and stir constantly to aerate the mixture and keep it from sticking together, until the granola is cool. Stir in the golden and dark raisins and the dates, if using. Other diced fruits, such as apricots, figs, and prunes, can be added or substituted if you want. Store the granola in an airtight glass canister or tightly wrapped earthenware bowl.

Makes about 18 cups.

Savory Potato Pancakes

These crispy golden pancakes with subtle hints of onion and rosemary are delicious country fare when served with Rosy Applesauce and grilled sweet Italian sausage.

6 large boiling potatoes, peeled

2 shallots, minced

2 tablespoons minced fresh rosemary

2 tablespoons unbleached all-purpose flour

1 large egg, lightly beaten

4 tablespoons heavy or whipping cream

Salt and freshly ground pepper to taste

Vegetable oil for frying

Rosy Applesauce (recipe follows)

1. Grate the potatoes with a hand grater or in a food processor fitted with the large shredding disk. Place them in the center of a clean dish cloth and squeeze tightly to extract as much liquid as possible.

2. Place the potatoes in a large mixing bowl and toss with the shallots, rosemary, and flour. With a large spoon beat in the egg, cream, salt and pepper until well blended. Cook this mixture as quickly as possible or the potatoes will begin to discolor.

3. Preheat the oven to 300°F.

4. Brush a large flat skillet all over with a few tablespoons of oil and heat over medium-high heat. Using your hands, form the potato mixture into patties 3 inches in diameter and ½ inch thick.

5. Place as many pancakes as will comfortably fit in the skillet and fry until crusty and golden brown, 3 to 4 minutes per side. Repeat with the remaining batter, adding more oil to the skillet as needed.

6. Keep the pancakes warm in the oven until all are cooked. Serve 2 to 3 pancakes per person accompanied by the applesauce and sausage.

Makes 16 to 18 pancakes.

Rosy Applesauce

Homemade applesauce, especially served warm, is real security food for me. I like to make my applesauce from a blend of freshly picked orchard apples—McIntosh, Macoun, and Jonathan, for example. I also leave the skins on the apples while simmering because I love the rich rosy hue they bring to the finished product.

3 pounds of your favorite apples, cored, unpeeled, and cut into chunks
1½ cups water
3 tablespoons Calvados or other brandy
1 tablespoon fresh lemon juice
½ cup (packed) brown sugar
1 tablespoon ground cinnamon
½ teaspoon grated nutmeg

1. Combine the apples, water, Calvados, and lemon juice in a large heavy soup kettle. Bring just to a boil over medium-high heat, then reduce to a simmer. Cook uncovered until the apples are quite soft, about 40 minutes. Stir in the brown sugar, cinnamon, and nutmeg. Remove from heat.

2. Press the mixture through a food mill to purée and remove the skins. Taste for flavor and adjust the sugar and spices if necessary. Serve at once or store covered in the refrigerator until ready to use.

Makes about 2 quarts.

Chicken and Apple Hash with Cider Cream

A fancy and updated version of hash with a woodsy flavor that makes it the perfect dish for an autumn brunch.

*4 tablespoons (½ stick)
    unsalted butter
1 large red onion, chopped
½ cup diced (½-inch
    pieces) fennel or celery
2 Granny Smith apples,
    cored, unpeeled, and
    thinly sliced*

*4 whole boneless, skinless
    chicken breasts,
    poached just until
    barely cooked (see
    Index)
2 cups cooked wild rice*

CIDER CREAM:
*4 tablespoons (½ stick)
    unsalted butter
2 tablespoons unbleached
    all-purpose flour
2 cups apple cider
3 tablespoons heavy or
    whipping cream*

*1 teaspoon ground coriander
½ teaspoon grated nutmeg
Salt and freshly ground
    pepper to taste*

1. Preheat the oven to 350°F. Butter a 12 x 9-inch casserole.

2. Melt the butter in a medium skillet over medium-high heat. Add the onion, fennel or celery, and apple slices and sauté, stirring occasionally, for 10 minutes. Remove from the heat and transfer to a medium mixing bowl.

3. Cut the chicken into irregular chunks, about ½ to 1 inch in size. Add them to the mixing bowl. Stir in the wild rice to blend.

4. Prepare the cider cream: Melt the butter in a medium saucepan over medium heat. Whisk in the flour and cook, stirring constantly, for 1 minute. Gradually whisk in the cider ½ cup at a time, whisking until smooth and thickened after each addition. When all of the cider has been added, whisk in the cream. Reduce the heat to low and continue to cook, stirring occasionally, for 10 minutes more. The sauce should be the consistency of a medium béchamel. Season with the coriander, nutmeg, salt and pepper. Remove from the heat.

5. Combine the cider cream with the chicken mixture, blending well. Transfer the mixture to the casserole. Bake just until the

hash is heated throughout, 20 to 25 minutes. Serve at once accompanied by a basket of your favorite breakfast breads.
    Makes 8 servings.

Breakfast Scallops

This dish is assembled the night before, so that you can wake up to an indulgent breakfast treat that tastes like a rich seafood quiche without the crust.

Butter for the baking pan
3 cups stale French bread
    cubes
1 pound fresh bay
    scallops
12 large eggs
½ cup heavy or whipping
    cream

2 teaspoons dried
    tarragon
Salt and freshly ground
    pepper to taste
10 ounces Cheddar
    cheese, shredded
2 teaspoons paprika

1. Coat an 11 x 8-inch baking pan with butter. Spread the cubed bread in the pan, then sprinkle the scallops evenly among the bread cubes.
    2. Beat the eggs, cream, tarragon, salt, and pepper together in a large bowl and pour over the bread and scallops. Sprinkle the Cheddar over the top, then sprinkle with the paprika. Cover the pan with plastic wrap and refrigerate overnight.

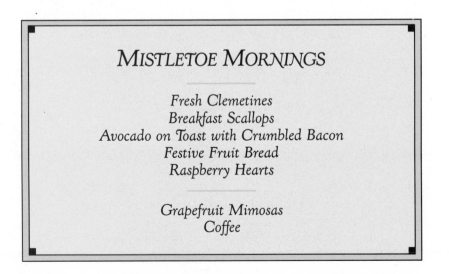

MISTLETOE MORNINGS

Fresh Clemetines
Breakfast Scallops
Avocado on Toast with Crumbled Bacon
Festive Fruit Bread
Raspberry Hearts

Grapefruit Mimosas
Coffee

3. The next morning, preheat the oven to 350°F.

4. Bake the scallop casserole for 30 minutes. Heat the broiler and broil the casserole 6 inches from the heat for 5 minutes. Serve hot.

Makes 6 to 8 servings.

Unbeatable Scrambled Eggs

Late one morning I was sitting in Harry's Bar in Venice. While I knew that in the true spirit of culinary adventure I should have been ordering cuttlefish in its own ink, I really craved the basic comfort of scrambled eggs. Their eggs were absolutely the most memorable I have ever eaten. The following recipe is my attempt to approximate Harry's eggs.

8 large eggs
3 ounces Montrachet
  goat cheese without
  ash, at room
  temperature
Salt and freshly ground
  pepper to taste

6 tablespoons (¾ stick)
  unsalted butter
2 tablespoons snipped
  fresh chives

1. Place a strainer over a medium mixing bowl. Break the eggs into the strainer and push them through, using the back of a wooden spoon. Add the goat cheese and push it through the strainer in the same manner. Whisk the eggs and cheese together and season to taste with salt and pepper.

2. The secret to making ever-so-creamy eggs is to cook them in a double boiler. Melt the butter in the top of a double boiler over simmering water.

3. When the butter is completely melted, add the egg mixture. Cook slowly over the simmering (not boiling) water, stirring constantly, especially around the sides, with a rubber spatula. Cook until the eggs are set as desired, 10 to 15 minutes. Stir in the chives.

4. Spoon the eggs onto 4 warmed plates and serve at once. If yo wish to be a touch more decadent, top each serving with a dollop of crème fraîche and a spoonful of good caviar.

Makes 4 servings.

Thanksgiving by the Sea

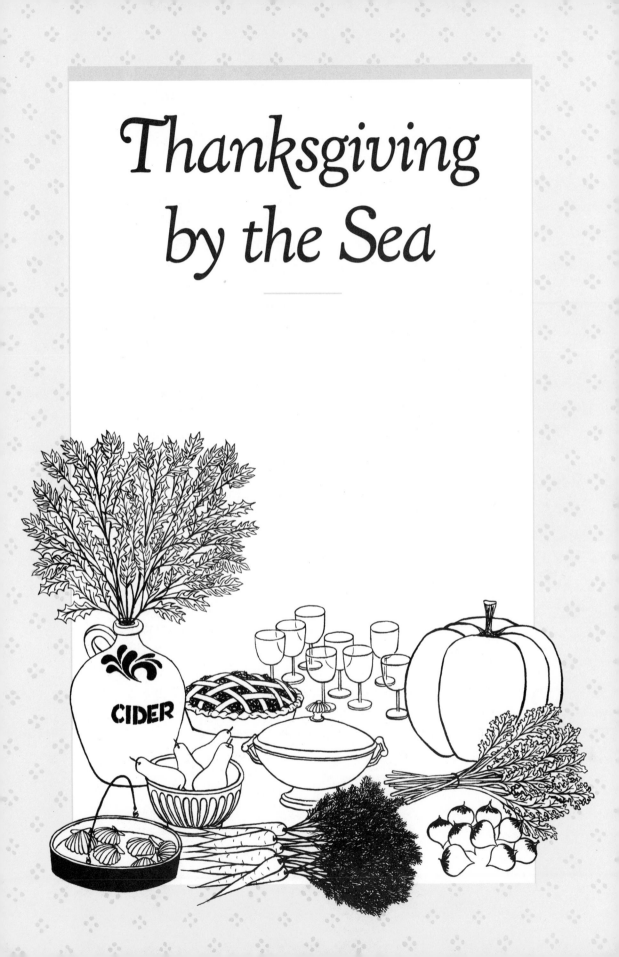

Savoring Thanksgiving on Nantucket is almost like going back in time to the Pilgrims' first Thanksgiving celebration at Plymouth Rock. Faded along with the autumn foliage and crimson moors are the sophisticated flourishes of the summer tourists as the island returns to the somber but cozy gray of its Quaker heritage. The raw, damp chill of the ocean is everywhere—piercing with a reminding shiver of what it must have been like in settlement days and sending the islanders scurrying back to their old sea-captain's houses to snuggle around eighteenth-century fireplaces.

Local scallopers fill the harbor at dawn every day as perfect testimony to Nantucket's ongoing reliance upon the bounty of the sea, while, at the stand on Main Street, salt-misted Brussels sprouts still on the stalk, turnips, kale, and cranberries signal the end of the farm season. A few of the more rugged summer residents return to brave one last family weekend in their un-heated cottages and mingle summer memories of easy living with struggles of contracting the local plumber and carpenter to drain the pipes and batten the shutters for winter. Yet, for all those that share in the experience of Thanksgiving on Nantucket, there is an overwhelm-ing sense of appreciation for the island's preservation of the best of Americana and its endowment of natural beauty. Indeed, the Thanksgiving meal is just one small token of all there is to be thankful for on the Atlantic-splashed shores of this special community.

Nantucket Scallop Bisque

This soup fulfills the platonic ideal of a perfect shellfish bisque. It is soothing, rich, and creamy and just a bit extravagant with its plentiful scallops and frail little wisps of saffron.

STOCK:

4 cups water
2 cups dry white wine
1 medium onion, sliced
2 carrots, sliced
2 cloves garlic, crushed
6 black peppercorns
2 sprigs parsley
1 teaspoon best-quality curry powder
1 teaspoon dried thyme
1 teaspoon fennel seeds

1¼ pounds fresh bay scallops
4 tablespoons (½ stick) unsalted butter
¼ cup unbleached all-purpose flour
2½ cups milk
½ cup dry white wine
1 cup heavy or whipping cream
1 teaspoon saffron threads
3 tablespoons Pernod
2 large egg yolks
Salt and freshly ground white pepper to taste

1. Place all the stock ingredients in a small stockpot and simmer uncovered for 20 minutes. Strain the stock, pressing the vegetables with the back of a spoon to extract as much liquid as possible. Discard the solids.

2. Return the stock to the pot and heat to a low boil. Add the bay scallops and poach just for 1 minute. Remove the scallops from the stock and reserve the scallops and the stock separately.

3. Melt the butter in a large pot over medium-high heat. Whisk in the flour and cook, stirring constantly, for 1 minute. Gradually add the stock, whisking until perfectly smooth. Whisk in the milk, wine, and ½ cup of the cream. Simmer uncovered, stirring occasionally, for 10 minutes.

4. Stir the saffron and Pernod into the soup. Whisk the remaining ½ cup cream and 2 egg yolks together in a small bowl. Gradually whisk ¾ cup of the hot soup into the egg yolk mixture. Whisk the mixture back into the soup. Be careful not to let the soup come to a boil from this point on, or it will curdle. Season the soup to taste with salt and white pepper. Return the scallops to the soup and heat through. Serve hot in small portions.

Makes 2 quarts.

Broiled Oysters with Cider Sabayon

When celebrating Thanksgiving in a seaside community, I believe one should pay homage to the bounty of the ocean in some form or another. These oysters are a rich and elegant way to begin the Thanksgiving festivities. I suggest serving each guest only one or two by a roaring fire just to tempt the appetite.

1 small white onion, minced
1 tablespoon cider vinegar
¾ cup plus 2 tablespoons apple cider
6 tablespoons (¾ stick) unsalted butter, cut into small pieces

3 tablespoons heavy or whipping cream
Salt and freshly ground pepper to taste
2 large egg yolks
18 fresh oysters on the half-shell
Sliced apples, for garnish

1. First, make the cider sabayon: Place the onion, vinegar, and ¾ cup cider in a small saucepan. Heat to boiling and continue to boil until just 1 tablespoon liquid remains. Whisk in the butter, 1 piece at a time, over the lowest possible heat. (The butter must emulsify the mixture rather than melt into it.) When all the butter has been added, whisk in the cream and season to taste with salt and pepper.

2. Whisk the egg yolks and remaining 2 tablespoons cider together in the top of a double boiler. Set the pan over simmering water and whisk constantly until the mixture is light, frothy, and doubled in volume, 3 to 4 minutes. Gently whisk into the butter mixture.

3. Preheat the broiler and arrange the rack or broiler pan 6 inches from the heat.

4. Place the oysters on a sturdy baking sheet. Spoon about 1½ tablespoons of the cider sabayon over each oyster. Broil the oysters until puffed and lightly browned, 3 to 4 minutes. Serve on small plates, garnished with a few apple slices, with cocktail forks.

Makes 18 oysters.

The Thanksgiving Menu

At Que Sera Sarah, we prepare everything for Thanksgiving except the turkey. Roast turkey just doesn't travel well, and the real pleasure of Thanksgiving is filling your own home for an entire day with the aroma of the bird as it cooks. The following is typical of the turkey accessories that the shop offers each year.

THANKSGIVING BY THE SEA

Nantucket Scallop Bisque
Broiled Oysters with Cider Sabayon
Harvest Crudités
Bay Scallop Gougère
Pumpkin Biscuits with Smoked Pheasant
and Beach Plum Jam

Cranberry-Orange Anadama Rolls
Savory Sausage-Apricot Stuffing

Shredded Brussels Sprouts with Prosciutto and Parmesan
Casserole of Sweet Potatoes and Pears
Classic Creamed Onions
Baked Julienne of Potatoes and Celeriac
Glazed Parsnips and Carrots
Whipped Turnips with Bacon and Caraway

Cranberry-Kumquat Relish
Confit of Cranberries, Figs, and Baby Onions

Deep-Dish Cranberry-Cassis Pie
Southern Pecan Pie
Golden Delicious Apple Tart
Pear and Parsnip Pie
Pumpkin Mousse

Harvest Crudités

It is traditional for many to serve celery sticks, carrot sticks, and olives before the big Thanksgiving feast. This recipe refines that notion with the inclusion of the warm Italian dipping sauce known as bagna cauda—my version is enriched with nutty ground hazelnuts.

HAZELNUT BAGNA CAUDA:

1 cup heavy or whipping cream

2 slices white bread, crusts removed

6 cloves garlic, peeled

8 anchovy fillets, drained

2 teaspoons grated lemon zest

⅔ cup hazelnuts, lightly toasted and skinned

½ cup light olive oil or hazelnut oil

4 tablespoons (½ stick) unsalted butter

1 cup light cream (see Index)

A pleasing assortment of autumn vegetables, cut for crudités, such as baby carrots, blanched Brussels sprouts, thinly sliced purple turnips, parsnip sticks, radicchio leaves, fresh wild mushrooms, and red and yellow bell pepper strips

1. Prepare the bagna cauda: Pour ¼ cup of the heavy cream over the bread in a small bowl. Let stand for 5 minutes, then wring out any excess liquid by squeezing the bread with your hands.

2. Place the bread, garlic, anchovies, lemon zest, and hazelnuts in a food processor fitted with the steel blade; process to a *very* smooth paste. With the machine running, pour the oil in a thin, steady stream through the feed tube; continue to process until well blended.

3. Melt the butter in a medium saucepan over low heat. Gradually whisk in the hazelnut purée. Cook, stirring constantly, over low heat for 5 minutes. Gradually whisk in the remaining ¾ cup heavy cream and the light cream. Be careful not to let the mixture boil or it will curdle. When the mixture is creamy and thick, transfer it to a heatproof serving bowl or chafing dish. Serve warm surrounded by the crudités.

Makes about 2½ cups dipping sauce.

Bay Scallop Gougère

This dramatic appetizer is a happy blending of the classic French gougère and some New England ingenuity.

GOUGERE DOUGH:

½ cup (1 stick) unsalted butter

2 cups milk

2 cups unbleached all-purpose flour

8 large eggs

2 cups Gruyère or Italian Fontina, cut into ¼-inch dice

1 tablespoon grainy mustard

1 teaspoon salt

1 teaspoon freshly ground pepper

FILLING:

4 tablespoons (½ stick) unsalted butter

1½ pounds bay scallops

1 medium red onion, chopped

½ cup tarragon vinegar

1 cup heavy or whipping cream

2 tablespoons Dijon mustard

1 tablespoon grainy mustard

2 tablespoons medium-dry sherry

Salt and freshly ground pepper to taste

1 cup grated Gruyère or Italian Fontina

1. The day before serving, prepare the gougère dough: Heat the butter and milk in a medium saucepan to boiling. Remove from the heat. Add the flour and stir until the mixture is smooth and cleans the side of the pan. Add the eggs, one at a time, beating well after each addition. Stir in the cheese, mustard, salt, and pepper. Cook, stirring constantly, over low heat just until the cheese melts.

2. Butter a 15 x 10-inch baking sheet. Spread the dough over the entire sheet, building up the sides and leaving just a thin layer of dough in the middle. Cover tightly with plastic wrap and refrigerate overnight.

3. The next day, prepare the filling: Melt the butter in a large skillet over medium-high heat. Add the scallops and sauté for just 1 minute. Remove the scallops with a slotted spoon and set aside.

4. Add the onion to the skillet and sauté for 2 minutes. Pour in the vinegar and heat until just 1 tablespoon remains. Pour in the cream, then stir in the mustards and sherry. Season with salt and pepper to taste. Continue to cook until the mixture is quite thick and reduced by about half. Remove from the heat and stir in the scallops.

5. Preheat the oven to 400°F.

6. Remove the gougère dough from the refrigerator. Spread the scallop mixture evenly over the dough. Sprinkle the grated cheese evenly over all. Bake the scallop gougère until puffed and golden brown, 40 to 45 minutes.

7. Let cool several minutes, then cut into bite-size squares and pass with cocktails.

Makes 10 to 12 servings.

Pumpkin Biscuits

When I make these biscuits for Thanksgiving, I like to cut them out with a pineapple-shaped cookie cutter. I then split them in half and fill them with a dab of the local Beach Plum Jam (see Index) and slivers of smoked pheasant. Both the jam and the pheasant celebrate Nantucket's native bounty, but feel free to make substitutions. The unadorned biscuits also make a nice addition to the Thanksgiving bread basket.

2½ cups unbleached
  all-purpose flour
1 tablespoon baking
  powder
1 teaspoon salt
2½ tablespoons brown
  sugar
½ cup (1 stick) unsalted
  butter, cold, cut into
  small bits

1 can (15 ounces)
  unsweetened pumpkin
  purée
2 teaspoons grated orange
  zest
2 tablespoons heavy or
  whipping cream

1. Preheat the oven to 400°F. Butter baking sheets.

2. Sift the flour, baking powder, salt, and brown sugar into a mixing bowl. Using a pastry blender, cut in the butter until the mixture resembles very coarse meal.

3. Stir in the pumpkin and orange zest to make a soft dough.

4. With floured hands and working on a well-floured surface, pat the biscuit dough ½ inch thick. Cut out using a floured decorative 2-inch cutter. Place the biscuits on the prepared baking sheets. Gather the scraps of dough, pat out ½ inch thick, and cut out as many biscuits as possible.

5. Using a pastry brush, brush the tops of the biscuits lightly with cream. Bake just until lightly browned, about 15 minutes.

Makes about 36 biscuits.

Cranberry-Orange Anadama Rolls

A few delicious liberties have been taken with this favorite old New England recipe. Lush ruby-colored cranberries abound in the bogs of Cape Cod and Nantucket throughout the fall and I can never resist tucking the berries into as many recipes as possible.

1½ cups cranberry juice
½ cup yellow cornmeal, plus additional for sprinkling the rolls
4 tablespoons (½ stick) unsalted butter, at room temperature
⅓ cup plus 2 tablespoons dark molasses
1 teaspoon salt
1 package (¼ ounce) active dry yeast

½ cup warm water
1 cup whole-wheat flour
2½ cups fresh cranberries
Finely chopped zest of 1 orange
4 to 5 cups unbleached all-purpose flour
1 large egg
1 tablespoon water

1. Heat the cranberry juice in a small saucepan to just below boiling and gradually stir in ½ cup cornmeal. Reduce the heat to low and stir the mixture constantly with a wooden spoon until the mixture is as thick and smooth as porridge, 5 to 7 minutes. Remove from the heat.

2. Immediately add the butter and stir until melted. Stir in ⅓ cup molasses and the salt. Let cool to room temperature.

3. Meanwhile, sprinkle the yeast over the warm water in a large bowl and let stand for 10 minutes. Stir in the whole-wheat flour and the cooled cornmeal mixture.

4. Place the cranberries, orange zest, and remaining 2 tablespoons molasses in a food processor fitted with the steel blade; process with on/off pulses just until the cranberries are coarsely chopped. Add the cranberry mixture to the dough and stir until thoroughly mixed.

5. If you have a heavy-duty mixer with a dough hook, place the dough in the mixer bowl and mix in the all-purpose flour. Or you may mix in the all-purpose flour, 1 cup at a time, using a wooden spoon and later your hands when the dough is too stiff to stir. The dough should be soft and pliable. Knead the dough on a lightly floured surface until smooth and elastic, about 10 minutes by hand. Shape the dough into a ball, place it in a buttered bowl, and turn the buttered side up. Cover loosely with plastic wrap and let rise in a warm spot until doubled in bulk, about 1½ hours.

6. Punch the dough down and turn out onto a lightly floured surface. Shape the dough into round rolls, about 3 inches in diameter. Place 2 inches apart on lightly greased baking sheets.

7. Cover the rolls loosely with dampened towels and let rise again until doubled in bulk, 30 to 45 minutes.

8. Preheat the oven to 375°F.

9. Beat the egg and water together and brush over the rolls. Sprinkle the tops lightly with cornmeal. Bake the rolls until golden brown, about 20 minutes. Serve warm with butter.

Makes 20 rolls.

Savory Apricot-Sausage Stuffing

Stuffing is my very favorite part of Thanksgiving. I love to make it and adore eating it even more. I have been known to sneak a little home a few days before Thanksgiving to relish in a dinner composed entirely of baked stuffing and a few flutes of chilled Champagne. You'll find that this recipe makes plenty of delectable stuffing for both a bit of private indulgence and the main event.

3 cups diced dried
  apricots
½ cup amaretto liqueur
1 cup Cognac or brandy
1½ cups (3 sticks)
  unsalted butter
1 very large yellow onion,
  chopped
1 bunch scallions, white
  bulbs and green stalks,
  sliced
6 ribs celery, coarsely
  chopped
1½ pounds Pepperidge
  Farm's herb stuffing
  crumbs

1 pound sweet Italian
  sausage, casings
  removed
12 ounces bulk pork
  sausage
2 cups chestnuts, peeled
  and coarsely chopped
1 ripe pear, cored and
  diced
3 tablespoons chopped
  fresh rosemary or 1
  tablespoon dried
3½ cups chicken stock,
  preferably homemade
Salt and freshly ground
  pepper to taste

1. Soak the apricots in the amaretto and ½ cup of the Cognac for 2 hours.

2. Melt ¾ cup of the butter in a large sauté pan or skillet over medium-high heat. Add the onion, scallions, and celery and cook, stirring occasionally, for 10 minutes. Transfer to a large mixing bowl and toss with the stuffing crumbs.

3. Add the Italian and bulk sausage to the same pan and cook, crumbling the meat with a fork or the back of a large spoon, over medium-high heat until the meat is no longer pink. Add the meat to the stuffing mixture and stir to combine.

4. Add the chestnuts, pear, and rosemary to the stuffing and toss to combine. Stir in the apricots with the liquid.

5. Heat the remaining ¾ cup butter with the chicken stock in a saucepan just until the butter is completely melted. Pour the butter mixture and the remaining ½ cup Cognac over the stuffing mixture. Mix the stuffing well and season to taste with salt and pepper.

6. Store the stuffing in the refrigerator until ready to cook the turkey. Any stuffing that won't fit in the bird can be placed in a buttered casserole and baked at 350°F for 40 minutes.

Makes enough to stuff a 22- to 24-pound turkey.

Shredded Brussels Sprouts with Prosciutto and Parmesan

This is an outrageously rich preparation for Brussels sprouts that can also be served solo as a luncheon entrée.

½ cup (1 stick) unsalted
   butter
6 cloves garlic, minced
4 ounces thinly sliced
   prosciutto, cut into
   thin slivers
2 pounds Brussels
   sprouts, trimmed and
   shredded by cutting
   each into several thin
   slices
3 tablespoons all-purpose
   flour

1½ cups heavy or
   whipping cream
1 cup light cream (see
   Index)
¼ cup sweet Marsala
1 teaspoon grated nutmeg
Salt and freshly ground
   pepper to taste
1½ cups freshly grated
   Parmesan cheese

1. Preheat the oven to 350°F.

2. Melt the butter in a large sauté pan or skillet over medium-high heat. Add the garlic and the prosciutto and cook, tossing with a spoon, for 4 minutes.

3. Add the Brussels sprouts and continue to cook, tossing constantly, for another 4 minutes. Stir in the flour and toss to coat the Brussels sprouts.

4. Gradually stir in the heavy cream, light cream, and Marsala. Reduce the heat and simmer until the Brussels sprouts are just barely tender, about 5 minutes. Add the nutmeg and season to taste with salt and pepper. Stir in 1 cup of the Parmesan and cook just until the cheese is melted. Remove from the heat. (You can prepare the gratin to this point the day before you are serving it and refrigerate covered overnight. Bring the gratin to room temperature before baking.)

5. Transfer the mixture to a shallow 9-inch-square gratin dish. Top with the remaining ½ cup Parmesan. Bake the gratin until bubbly and the top is slightly browned, about 20 minutes. Serve hot.

Makes 10 to 12 servings.

Casserole of Sweet Potatoes and Pears

A successful combination that celebrates autumn in color and flavor.

6 large sweet potatoes,
    peeled and sliced ½
    inch thick
6 ripe pears, peeled,
    cored, and cut into 8
    wedges each
⅓ cup pear brandy

½ cup orange juice
¾ cup (packed) brown
    sugar
4 tablespoons (½ stick)
    unsalted butter
½ cup golden raisins
Salt to taste

1. Place the sweet potato slices in a pot and add water to cover. Heat to boiling. Reduce the heat and simmer uncovered just until barely tender, 12 to 15 minutes. Drain well.

2. Preheat the oven to 375°F.

3. Arrange the sweet potatoes and pears in alternate layers in a medium-size casserole.

4. Combine the pear brandy, orange juice, brown sugar, butter, and raisins in a small saucepan. Heat over medium heat until the sugar is dissolved and the butter melted. Season with a little salt. Pour the sauce over the sweet potatoes and pears, stirring to distribute evenly.

5. Bake the casserole until lightly browned and bubbly, about 30 minutes. Serve hot.

Makes 10 to 12 servings.

Classic Creamed Onions

Creamed onions are definitely one of the more time-consuming dishes to make at Thanksgiving, but I think the results are well worth the somewhat tearful labor.

3 pounds small white
   onions, peeled
1½ cups water, plus
   additional if needed

1 cup dry white wine
4 tablespoons (½ stick)
   unsalted butter

BECHAMEL:
4 tablespoons (½ stick)
   unsalted butter
¼ cup unbleached
   all-purpose flour
1 cup cooking liquid from
   the onions
1 cup milk
½ cup heavy or whipping cream

1 tablespoon chopped
   fresh tarragon or
   2 teaspoons dried
Pinch grated nutmeg
Salt and freshly ground
   pepper to taste

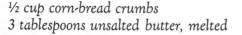

½ cup corn-bread crumbs
3 tablespoons unsalted butter, melted

1. Drop the onions into a large pot of boiling water and blanch for 1 minute. Drain, cool, and slip off the skins.

2. Place the onions in a medium saucepan and add the water, wine, and butter. Heat to boiling. Reduce the heat and simmer uncovered, stirring occasionally, until just barely tender, 15 to 20 minutes. Add more water if needed during cooking. Drain the onions, reserving 1 cup of the cooking liquid.

3. Prepare the béchamel: Melt the butter in a small saucepan over medium heat. Whisk in the flour and cook, stirring constantly, until the mixture turns light golden, about 2 minutes. Gradually whisk in the cooking liquid to make a thick and smooth sauce. Then gradually whisk in the milk and cream to make a smooth sauce. Season with the tarragon, nutmeg, salt, and pepper. Simmer, stirring occasionally, over low heat to allow the flavors to blend, 10 to 15 minutes.

4. Preheat the oven to 350°F.

5. Combine the béchamel and onions and transfer to a buttered gratin dish large enough to hold the onions in a single layer. Mix the corn-bread crumbs with the melted butter and sprinkle evenly over the dish. (You can prepare the creamed onions to this point the day before you are serving them and refrigerate covered overnight. Bring the onions to room temperature before baking.)

6. Bake the onions until the sauce begins to bubble and the onions are heated through, 20 to 25 minutes. Serve hot.

Makes 12 servings.

Baked Julienne of Potatoes and Celeriac

This is one of my favorite vegetable combinations baked into an irresistible looking and tasting gratin. The dish contrasts nicely with the traditional Thanksgiving vegetable purées.

4 large boiling potatoes, peeled and cut into thin julienne strips
3½ cups julienned celeriac, canned or fresh
1 medium onion, chopped
3 large eggs
1 cup heavy or whipping cream

1 cup milk
5 ounces St. André cheese
1 teaspoon celery seeds
Salt and freshly ground pepper to taste
4 tablespoons (½ stick) unsalted butter, melted

1. Preheat the oven to 375°F.

2. Place the julienned potatoes and celeriac in a clean kitchen towel and squeeze out as much moisture as possible. Toss the potatoes, celeriac and onion together in a mixing bowl.

3. Beat the eggs, cream, milk, and cheese in a small bowl until smooth. Season with the celery seeds, salt, and pepper.

4. Coat the bottom of a large gratin dish with the melted butter. Spread the potato, celeriac, and onion mixture evenly in the dish and pour the egg mixture evenly over all.

5. Bake the gratin until the vegetables are tender and the top is crusty and brown, 55 to 60 minutes. Let cool several minutes, then serve.

Makes 10 to 12 servings.

Glazed Parsnips and Carrots

This simple vegetable preparation exudes the colors and flavors of autumn harvest. I like to make it with a choice friend's native Nantucket honey.

1 pound thin parsnips, peeled and cut lengthwise in half	2 tablespoons fresh orange juice
12 ounces baby carrots, peeled and trimmed	3 tablespoons honey
3 tablespoons unsalted butter	1 teaspoon best-quality curry powder
	Salt and freshly ground pepper to taste

1. Preheat the oven to 400°F.

2. Cook the parsnips and carrots separately in boiling water to cover just until barely tender, about 8 minutes for the parsnips and 10 to 12 minutes for the carrots. Drain the vegetables well and combine them in a shallow gratin dish.

3. Melt the butter in a small saucepan. Stir in the orange juice, honey, and curry powder. Heat to boiling, then pour the mixture over the parsnips and carrots. Sprinkle with salt and pepper to taste.

4. Bake the vegetables until lightly glazed, 15 to 20 minutes. Serve hot.

Makes 8 to 10 servings.

Whipped Turnips with Bacon and Caraway

Of the many aromas of Thanksgiving, the smell of turnips cooking is my very favorite. My aunt invented this savory turnip combination and has served it at every one of the splendid Thanskgiving dinners I have shared in at her old sea-captain's house on Nantucket.

4 pounds yellow turnips (rutabagas), peeled and cut into 2-inch chunks	1 teaspoon sugar
	Salt and freshly ground pepper to taste
4 tablespoons (½ stick) unsalted butter	8 slices bacon, cooked crisp and drained
½ cup sour cream	Paprika
2 teaspoons caraway seeds	

1. Preheat the oven to 350°F. Butter a 13 x 11-inch gratin dish.

2. Place the turnips in a pot and add water to cover. Heat to boiling over high heat. Reduce the heat and simmer until very tender, 25 to 30 minutes. Drain the turnips well and place in a mixing bowl.

3. Beat the turnips with an electric mixer. Add the butter and sour cream and beat until the mixture is fluffy but still retains some texture. Beat in the caraway seeds and sugar, then season to taste with salt and pepper.

4. Transfer the mixture to the prepared dish. Chop the bacon into small pieces and sprinkle over the top of the casserole. Sprinkle lightly with paprika. (The casserole can be stored in the refrigerator at this point. Warm to room temperature before baking.) Bake the casserole until heated through, about 20 minutes. Serve hot.

Makes 10 to 12 servings.

Cranberry-Kumquat Relish

This unusual rendition of Thanksgiving relish keeps in the refrigerator for at least two weeks. Once the turkey has disappeared, the relish makes for a refreshing surprise tucked into sandwiches or served as a condiment with roast pork, lamb, or turkey.

2 packages (12 ounces each) fresh cranberries
1 orange
1 lemon
½ cup granulated sugar
½ cup (packed) brown sugar

10 bottled or fresh kumquats, seeded and diced
⅓ cup pine nuts, lightly toasted
⅓ cup cranberry liqueur

1. Place the cranberries in a food processor fitted with the steel blade; process with on/off pulses just until very coarsely chopped. Be careful not to overprocess the cranberries. Transfer to a mixing bowl.

2. Seed both the lemon and orange and cut into small chunks. Process in the food processor until finely diced. Add to the cranberries. Add both sugars and stir until thoroughly mixed.

3. Return about one-third of the cranberry mixture to the food processor and process until finely minced. Stir into the remaining mixture in the bowl.

4. Stir in the kumquats, pine nuts, and liqueur. Refrigerate the relish several hours to allow the flavors to mellow and blend.

Makes about 2 quarts.

Confit of Cranberries, Figs, and Baby Onions

A delicious and unusual mélange to serve in place of or, better yet, in addition to traditional cranberry relish.

8 ounces dried figs,
    quartered
1 cup boiling water
5 tablespoons unsalted
    butter
2 dozen small white
    onions (about 1 inch
    in diameter), blanched
    in boiling water 1
    minute, trimmed, and
    peeled

¼ cup sugar
4 tablespoons balsamic
    vinegar
2 cups dry white wine
1 package (12 ounces)
    fresh cranberries

1. Soak the figs in boiling water in a small bowl for 15 minutes.

2. Melt the butter in a heavy saucepan over medium-high heat. Add the onions and stir to coat with butter. Stir in the sugar and 1 tablespoon of the vinegar. Cook, stirring constantly, just until the sugar caramelizes, about 2 minutes.

3. Stir in the remaining 3 tablespoons vinegar, 1 cup of the wine, and the figs with liquid. Heat to boiling. Reduce the heat to low and simmer, stirring occasionally, for 30 minutes. Stir in another ½ cup wine and cook 15 minutes longer.

4. Stir in the cranberries and the remaining ½ cup wine. Simmer, stirring occasionally, for 25 minutes. Let cool to room temperature before serving. The confit can be stored in the refrigerator; let warm to room temperature before serving.

Makes about 1 quart.

Deep-Dish Cranberry-Cassis Pie

The affinity of flavors in this pie makes it a most fitting conclusion to a day of Thanksgiving delights.

CRUST:

2½ cups unbleached
   all-purpose flour
5 tablespoons (packed)
   brown sugar
1 tablespoon ground
   ginger
Pinch salt
6 tablespoons (¾ stick)
   unsalted butter, cold,
   cut into small pieces

6 tablespoons unsalted
   margarine, cold, cut
   into small pieces
4 to 5 tablespoons apple
   cider, cold

FILLING:

8 cups fresh cranberries
Grated zest of 2 oranges
1 cup cassis liqueur
½ cup Grand Marnier
1¾ cups granulated
   sugar

⅓ cup cornstarch
½ cup minced candied
   ginger
1 large egg
1 tablespoon water

1. One day before you plan to serve the pie, make the crust and marinate the filling. For the crust: Place the flour, brown sugar, ginger, salt, butter, and margarine in a food processor fitted with the steel blade; process until the mixture resembles coarse meal. With the machine running, pour the cider through the feed tube and process just until the mixture begins to form a ball. Wrap in plastic wrap and refrigerate overnight.

2. Marinate the filling: Place the cranberries in a large bowl. Add the orange zest, cassis, and Grand Marnier and toss to combine. Cover and let marinate at room temperature overnight.

3. The next day, drain the liquid from the cranberries into a medium saucepan. Stir in the sugar and cornstarch. Heat, stirring constantly, over medium-high heat until thick and translucent. Pour the sauce over the cranberries and stir in the candied ginger.

4. Preheat the oven to 350°F.

5. Divide the dough in half. Roll out one-half into an 11-inch circle on a lightly floured surface. Line a 9-inch pie pan with the

dough; trim and crimp the edges decoratively. Pour the cranberry filling into the pie shell.

6. Roll out the remaining dough ⅛ inch thick. Cut into ½-inch-wide strips and arrange in a lattice pattern on the top of the pie. Trim the edges. Beat the egg and water in a small bowl and brush over the pastry. Place the pan on a baking sheet to catch any drips.

7. Bake the pie until the crust is golden brown and the filling is bubbling, 50 to 60 minutes. Let cool to room temperature before serving.

Makes 8 servings.

Southern Pecan Pie

My family recipe for this traditional American dessert.

Pastry for 9-inch pie shell
(see Lemon Chiffon Pie
in Index)
½ cup unsalted butter, at
room temperature
½ cup sugar
¾ cup light corn syrup
¼ cup honey

3 large eggs, lightly
beaten
1 teaspoon vanilla extract
1 cup coarsely chopped
pecans
1 cup pecan halves
Whipped cream for
serving

1. Line a 9-inch pie plate with the pastry; trim and crimp the edges decoratively. Refrigerate the pie shell while preparing the filling.

2. Preheat the oven to 350°F.

3. Using an electric mixer, cream the butter and sugar in a mixing bowl. Beat in the corn syrup and honey, then beat in the eggs and vanilla. Stir in the pecan pieces.

4. Pour the mixture into the pie shell. Arrange the pecan halves in concentric circles over the filling.

5. Bake the pie until the top is golden brown and firm when lightly pressed in the center, about 55 minutes. Serve accompanied by a bowl of whipped cream.

Makes 8 to 10 servings.

Golden Delicious Apple Tart

T his tart always wins rave reviews. It has the look of the most exquisite of French pastries and the homey flavor of old-fashioned American pie. I like to serve it for dessert after the sumptuous Thanksgiving repast because it is lighter than most traditional desserts.

CRUST:

6 tablespoons (¾ stick) unsalted butter, cold, cut into small pieces
1 cup unbleached all-purpose flour

2 tablespoons sugar
2 tablespoons (or as needed) cold water

FILLING:

5 Golden Delicious apples
5 tablespoons sugar
4 tablespoons (½ stick) unsalted butter

Pinch ground cinnamon
1½ tablespoons Calvados

GLAZE:

3 tablespoons apricot jam   1 tablespoon water

1. Prepare the crust: Place the butter, flour, and sugar in a food processor fitted with the steel blade; process just until the mixture resembles coarse meal. With the machine running, pour enough cold water through the feed tube to form a dough. Wrap in plastic wrap and refrigerate at least 1 hour.

2. Roll out the dough into a 10½-inch circle on a lightly floured surface. Line a 9-inch tart pan with a removable bottom with the dough; trim and crimp the edges decoratively. Place the tart pan in the freezer while making the filling.

3. Prepare the filling: Peel the apples, then cut them in half from top to bottom. Core the apple halves. Place 1 half flat on a cutting board and cut into thin slices without separating the slices. Maintain the shape of the apple half as best you can. Repeat with the remaining apples.

4. Preheat the oven to 375°F.

5. Remove the tart shell from the freezer and arrange the apples inside by fanning each half from the outer edge of the shell toward the center. Fill any gaps with extra apple slices. The tart should look like one big flower blossom.

6. Sprinkle the sugar evenly over the apple slices and dot with the butter. Sprinkle with cinnamon and the Calvados.

7. Bake the tart until light golden brown, about 45 minutes.

8. While the tart is baking, heat the apricot jam and the water in a small pan until the jam is melted. Brush the glaze evenly over the baked warm apple tart. Serve the tart warm or at room temperature.

Makes 6 to 8 servings.

Pear and Parsnip Pie

I prefer the delicate flavor of this custardy pie to the more traditional pumpkin pie.

Pastry for 9-inch pie shell
  (see Lemon Chiffon Pie
  in Index)
5 cups sliced peeled
  parsnips
2 tablespoons unsalted
  butter
2 ripe large Anjou pears,
  peeled and diced
3 tablespoons Calvados
4 large eggs
½ cup honey
½ cup (packed) brown
  sugar

⅔ cup heavy or whipping
  cream
1 tablespoon ground
  ginger
2 teaspoons ground
  cinnamon
½ teaspoon grated
  nutmeg
Whipped cream flavored
  with several
  tablespoons Poire
  Williams or other pear
  brandy (optional)

1. Line a 9-inch pie plate with the pastry; trim and crimp the edges decoratively. Refrigerate the pie shell while preparing the filling.

2. Place the parsnips in a medium saucepan and add water to

cover. Cook uncovered over medium heat until very tender, about 20 minutes. Drain.

3. While the parsnips are cooking, melt the butter in a skillet over medium-high heat. Add the pears and sauté for several minutes. Stir in 2 tablespoons of the Calvados and simmer the pears, stirring occasionally, until they are quite soft, 12 to 15 minutes.

4. Preheat the oven to 375°F.

5. Place the parsnips and pears in a food processor fitted with the steel blade; process until very smooth. Let cool to room temperature.

6. Beat the eggs, honey, sugar, and cream together in a mixing bowl. Add the cooled parsnip purée and whisk until well blended. Whisk in the ginger, cinnamon, and nutmeg. Pour the filling into the pie shell.

7. Bake the pie until the top is golden and the center is set, 50 to 60 minutes. Serve at room temperature with flavored whipped cream, if desired.

Makes 6 to 8 servings.

Pumpkin Mousse

Since I have never been a fan of pumpkin pie, I prefer to fill my Thanksgiving pumpkin quota with this lighter and more glamorous mousse.

1 envelope unflavored gelatin
¼ cup amber-colored rum
4 large eggs
⅔ cup sugar
1 cup canned unsweetened pumpkin purée
2 teaspoons ground cinnamon
2 teaspoons ground ginger

½ teaspoon grated nutmeg
½ teaspoon ground cloves
2 teaspoons grated orange zest
1 cup heavy or whipping cream, cold
Toasted slivered almonds and whipped cream (optional)

1. Sprinkle the gelatin over the rum in a heatproof small bowl. Place the bowl in a pan and pour in simmering water to come half-way up the side of the bowl. Stir to dissolve the gelatin. Remove from the heat and let cool to room temperature.

2. Beat the eggs in a large mixing bowl until thick. Gradually beat in the sugar and continue beating until the mixture is very light and lemon colored, about 5 minutes. Stir in the pumpkin, spices, and orange zest thoroughly, then stir in the cooled gelatin.

3. Using clean beaters, whip the cream in another mixing bowl until stiff. Gently fold the cream into the pumpkin mixture. Spoon the mousse into individual glasses and refrigerate at least 3 hours before serving. Garnish with toasted almonds and dollop of whipped cream, if desired.

Makes 8 servings.

A
Christmas
Stroll

December on Nantucket brings a flurry of holiday activity and the denouement of the island's prolific entertaining season. While there is one last inundation of tourists arranged by the Chamber of Commerce and known as Nantucket's Christmas Stroll, those who truly love the island celebrate the season with quieter parties that revolve around the warm and welcoming hospitality of an open house.

The treasured historic demeanor of the town takes on a special glow with doorways and window sashes garlanded in a mix of evergreen and island-inspired decorations. As the first snowflakes mingle with the froth of the winter waves at the ocean's edge, Christmas shopping among locals tends to mellow into a pleasant gathering with neighbors and friends. Those who have lingered long enough to flirt with a winter's hibernation on the island develop a natural sense of camaraderie that is also evident in the relaxed style of entertaining.

The recipes that make up this final chapter are an assortment of end-of-the-season inspirations and traditional family recipes. They are foods that are at once festive and flexible—one last splurge of savories and sugarplums before the quiet, cozy, and contemplative months commence with a long-awaited island lullaby.

Lobster Fritters with Rouille

The extravagance of these puffy little fritters is well suited to the festive glitter of holiday entertaining. The lobster-colored rouille—a spicy provençal sauce of roasted red peppers, garlic, and olive oil—adds just the right splash of contrast to the cheese and seafood-rich flavor of the fritters.

ROUILLE:

½ cup fresh bread crumbs
1 large egg yolk
4 cloves garlic, minced
1 roasted red pepper (see Index), seeded and chopped
2 tablespoons fresh lemon juice
½ teaspoon hot red pepper flakes, or to taste
1 cup fruity olive oil
Salt to taste

4 large boiling potatoes, peeled
6 tablespoons (¾ stick) unsalted butter
1 bunch scallions, white bulbs and green stalks, minced
2 cloves garlic, minced
3 large eggs yolks
3 tablespoons heavy or whipping cream
1¼ pounds fresh cooked lobster meat, finely diced
2 cups shredded sharp white Cheddar cheese
3 tablespoons chopped fresh parsley
1 tablespoon crumbled dried tarragon
Salt and freshly ground pepper to taste
½ cup unbleached all-purpose flour
2 large eggs, beaten
3 cups fresh bread crumbs
Vegetable oil for frying
Fresh parsley sprigs and lime slices, for garnish

1. Prepare the rouille: Place the bread crumbs, egg yolk, garlic, roasted pepper, lemon juice, and red pepper flakes in a food processor fitted with the steel blade. Process until smooth. With the machine running, pour in the olive oil in a thin, steady stream through the feed tube. Process until thick. Season to taste with salt. Refrigerate the rouille until ready to use.

2. Place the potatoes in a medium saucepan, add water to cover, and boil until tender, 20 to 25 minutes.

3. Melt 2 tablespoons of the butter in a small skillet, add the scallions and garlic, and sauté over medium high heat, stirring constantly, for 5 minutes.

4. Drain the potatoes and place in a large bowl. Add the remaining 4 tablespoons butter, the scallion mixture, egg yolks, and heavy cream and mash together with a hand mixer.

5. Add the lobster, cheese, parsley, and tarragon to the mashed potatoes and stir to combine. Season to taste with salt and pepper.

6. Form the mixture into small patties. Dip each patty first in flour, then in beaten egg, and finally in the bread crumbs to coat. (The fritters may be made in advance to this point and stored in a single layer in the refrigerator.)

7. Heat oil in a deep-fat fryer to 375°F or, pour oil to ½ inch depth in a large skillet and heat over medium-high heat. Fry the fritters in batches until golden brown all over and drain on paper towels. Keep warm in a low oven while cooking the rest.

8. Top each fritter with a dollop of the rouille and a small sprig of parsley. Arrange on a serving platter garnished with lime slices and serve at once.

Makes 4 dozen fritters.

Oysters with Bacon and Balsamic Beurre Blanc

While balsamic vinegar may be the greatest food discovery of the past decade, the affinity that the vinegar has with oysters has got to be the second greatest discovery. Just the aroma of this oyster preparation makes me swoon.

½ cup balsamic vinegar
⅓ cup dry red wine
2 shallots, minced
1¼ cups (2½ sticks) unsalted butter, cold, cut into tablespoons
Salt and freshly ground pepper to taste

36 fresh oysters, on the half-shell
¾ pound bacon, partially cooked, but browned
Parsley and lemon wedges, for garnish

1. Combine ¼ cup of the vinegar, the red wine, and the shallots in a small, non-aluminum skillet. Reduce over medium heat until only 2 tablespoons of liquid remain. Whisk in the butter, tablespoon by tablespoon, over very low heat so it blends rather than melts into the vinegar mixture. When all the butter has been incorporated, remove the skillet from the heat and season to taste with salt and pepper.

2. Preheat the broiler.

3. Spoon a scant 2 teaspoons of the balsamic beurre blanc on top of each oyster. Top with a strip of bacon cut 1½ to 2 inches long. Place the oysters on a baking sheet. Drizzle the remaining ¼ cup of vinegar over the oysters.

4. Place the oysters 6 inches from the heat and broil for 2 minutes. Raise the broiler tray 2 inches and cook just until the bacon is well crisped, about 30 seconds more. Spoon any juices that have accumulated on the baking sheet over the oysters and garnish with parsley sprigs and lemon wedges. Serve at once with cocktail forks.

Makes 3 dozen.

Christmas Sushi Roll

Nantucket bay scallops are at their most plump and best throughout the holiday season. They are so sweet raw that it often seems a shame to cook them.

2 pounds very fresh bay
   scallops
1½ cups fresh lemon juice
2 tablespoons chopped
   fresh ginger
3 unwaxed medium
   cucumbers, as straight
   as possible

1 jar (4 ounces) Japanese
   pickled ginger, cut into
   thin strips
1 cup soy sauce
Wasabi paste (Japanese
   horseradish)

1. Place the bay scallops in a shallow dish and cover with the lemon juice. Stir in the ginger. Cover and let marinate in the refrigerator for 3 hours.

2. Drain the scallops thoroughly. Slice the cucumbers length-wise as thinly as possible. (A meat slicer is ideal for this task; otherwise a very sharp knife and steady hand are recommended.) Cut each of the strips lengthwise in half, so that you end up with strips about 6 inches long, ½ inch wide, and ⅛ inch thick.

3. Wrap each scallop in a cucumber strip and secure with a toothpick. Place the rolls on serving platters and place a little strip of the pickled ginger on the center of each scallop. Refriger-ate until ready to serve.

4. Serve the scallops with a bowl of soy sauce and a mound of wasabi paste on a small plate for dipping.

Makes about 100 rolls.

Phyllo Flowers

These delicious little hors d'oeuvres look like miniature pink poinsettias. The garnish of glistening salmon caviar adds just the right sparkle to the seasonal festivities.

8 ounces Montrachet
   goat cheese without the
   ash, at room
   temperature
8 ounces cream cheese, at
   room temperature
2 large eggs
½ cup heavy or whipping
   cream
8 ounces smoked salmon,
   finely minced

3 tablespoons chopped
   fresh dill
Salt and freshly ground
   pepper to taste
8 ounces phyllo dough
Melted unsalted butter,
   as needed
1 jar (¾ ounce) salmon
   caviar, for garnish

1. Beat the goat cheese and cream cheese together in a mixing bowl until fluffy. Beat in the eggs, one at a time, beating well after each addition. Stir in the cream until well blended. Stir in the smoked salmon and dill and season with salt and pepper.

2. Lay out the phyllo dough on a clean work surface and cut into 3-inch squares. Keep the phyllo covered with a dampened towel to prevent it from drying out.

3. Preheat the oven to 350°F. Lightly brush 1½-inch minia-ture muffin cups with butter.

4. Lightly brush 2 phyllo squares with melted butter and lay, overlapping, on a muffin cup. Brush 2 more squares and arrange

overlapping the first 2 squares at a 90° angle. Gently ease the dough into the muffin cup. It should resemble the cup of a flower. Spoon the salmon mixture into the phyllo, filling it to the top. Repeat with the remaining phyllo and filling.

5. Bake the filled phyllo cups until the filling is lightly puffed and the phyllo is golden, about 20 minutes. Let cool slightly and gently remove from the pans. Top each cup with a little spoonful of salmon caviar and serve hot. (These can be baked in advance, removed from the pans, and reheated on a baking sheet for 10 to 15 minutes in a 350°F oven.)

Makes about 72 hors d'oeuvres.

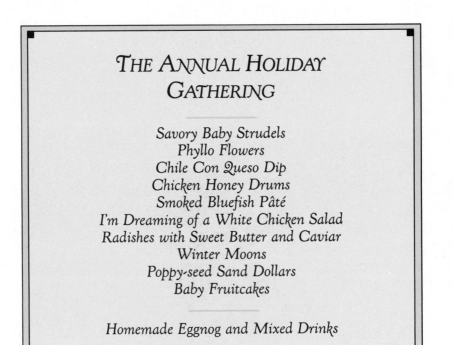

THE ANNUAL HOLIDAY GATHERING

Savory Baby Strudels
Phyllo Flowers
Chile Con Queso Dip
Chicken Honey Drums
Smoked Bluefish Pâté
I'm Dreaming of a White Chicken Salad
Radishes with Sweet Butter and Caviar
Winter Moons
Poppy-seed Sand Dollars
Baby Fruitcakes

Homemade Eggnog and Mixed Drinks

Sausages with Warm Cranberry Cumberland Sauce

Ruby-colored cranberries blend wonderfully with the classic cumberland sauce to make a tart, Christmas-colored condiment for dipping favorite sausages.

2 cups fresh cranberries
¾ cup red currant jelly
½ cup sugar
2 tablespoons fresh lemon
    juice
3 tablespoons port
1 tablespoon Dijon
    mustard
1 shallot, finely minced

Finely grated zest of
    1 lemon
Finely grated zest of
    1 orange
2½ pounds kielbasa or
    sweet Italian sausage,
    cut into bite-size pieces
    and cooked until well
    browned

1. Place the cranberries, currant jelly, and sugar in a small saucepan and simmer over medium heat until the cranberry skins pop and the jelly melts, 15 minutes.

2. Place the cranberry mixture in a blender and add the lemon juice, port, mustard, shallot, and lemon and orange zest; blend until smooth. Transfer the mixture to a small chafing dish to keep warm.

3. Arrange the sausages on a platter and spear with toothpicks, so guests can dip them into the warm cumberland sauce.

Makes 10 to 12 hors d'oeuvre servings; about 2½ cups cumberland sauce.

Radishes with Sweet Butter and Caviar

A miniature Christmas-colored hors d'oeuvre that is crunchy and sophisticated.

48 red radishes
1 cup (2 sticks) unsalted
    butter, at room
    temperature, whipped

1 jar (4 ounces) salmon
    or sturgeon caviar
Fresh dill sprigs

1. Several hours before serving, trim the radish bottoms so they can stand upright. Scoop out some of the top center portion of each radish and cut the top of the shell into a zigzag flower shape. Refrigerate in a bowl of ice water for several hours to crisp.

2. Drain the radishes and pat dry. Spoon the butter into a pastry bag fitted with a star tip and pipe about 1 teaspoon butter into the center of each radish flower. Arrange the radishes on a serving tray.

3. Spoon a little cluster of caviar eggs on top of the butter on each radish flower. Garnish with a tiny sprig of dill and serve.

Makes 48 hors d'oeuvres.

Savory Baby Strudels

These are a unique variation on the rather commonplace phyllo triangle party hors d'oeuvre. Smoky sausage blended with fruity apples, raisins, and crunchy caraway seeds give these the condensed flavor of an Alsatian Choucroute Garni.

4 tablespoons (½ stick) unsalted butter

3 medium leeks (including two-thirds of green tops), rinsed, dried, and minced

3 cloves garlic, minced

½ cup diced hard Italian sausage

2 medium apples, peeled, cored, and cut into ½-inch dice

3 tablespoons golden raisins

3 tablespoons dry white wine

1 tablespoon caraway seeds

6 ounces shredded sage Cheddar cheese (see Note)

Salt and freshly ground pepper to taste

8 ounces phyllo dough

Melted unsalted butter, as needed

1. Make the strudel filling: Melt the butter in a medium skillet over medium-high heat. Add the leeks and garlic and sauté, stirring constantly, for 10 minutes.

2. Stir in the diced sausage, apples, raisins, wine, and caraway seeds. Reduce the heat to medium and simmer, stirring occasionally, for 10 minutes. Remove from the heat and let cool for 15 minutes.

3. Stir in the Cheddar. Season to taste with salt and pepper.

4. Lay out the phyllo dough on a clean work surface and cut crosswise into 2½-inch-wide strips. Keep the dough covered with a dampened towel to prevent it from drying out.

5. Preheat the oven to 350°F. Butter 2 baking sheets.

6. Lightly brush 2 strips with melted butter and place exactly on top of one another. Place a heaping teaspoon of filling at the end of the doubled strip and roll up tightly like a scroll. Repeat with the remaining phyllo and filling. Place the baby strudels, seam-sides down, 1 inch apart on the prepared baking sheets.

7. Brush the tops and sides of the strudels lightly with more butter. Bake until golden brown, 20 to 25 minutes. Let cool slightly and transfer to a serving platter. (The strudels can also be slightly underbaked and refrigerated or frozen until needed. Bake in a 350°F oven until golden brown.)

Makes about 36 baby strudels.

Note: If you can't find sage Cheddar cheese, use regular Cheddar and add ½ teaspoon ground sage

I'm Dreaming of a White Chicken Salad

As yet another example of quintessential blond food, this is a great chicken salad to make during the winter months when the usual fruit and vegetable mix-ins for chicken salad are not at their peak. This makes a sensational holiday hors d'oeuvre when spooned into the hollow of a radicchio leaf or endive spear.

3 pounds boneless, skinless chicken breasts, poached and cooled (see Index)

1 can (8 ounces) water chestnuts, rinsed, drained, and cut into 3 slices each

2½ cups canned or fresh thin celeriac strips

1 can (14 ounces) hearts of palm, drained and sliced ½ inch thick

½ cup sliced almonds, lightly toasted

GINGER MAYONNAISE:

2 large egg yolks

2 teaspoons Dijon mustard

1 tablespoon fresh lemon juice

2½ tablespoons finely minced fresh ginger

2 cups vegetable oil

2 teaspoons ground ginger

Salt to taste

1. Cut the chicken into ¾-inch chunks. Combine the chicken, water chestnuts, celeriac, hearts of palm, and toasted almonds in a large mixing bowl.

2. Prepare the ginger mayonnaise: Process the egg yolks, mustard, lemon juice, and fresh ginger in a food processor fitted with the metal blade. With the motor running, add the oil in a thin, steady stream. Add the ground ginger and salt and continue processing until the mayonnaise is thick and smooth.

3. Add the mayonnaise to the chicken salad and toss to coat. Refrigerate the salad for several hours to allow the flavors to blend.

Makes about 2 quarts.

Chicken Honey Drums

The crunchy pecans, sharp mustard, and sweet honey coating on these chubby little chicken legs make them festive finger food for buffet nibbling.

16 chicken drumsticks	*½ cup fresh bread crumbs*
4 tablespoons (½ stick) unsalted butter	*½ cup pecans, finely chopped*
¼ cup honey	*Salt and freshly ground pepper to taste*
2 tablespoons Dijon mustard	

1. Preheat the oven to 350°F. Arrange the chicken drumsticks in rows on a baking sheet lined with parchment paper or aluminum foil.

2. Melt the butter in a small saucepan over medium heat. Stir in the honey and the mustard and simmer, stirring occasionally, for 5 minutes. Remove from the heat.

3. Using a pastry brush, brush each drumstick generously and all over with the honey mixture. If there is any remaining, reserve it. Combine the bread crumbs and pecans and sprinkle generously all over the drumsticks.

4. Bake the drumsticks until the meat is tender and the coating is nicely browned, 50 to 60 minutes. Drizzle with the remaining honey mixture. Arrange the drumsticks on a platter and serve warm.

Makes 16 drumsticks.

Que Sera Christmas Torta

If you are a devotee of the incredibly sensuous Italian cheese tortas as I am, you have probably experienced extended periods of deprivation due solely to the inherently capricious nature of Italian cheese makers and shippers. I decided to try making my own after one particularly long spell without a single mouthful of my favorite Peck's Basil Torta. Modesty aside, I thought the result was stunning and the red, white, and green colors are most suited to holiday festivities.

1¼ pounds cream cheese, at room temperature
¾ cup (1½ sticks) unsalted butter, at room temperature
5 ounces Montrachet goat cheese without ash, at room temperature

1 pound sliced Italian Fontina or Provolone
1 cup good-quality pesto
12 sun-dried tomatoes packed in oil, drained
⅓ cup pine nuts, lightly toasted

1. One day before serving, line a 9 x 5-inch loaf pan with a double thickness of slightly dampened cheesecloth.

2. Beat the cream cheese, butter, and goat cheese together in a mixing bowl until very smooth.

3. To assemble the torta, arrange a layer of the sliced cheese on the bottom of the lined loaf pan. Trim the edges of the cheese to fit if necessary. Spread a layer of the cheese mixture evenly on top with a rubber spatula. Top with a thin layer of pesto and top the pesto with another layer of the sliced cheese. Spread a layer of the cheese mixture on top of the sliced cheese. Top with a layer of sun-dried tomatoes and a sprinkling of the pine nuts. Continue to layer the ingredients in the pan, alternating the pesto and sun-dried tomatoes.

4. Cover the top with a layer of lightly dampened cheesecloth and press the torta gently with the palm of your hand to compress the layers. Refrigerate overnight.

5. When you are ready to serve, remove the cheesecloth from the top and unmold the torta onto a serving platter. Remove the cheesecloth liner. Arrange crackers or sliced fresh French bread around the torta. Garnish the top with a few sprigs of holly leaves, if desired.

Makes 25 to 30 servings.

Chile Con Queso Dip

This warm dipping sauce is a sort of Mexican fondue. The creamy pink color flecked with the red and green of the minced peppers is well suited to Christmastime. I like to offer with it a variety of dippers—nacho chips, sautéed chorizo sausage, corn bread, and an assortment of raw vegetables.

3 tablespoons olive oil
2 bunches scallions, white bulbs and green stalks, minced
3 fresh jalapeño peppers, or to taste, seeded and minced
1 red bell pepper, seeded and minced
1 can (17 ounces) plum tomatoes, drained and chopped

2 cups light cream (see Index)
6 ounces cream cheese
8 ounces Monterey Jack cheese, shredded
8 ounces sharp Cheddar cheese, shredded
2 tablespoons all-purpose flour
1 tablespoon cumin
Salt and freshly ground pepper to taste

1. Heat the oil in a medium saucepan over medium-high heat. Add the scallions, jalapeños, and bell pepper; sauté, stirring frequently, until the vegetables are softened, 5 to 7 minutes.

2. Stir in the tomatoes and simmer 5 minutes. Stir in the cream and heat the mixture just to boiling, then remove from the heat.

3. Break the cream cheese into small pieces and add to the hot cream mixture. Stir until completely melted. Toss the shredded cheeses with the flour and stir into the hot mixture, one handful at a time, until all is completely melted.

4. Return the mixture to low heat and stir until heated through. Season with the cumin, salt, and pepper. Transfer the mixture to a chafing dish and serve warm with a selection of the suggested dippers.

Makes about 1 quart.

Festive Fruit Bread

In my opinion, there should always be some extravagant fruit bread to make the holiday table complete. This recipe yields a generous four loaves, so you may want to tuck extras in holiday gift baskets and share them with friends.

1 cup diced dried apricots
1 cup diced mixed
   candied fruits
1 cup diced dried figs
½ cup golden raisins
¾ cup amaretto liqueur
3 packages (¼ ounce
   each) active dry yeast
½ cup warm water
2 cups milk
1 cup (2 sticks) unsalted
   butter
¾ cup granulated sugar
1 teaspoon saffron
   threads

1 teaspoon almond
   extract
Grated zest of 1 lemon
Grated zest of 1 orange
1 teaspoon salt
9½ to 10 cups
   unbleached all-purpose
   flour
4 large eggs
¾ cup pine nuts
1 tablespoon water
Confectioners' sugar,
   optional, for garnish

1. The night before making the bread, combine the apricots, candied fruit, figs, raisins, and amaretto in a mixing bowl. Let marinate overnight.

2. Sprinkle the yeast over the warm water in a large mixing bowl; let stand 5 to 10 minutes to dissolve. Place the milk, butter, sugar, saffron, almond extract, lemon and orange zests, and salt in a medium saucepan. Heat over low heat, stirring occasionally, just until the butter is melted (this mixture should get no warmer than 115°F).

3. Add the milk mixture to the yeast and stir to blend. Stir in 4 cups of the flour and 3 of the eggs. Beat vigorously with a wooden spoon until smooth. Mix in enough of the remaining flour to make a moderately stiff dough. Turn the dough out onto a floured surface and knead until smooth and satiny, 10 to 15 minutes. Transfer to a buttered very large bowl. Turn the dough so that it is buttered-side up. Cover with a dampened towel and let rise in a warm place until doubled in bulk, about 1½ hours.

4. Stir the pine nuts into the marinated fruit

mixture. Punch the dough down and turn out onto a floured work surface. Very gently knead the marinated fruit and nuts into the dough until all are well distributed in the dough. Return the dough to the buttered bowl. Cover with a dampened towel and let rise again until doubled in bulk, about 1½ hours.

5. Punch the dough down and divide it into 4 equal parts. Roll out each piece into a 18 x 12-inch rectangle and roll up each from a short side into a baguette-shaped loaf. Place the loaves at least 4 inches apart on greased large baking sheets. Cover with dampened towels and let rise once again until doubled in size, about 1 hour.

6. Preheat the oven to 375°F.

7. Beat the remaining egg and 1 tablespoon water together in a small bowl. Brush the tops of the loaves with the egg wash. Bake the bread until golden brown, 40 to 45 minutes. Let cool completely. Sift confectioners' sugar over the tops just before serving, if desired.

Makes 4 long loaves.

Tahitian Vanilla Nuts

With Tahitian vanilla beans a current flavoring rage, these exotic sounding nuts make a fashionable fireside nibble or midnight snack certain to ensure dreamy visions of sugarplums. If you can resist hoarding all the nuts for yourself, they make a welcome Christmas gift for a host or hostess.

¾ pound shelled brazil or
  macadamia nuts
2 tablespoons vegetable
  oil
2 tablespoons Cointreau
¼ cup sugar
1 whole vanilla bean
  (preferably Tahitian),
  pulverized in a blender
  or minced as finely as
  possible by hand

2 teaspoons ground
  cinnamon
½ teaspoon ground
  nutmeg
½ teaspoon ground cloves
Salt to taste

1. Preheat the oven to 350°F.

2. Blanch the nuts in boiling water for 1 minute and drain thoroughly.

3. Whisk the oil, Cointreau, and sugar together in a bowl. Add the nuts, stir to coat, and let marinate for 15 minutes.

4. Spread the nuts into a 9-inch-square baking pan and toast in the oven until light golden brown, 25 to 30 minutes.

5. In a clean bowl, mix the vanilla, cinnamon, nutmeg, and cloves together. Toss the hot nuts in the spice mixture to coat well. Sprinkle with salt. Lay the nuts out on a double thickness of paper towels to absorb any excess oil and cool completely. Store in an airtight tin until serving time.

Makes about 2½ cups.

Polish Poppy-Seed Bread

This bread is my personal favorite of the traditional holiday foods my family makes at Christmas.

2 packages (¼ ounce each) active dry yeast
5 to 6 cups unbleached all-purpose flour
1½ cups milk
½ cup (1 stick) unsalted butter
⅓ cup sugar

2 teaspoons ground cardamom
2 teaspoons grated lemon zest
1 teaspoon salt
3 large eggs
1 can (12 ounces) poppy-seed filling

1. Combine the yeast and 2 cups of the flour in a large mixing bowl. Heat the milk, butter, sugar, cardamom, lemon zest, and salt in a saucepan just until warm, stirring to melt the butter. Add the milk mixture and the eggs to the yeast and flour. Beat at low speed 30 seconds, scraping the bowl constantly. Increase the speed to high and beat 3 minutes longer.

2. Stir in enough of the remaining flour by hand, to make a moderately stiff dough. Turn the dough onto a floured surface and knead until smooth and satiny, 5 to 10 minutes. Transfer the dough to a lightly buttered large bowl and turn the buttered-side up. Cover with a dampened towel and let rise in a warm place until doubled in bulk, about 1½ hours.

3. Punch the dough down and divide in half. Let rest 10 minutes. Roll out half the dough into a 24 x 8-inch rectangle on a lightly floured surface. Leaving a 1-inch border on all sides, spread half the poppy-seed filling over the dough. Roll up, starting at one short side; seal the ends and place seam-side down in a butterd 9 x 5 x 3-inch loaf pan. Repeat with the remaining dough. Cover the loaf pans with dampened towels and let rise in a warm place until doubled in bulk, about 45 minutes.

4. Preheat the oven to 350°F.

5. Bake the loaves until nicely browned, 40 to 45 minutes. Cool in the pans for 10 minutes, then turn out onto a wire rack to cool completely. Slice and serve with whipped butter.

Makes 2 loaves.

Baby Fruitcakes

These are the ideal accompaniment to steaming cups of tea or after-dinner snifters of Cognac.

½ cup (1 stick) unsalted
 butter, at room
 temperature
½ cup granulated sugar
2 large eggs
1¼ cups finely diced
 mixed candied fruit

2 tablespoons
 orange-flavored liqueur
1¾ cups unbleached
 all-purpose flour
1 teaspoon baking powder
½ teaspoon ground
 cardamom

GLAZE:
1 cup sifted confectioners'
 sugar
3 tablespoons
 orange-flavored liqueur

1 teaspoon grated orange
 zest
¼ cup sliced almonds,
 toasted, for garnish

1. Preheat the oven to 350°F. Lightly butter 1½-inch miniature muffin cups.

2. Cream the butter and granulated sugar in a mixing bowl until light and fluffy. Beat in the eggs, one at a time, beating well after each addition. Stir in the candied fruit and liqueur.

3. Sift the flour, baking powder, and cardamom together into a medium bowl, then gently stir into the batter until well blended.

4. Fill each cup two-thirds full with batter. Bake until the fruitcakes spring back when pressed lightly in the center, 15 to 20 minutes. Cool slightly, then turn out onto wire racks to cool completely.

5. Prepare the glaze: Stir the confectioners' sugar, liqueur, and orange zest in a small bowl until smooth. Dip the top of each baby fruitcake in the glaze and top with 1 almond slice each. Return to the wire racks to let the glaze set. Store the fruitcakes in airtight containers up to 1 week.

Makes about 40 cakes.

Orange Shortbread

This is the cookie I look forward to most each holiday season.

2 cups (4 sticks) unsalted butter, at room temperature	Pinch salt
	Finely grated zest of 2 oranges
1½ cups (packed) brown sugar	2 large eggs
4 cups unbleached all-purpose flour	2 tablespoons water

1. Cream the butter and brown sugar in a mixing bowl. Gradually beat in the flour and salt to make a fairly stiff dough. Stir in the orange zest. Wrap the dough in plastic wrap and refrigerate at least 2 hours.

2. Preheat the oven to 350°F. Line baking sheets with parchment paper.

3. Roll out the dough ½ inch thick on a lightly floured surface. Cut out the dough with an assortment of 1½- to 2-inch cookie cutters. Place the cookies on the prepared baking sheets.

4. Beat the eggs and water together in a small bowl and brush lightly over the cookies. Bake until light golden brown, 15 to 20 minutes. Let cool on wire racks, then store in airtight containers until ready to serve.

Makes about 60 cookies.

THE FIRE IS SO DELIGHTFUL. . . .

Que Sera Christmas Torta
Tahitian Vanilla Nuts
Oysters with Bacon and Balsamic Beurre Blanc
Lobster Fritters with Rouille
Sausages with Warm Cranberry Cumberland Sauce
Polish Cream Cheese Cookies
Orange Shortbread

Rosé Champagne

Polish Cream Cheese Cookies

One final Christmas recipe from my polish grandmother. The delicate cream cheese crust and tart little mouthful of apricot filling make these cookies an ideal conclusion to a day of feasting.

½ pound cream cheese, cold, cut into small bits
1 cup (2 sticks) unsalted butter, cold, cut into tablespoons
2 cups unbleached all-purpose flour

1 cup dried apricots
3 cups water
¼ cup granulated sugar
1 tablespoon fresh lemon juice
Confectioners' sugar for dusting

1. Prepare the dough at least 3 hours in advance or the day before: Place the cream cheese, butter, and flour in a food processor fitted with the steel blade. Process just until the ingredients begin to form a ball. Wrap the dough in plastic wrap and refrigerate.

2. One hour before you are ready to bake the cookies, place the apricots in a heavy saucepan and cover with the water. Bring to a boil, then lower the heat and simmer uncovered until the

apricots are very tender, about 45 minutes. Add more water as needed to keep the apricots covered. Drain and purée the apricots with the sugar and lemon juice in a food processor until smooth.

3. Preheat the oven to 350°F. Line baking sheets with parchment paper.

4. Roll the cream cheese pastry out to ⅛-inch thickness on a lightly floured surface. With a pastry wheel, cut the dough into 2-inch squares.

5. Place a dab of apricot filling near one corner of each dough square. Fold the dough over to make a triangle and seal the edges together by pressing lightly with the tines of a fork. Place the cookies 1 inch apart on the lined baking sheets.

6. Bake the cookies just until light golden brown, 12 to 15 minutes. Cool on wire racks and store the cookies in an airtight container in the refrigerator. Just before serving, sprinkle each cookie with a light dusting of confectioners' sugar.

Makes about 36 cookies.

Poppy-Seed Sand Dollars

I love creating food around themes; these tasty little cookies are the result of once creating a whole shoreline of Christmas cookies.

8 ounces cream cheese, cold, broken into small pieces
1 cup (2 sticks) unsalted butter, cold, cut into small pieces
½ cup granulated sugar
3 cups unbleached all-purpose flour
1 teaspoon almond extract
1 can (12½ ounces) poppy-seed filling
Confectioners' sugar

1. Place the cream cheese, butter, granulated sugar, flour, and almond extract in a food processor fitted with the steel blade; process just until the dough starts to gather into a ball. Wrap the dough in plastic wrap and refrigerate several hours or overnight.

2. Preheat the oven to 350°F. Line baking sheets with parchment paper.

3. Divide the dough into 4 equal pieces. Roll out one piece at a time ⅛ inch thick on a lightly floured surface. Cut out with a 2-inch-round cookie cutter.

4. Place half the dough circles ½ inch apart on the lined baking sheets. Place 1 teaspoon of the poppy-seed filling in the center of each circle. Top each cookie with another dough circle and press the edges together with your fingers. Cut a small X in the center of each cookie with a sharp knife. Repeat until all the dough and scraps have been used.

5. Bake the cookies just until very slightly browned, about 8 minutes. Cool on wire racks, then dust heavily with sifted confectioners' sugar. Store in airtight containers up to 1 week.

Makes about 80 cookies.

Raspberry Hearts

Luxurious raspberry jam sparkles like Christmas tree ornaments in the center of this linzer-type cookie.

2 cups unbleached
   all-purpose flour
¼ cup (packed) brown
   sugar
¾ cup (1½ sticks)
   unsalted butter, at
   room temperature, cut
   into small pieces
2 large egg yolks
2 hard-cooked egg yolks,
   pressed through fine
   sieve

Finely grated zest of 1
   lemon
2 teaspoons ground
   cinnamon
Pinch salt
8 ounces best-quality
   raspberry jam
2 large eggs
2 tablespoons water

1. Place the flour, sugar, butter, egg yolks, lemon zest, cinnamon, and salt in a mixing bowl. Mix with your hands until the dough holds together and all the ingredients are well blended. Wrap the dough in plastic wrap and refrigerate at least 2 hours.

2. Roll out the dough ¼ inch thick on a lightly floured surface. Using a 2½- to 3-inch heart-shaped cookie cutter, cut out as many hearts as possible. Gather the dough scraps, reroll, and cut out more hearts. Using a smaller heart-shaped cookie cutter, cut out the centers of half the cookies.

3. Preheat the oven to 350°F. Line baking sheets with parchment paper.

4. Spread each whole heart with a thin coating of raspberry jam. Top with a heart frame. Repeat until all the dough has been used. Place the hearts 1 inch apart on the lined baking sheets. Beat the 2 eggs with water in a small bowl and brush lightly over the cookie frames.

5. Bake the cookies just until light golden brown, 12 to 15 minutes. Cool on wire racks and store in the freezer or in an airtight container until ready to serve.

Makes about 24 cookies.

Winter Moons

Crisp and crunchy hazelnut crescent cookies dusted lightly with snowy confectioners' sugar.

1 cup (2 sticks) unsalted
    butter, at room
    temperature
1½ cups hazelnuts,
    lightly toasted,
    skinned, and finely
    ground
2 teaspoons vanilla
    extract

1 teaspoon grated lemon
    zest
⅔ cup granulated sugar
2½ cups unbleached
    all-purpose flour, sifted
Confectioners' sugar

1. Preheat the oven to 325°F.

2. Beat the butter in a large mixing bowl until fluffy. Gradually beat in the hazelnuts, vanilla, and lemon zest. Beat in the granulated sugar.

3. Using a wooden spoon, gradually stir in the flour until all is well blended.

4. Roll out the dough ¼ inch thick on a lightly floured surface. Cut out the dough with a 2½-inch crescent-shaped

cookie cutter. Bake the cookies on ungreased baking sheets until lightly browned, 12 to 15 minutes. Let cool on wire racks.

5. When the cookies are cooled, sift confectioners' sugar over them.

Makes about 48 cookies.

Grapefruit Curd Tarts

G rapefruit is at its peak during the winter months and I love to experiment with its tart and slightly bitter flavor. This curd recipe is a delicious variation on the traditional lemon flavor and it makes a good, light finale to rich holiday feasting. The combination of the sunny yellow grapefruit curd set against the crisp and snowy white meringue tart shells dissipates all of winter's bleakness.

MERINGUE TARTS:
8 large egg whites, at room temperature
½ teaspoon cream of tartar

1½ cups superfine sugar
1½ tablespoons orange-flavored liqueur

GRAPEFRUIT CURD:
1½ cups fresh grapefruit juice
8 large egg yolks
1¼ cups granulated sugar

½ cup plus 2 tablespoons (1¼ sticks) unsalted butter, cut into tablespoons
Finely shredded zest of 1 grapefruit

Pink grapefruit sections or fresh mint sprigs, for garnish

1. Beat the egg whites with an electric mixer in a large bowl until foamy. Add the cream of tartar and continue beating until the whites form soft peaks. Beat in the superfine sugar, tablespoon by tablespoon, until all is added and the mixture holds very stiff peaks.

2. Preheat the oven to 225°F. Line two 15 x 12-inch baking sheets with parchment paper.

3. Spoon the meringue into a pastry bag fitted with a star tip. Pipe onto the lined baking sheets in 3-inch circles that are ½ inch

thick. Place 8 tarts on each baking sheet. Pipe a ring of meringue, 1½ inches high around the edge of each circle to form the side of the tarts.

4. Bake in the oven until the meringues are firm and dry, about 2 hours. Cool, then remove the meringues from the baking sheets with a metal spatula. If not filling the shells immediately, store in an airtight container in a cool, dry spot.

5. While the meringue bakes prepare the grapefruit curd: Place the grapefruit juice in a small saucepan and reduce over high heat to ¾ cup. Cool to room temperature.

6. In a heavy saucepan, beat the egg yolks, sugar, and reduced grapefruit juice together. Place over medium-low heat and whisk constantly until the mixture thickens to custard consistency, 12 to 15 minutes. (Do not allow the mixture to boil or it may curdle.) Remove from the heat and whisk in the butter, 1 tablespoon at a time, until each is melted and the mixture is smooth. Stir in the grapefruit zest and store in the refrigerator until ready to serve.

7. Just before serving, spoon or pipe the grapefruit curd into the center of each meringue tart. Garnish with pink grapefruit sections or mint sprigs.

Makes sixteen 3-inch tarts.

Bûche de Noël

A rich chocolate and coffee version of this traditional French Christmas specialty.

CAKE:
1 cup sifted cake flour
¼ cup unsweetened cocoa
   powder
1 teaspoon baking powder
¼ teaspoon salt

3 large eggs
1 cup granulated sugar
½ cup water
1 teaspoon vanilla extract
Confectioners' sugar

COFFEE CREAM FILLING:
1 cup heavy or whipping
   cream, very cold
1½ tablespoons instant
   coffee powder

½ cup sifted
   confectioners' sugar

CHOCOLATE ICING:

4 tablespoons (½ stick) unsalted butter	¼ cup sour cream
2 ounces unsweetened chocolate	2 tablespoons coffee-flavored liqueur
2½ cups sifted confectioners' sugar	¼ cup chopped, shelled pistachio nuts

1. Preheat the oven to 375°F. Butter a 15 x 10-inch jelly-roll pan. Line with a piece of waxed paper ½ inch smaller than the pan; butter the paper.

2. Prepare the cake: Sift the cake flour, cocoa, baking powder, and salt together onto a large sheet of waxed paper. Set aside.

3. Beat the eggs in a medium mixing bowl until thick and creamy. Beat in the sugar, 1 tablespoon at a time; continue beating until the mixture is very thick. Stir in the water and vanilla. Using a large rubber spatula, quickly fold in the flour mixture just until thoroughly combined. Pour the batter into the prepared pan and spread evenly. Bake until the cake pulls away from the sides of the pan and springs back when touched lightly in the center, 12 to 15 minutes.

4. Using a sharp knife, trim ¼ inch cake from all sides. Invert the cake onto a clean kitchen towel dusted lightly with confectioners' sugar. Peel off the waxed paper and starting with a short side, roll up the cake in the towel like a jelly roll. Let cool completely on a wire rack.

5. Prepare the coffee cream filling: Beat the cream, coffee, and confectioners' sugar in a cold mixing bowl until quite stiff. Carefully unroll the cake and spread evenly with the filling. Roll up the cake and place on a serving plate. Refrigerate while making the icing.

6. Prepare the icing: Melt the butter and chocolate in the top of a double boiler over simmering water. Cool slightly. Beat the confectioners' sugar, sour cream, and liqueur together in a mixing bowl. Gradually beat in the melted chocolate to make a smooth, spreadable frosting.

7. To finish the *bûche,* cut a diagonal slice, 1½ inches deep, from one end of the cake roll. Place the slice about one-third of the way down the roll to resemble a knot on a log. Spread the top and sides of the cake with the chocolate icing. Using the tines of a fork, draw lines in the icing to resemble the bark on a tree. Sprinkle with the pistachios and sift confectioners' sugar very lightly over the top. Store in the refrigerator until ready to serve.

Makes 8 to 10 servings.

Index